Mediating the Vote

The Changing Media Landscape in U.S. Presidential Campaigns

Michael Pfau, J. Brian Houston, and Shane M. Semmler

ROWMAN & LITTLEFIELD PUBLISHERS, INC.
Lanham • Boulder • New York • Toronto • Plymouth, UK

ROWMAN & LITTLEFIELD PUBLISHERS, INC.

Published in the United States of America
by Rowman & Littlefield Publishers, Inc.
A wholly owned subsidiary of The Rowman & Littlefield Publishing Group, Inc.
4501 Forbes Boulevard, Suite 200, Lanham, Maryland 20706
www.rowmanlittlefield.com

Estover Road
Plymouth PL6 7PY
United Kingdom

Copyright © 2007 by Rowman & Littlefield Publishers, Inc.

All rights reserved. No part of this publication may be reproduced, stored
in a retrieval system, or transmitted in any form or by any means, electronic,
mechanical, photocopying, recording, or otherwise, without the prior permission
of the publisher.

British Library Cataloguing in Publication Information Available

Library of Congress Cataloging-in-Publication Data

Pfau, Michael.
  Mediating the vote : the changing media landscape in U.S. presidential campaigns / Michael Pfau, J. Brian Houston, and Shane M. Semmler.
    p. cm. — (Communication, media, and politics)
  Includes bibliographical references and index.
  ISBN-13: 978-0-7425-4143-6 (cloth : alk. paper)
  ISBN-10: 0-7425-4143-6 (cloth : alk. paper)
  ISBN-13: 978-0-7425-4144-3 (pbk. : alk. paper)
  ISBN-10: 0-7425-4144-4 (pbk. : alk. paper)
  1. Political campaigns—United States. 2. Communication in politics—United States. 3. Mass media—Political aspects—United States. 4. Presidents—United States—Election—2004. I. Houston, J. Brian, 1973- II. Semmler, Shane M., 1972- III. Title. IV. Series.
JK2281.P43 2007
324.7'30973—dc22

2006014124

Printed in the United States of America

∞™ The paper used in this publication meets the minimum requirements of American National Standard for Information Sciences—Permanence of Paper for Printed Library Materials, ANSI/NISO Z39.48-1992.

Contents

Acknowledgments		vii
Introduction		1
1	The Changing Communication Landscape	7
2	Communicating along Party Lines	29
3	Political Communication, Emotions, and the Intellect	49
4	Perceiving Presidential Candidates	81
5	The Media Landscape and Democratic Engagement	107
Appendix: Design of the Studies		131
References		145
Index		165
About the Authors		177

Acknowledgments

We owe a debt of gratitude to Dr. Mary Outwater, coordinator of the University of Oklahoma Public Opinion Learning Laboratory, for conducting the two surveys employed in this investigation. Dr. Outwater, who conducts numerous polls for clients, most much less demanding than these, was delightful to work with on this project. She was accommodating of our insistence on the considerable length of both survey instruments.

We thank the Department of Communication at the University of Oklahoma for its support for this project. The Department provided monetary support for the data collection effort and offers an atmosphere of intellectual stimulation and encouragement for all academic pursuits.

A number of individuals have helped shape our thinking about this project, including Kathleen Hall Jamieson, professor and the former dean, and Michael Delli Carpini, professor and present dean, Annenberg School for Communication at the University of Pennsylvania; Jack M. McLeod, Professor Emeritus, School of Journalism and Mass Communication, the University of Wisconsin—Madison; Thomas Patterson, Bradlee Professor of Government and the Press at the Shorenstein Center, Harvard University; Roderick P. Hart, Shivers Chair in Communication, professor of government, and dean of the College of Communication, University of Texas at Austin; and Diana Owen, associate professor of political science, Georgetown University. Their ideas have contributed to our understanding of communication use and politics, and their scholarship continues to inspire us.

Michael Pfau thanks Kristi Wright, his administrative assistant in the Department of Communication at the University of Oklahoma, who, thanks to her excellent work, has made it possible to chair a department and continue scholarly pursuits. In addition, Pfau thanks the many dedicated doctoral students he has been privileged to direct since moving from the University of

Wisconsin—Madison to the University of Oklahoma in the fall of 2001. Their dedication, enthusiasm, and raw potential make academic life fulfilling.

J. Brian Houston thanks his parents, who have always provided great encouragement and support for all of his endeavors. Houston also thanks his grandfather, Anthony Robert Kahmann, for passing on an insatiable curiosity about the world. And, most important, Houston thanks his wife, Jennifer, who has made him a much better person than he ever would have been on his own.

Shane Semmler extends his appreciation to those who have guided, nurtured, and inspired his pursuit of disciplined academic inquiry. In particular, he thanks his dissertation adviser, Dr. Michael Pfau; other graduate faculty in the Department of Communication at the University of Oklahoma; and members of his M.A. thesis committee at the University of South Dakota: Dr. Terry Robertson, Dr. Michael Turchen, and Dr. Bill Richardson. He also thanks his college debate coach, Dr. Charles Follette, and undergraduate adviser, Dr. Dennis Stevens. Finally and most important, he thanks those in his personal life who have graced him with their love and support, namely, his wife, Kelly McKay-Semmler, and his mom, Toni Binkerd.

As with most large-scale projects, the results of one phase of this study previously appeared in a different venue. Results of the effects of communication use on normative outcomes appeared in *American Behavioral Science*'s special issue on the 2004 campaign. Otherwise, all results of both surveys are being reported for the first time.

Introduction

> If the modern media landscape is fragmented and diversified, and if political knowledge is no longer the result of many people using the same media for the same purpose, then what implications does this sea change carry for the ways in which political candidates are evaluated and ultimately elected, for the ways in which we think and feel about those candidates, and, perhaps most importantly, for America's civic health, which involves the ideas we have about the process and prospect for democracy in the United States?
>
> —Michael Pfau, J. Brian Houston, and Shane M. Semmler, 2006

Political communication scholars maintain that politics is shaped by the nature of the communication forms that people use to receive political information (Chaffee, 1981; Geer & Lau, 1998; McLeod, Kosicki, & McLeod, 1994; Owen, 1991; Pfau, Cho, & Chong, 2001). We use communication "form" to characterize distinct venues or conduits for the transmission of political communication to prospective voters. The word "form" is more precise than "media" because we want to assess the influence of some forms across media (for example, newspapers and political talk radio), but we also want to distinguish the impact of potential forms that transmit political campaign content to citizens via a single medium (for example, network television news, local television news, televised advertising, television talk shows, television entertainment talk shows, prime-time television political drama, television comedic programming, television newsmagazines, and televised candidate debates).

 This book is about the relative influence of communication forms on people's perceptions of candidates and the democratic process. This is an important inquiry because, as James Carey (1995) observes, ultimately "democracy depends on the forms of communication by which we conduct our politics" (pp. 378–379). Throughout much of the twentieth century, people relied on a truly "mass" media for information about national campaigns and candidates. Early in the twentieth century, they used newspapers; by the 1920s and 1930s, they employed a combination of newspapers, newsmagazines, and radio news; finally, by the 1960s, they relied most heavily on network television news but supplemented it with newspapers, newsmagazines, and radio news.

However, by the 1990s, Americans increasingly turned away from these standard "mass" media forms as primary sources of information about campaigns and candidates. By the end of the century, daily newspaper readership had fallen to just over 50 percent, a trend that will accelerate in the years ahead because readership is declining most precipitously among younger people (Hoenisch, 1991; Norris, 2000). Between the 1960s and 1980s, network television news was the dominant source of information about campaigns and candidates for Americans, attracting approximately 70 percent of the viewing audience (Roper Organization, 1981). However, in recent years, network television news viewership has declined dramatically. Today, viewership is less than 40 percent and continues to fall (Norris, 1999, 2000). Pew Research Center for the People and the Press surveys indicate that the proportion of Americans who say that they "regularly" watch network news declined by half between 1994 and 2000 (Pennington, 2002), a development that Norris (1999) termed "a dramatic hemorrhage of viewers" (p. 77).

SCOPE OF THE BOOK

Given the precipitous decline in American's use of newspapers and network television news, where are people now turning for information about politics? Following the proliferation of cable television and, more recently, the explosion of the Internet, we anticipate that involved partisans are turning to specialized media that reflect their particular political predispositions. In addition, we expect that less politically involved citizens—the people Neuman (1986) calls "the marginally-attentive public" (p. 170), who may go to the polls on Election Day but are not cognitively engaged in politics and public affairs—have found it easier to tune out political content. However, they do consume some political content, "albeit inadvertently," in that their exposure is wholly secondary to their primary motivation for using media, which is diversionary (Blumler, 1999). They absorb political content while viewing Jay Leno's monologues or while watching *Saturday Night Live*. The *Cook Political Report* advises that entertainment is the only way for campaigns to reach "an important slice of swing voters who don't watch the news, . . . don't read newspapers, [and] . . . don't pay attention to politics on a day-to-day basis" (Robertson, 2000, p. 11).

The broader question is how changes in the media landscape affect American political campaigns. This is a book about the sea change taking place in communication use and its implications for people's perceptions of candidates in presidential campaigns and for fundamental democratic values. Increasingly, mass media feature many diverse venues, and this book examines "what all the media have to say" (Page, 1996, p. 7). In today's diversified media landscape, people get political information from many forms, and this book seeks to determine which communication forms Americans turned to for information about the candidates during the 2004 presidential campaign, the relative influence of communication forms on people's perceptions about candidates and about the democratic process, and the implications of communication use for American democracy.

The book features data drawn from two national public opinion surveys that were conducted during different phases of the 2004 presidential campaign. Correlation and regression analyses are employed to assess the relative influence of people's use of seventeen distinct communication forms: from traditional venues, such as newspapers, newsmagazines, network and local television news, televised candidate debates, radio news, and televised ads, to alternative communication forms, including political talk radio, movies/DVDs, television talk shows, television entertainment talk shows, television comedic shows, prime-time television political drama, television newsmagazines, the World Wide Web, and others.

The book systematically explores a number of questions important to democratic engagement. Are Democratic and Republican partisans increasingly turning to different communication forms for information about candidates and campaigns, and, if so, what does this mean for political discourse? What communication forms do the marginally attentive use, and, if entertainment is becoming their primary source of information, what does this suggest for the future of American democracy? Do communication forms differ in their affective and cognitive proclivities, and, if they do, what are the implications for assumptions about democratic engagement? What communication forms exerted the greatest impact on people's perceptions of the presidential candidates early and late in the 2004 general election campaign? Did overall impact of communication, relative to sociodemographic factors such as party identification, grow over the course of the presidential election campaign? And how do different communication forms vary in terms of their influence on normative outcomes? Do some communication forms elevate, whereas others "strain against, rather than with, the grain" of basic democratic values (Blumler & Gurevitch, 1995, p. 203)? This investigation probes these questions. We are convinced that the pattern of the results contributes to "a more nuanced, integrated and, ultimately, accurate picture of how media affects democratic engagement" (Delli Carpini, 2004, p. 423).

THE FOCUS OF INDIVIDUAL CHAPTERS

Specifically then, chapter 1, "The Changing Communication Landscape," argues that the mass media are a product of the dominant technology of an era and that, over time, changes in technology affect the look of media and, subsequently, the nature and impact of campaign communication. The chapter overviews the nature of these changes over the course of American history. It concludes by initiating the argument that the contemporary media landscape is in the midst of significant changes that carry important implications for political campaign communication.

Chapter 2, "Communicating along Party Lines," explores the growing trend among political partisans from opposite ends of the ideological spectrum to use different communication forms for political information. The evidence is unmistakable that both Democratic and Republican partisans are drawn to communication forms that reflect their unique ideological predispositions. The chapter explores what this means for political discourse. In addition, the chapter examines the changing communication use patterns of people that Neuman (1986) calls "marginally attentive" and probes the implications for American democracy of their increasingly reliance on entertainment-based forms for information about candidates and campaigns.

Chapter 3, "Political Communication, Emotions, and the Intellect," discusses the ways in which communication forms differ in their proclivities to elicit affective versus cognitive responses to candidates. Previous research on the influence of communication forms has tended to examine the impact of media on political attitudes generally, not seeking to distinguish between the affective and cognitive components of an attitude. This chapter takes another path to understanding the media's influence on attitudes by examining the specific impact of each communication form on both the affective and the cognitive bases of political attitudes.

Chapter 4, "Perceiving Presidential Candidates," takes a macro approach to the question of how communication forms influence perceptions of candidates and treats the influence of each form in a natural environment. That is, this chapter does not focus on each communication form's influence on candidate evaluations in isolation but instead focuses on exploring the impact of each form while accounting for all other communication forms present in the modern media environment.

Finally, chapter 5, "The Media Landscape and Democratic Engagement," examines the impact of the new media landscape on perceptions of values inherent to a democracy. The questions addressed here seek to provide an understanding about how the use of different communication forms influences users' level of political expertise, attitude about the democratic process overall, and how it impacts users' likelihood of participating in the political process. The chapter seeks to understand whether some communication forms elevate basic democratic values, whereas other forms erode basic values.

The appendix describes the design of the study. It discusses the national surveys that were conducted to shed light on the nature of the current American media landscape. It then details the variables and measures featured in the surveys and the data analysis techniques used to assess expectations.

Ultimately, this book seeks to understand the change that is taking place in the American political media landscape. But beyond a simple documentation of media use lies a deeper question: If the modern media landscape is fragmented and diversified, and if political knowledge is no longer the result of many people using the same media for the same purpose, then what implications does this sea change carry for the ways in which political candidates are evaluated and ultimately elected, the ways in which we think and feel about those candidates, and, perhaps most important, America's civic health, which involves the ideas we have about the process and prospect of democracy in the United States?

CONCLUSION

Politics is about the nature of communication forms that people use to receive political information. However, we are well into a watershed period in which people's use of truly "mass" media to receive information about political candidates and campaigns is giving way to much more specialized media.

This investigation probes how changes in the mass media landscape are affecting presidential campaigns. It examines the communication forms that people relied on for information about the candidates in the 2004 presidential campaign, whether Democratic and Republican partisans and less interested citizens increasingly are turning to different communication forms, whether communication forms differ in their proclivity to elicit cognitive or affective responses to candidates, and what communication forms exerted the most impact on people's perceptions of presidential candidates early and late in the campaign. This book seeks the answers to these questions and probes their implications for political campaign communication.

Chapter One

The Changing Communication Landscape

> Politically-relevant information can take many forms . . . , emanate from many sources, . . . and have many different impacts.
>
> —Michael Delli Carpini (2004, p. 4),
> Annenberg School for Communication,
> University of Pennsylvania

This book is about the influence of changes in mass media communication on the way America elects its presidents. Aside from America's entrenched two-party political system and the pressures it exerts on candidate choice, communication is the most distinctive characteristic of presidential elections. Communication is a process that uses verbal and nonverbal symbols to symbolically transact understanding. Communication is the tool—the instrument—that candidates utilize in an effort to convince perusable potential voters to support them on Election Day. But communication is ineffectual unless it can reach its intended audience. Today the mass media are the primary conduit, or vehicle, for the dissemination of political communication. The symbiotic relationship between communication and mass media can perhaps be captured in an analogy: the relationship between bullets and a gun. Bullets are impotent absent the gun, which functions as the tool for their disbursement. So it is with political communication. In vast, populated areas such as the United States, face-to-face campaigning is an anachronism, relegated to the purposes of fund-raising or to showcase enthusiastic crowds as a backdrop for prepackaged sound bites that consist of memorable phrases that candidates and their handlers hope will be picked up by media news and transmitted to a large, national audience.

The mass media make up the principal vehicle for the dissemination of contemporary political messages. Most prospective voters have no direct contact with presidential candidates, instead basing their perceptions on political party affiliations, retrospective judgments about the past performances of candidates or parties, and/or on information gleaned from mass media reports. For most Americans, the mass media *constitute* their link to the political world—their window to presidential candidates.

However, even more so than most things, the mass media are a product of the dominant technology of an era. As a result, change is an intrinsic characteristic of mass media. Over time, changes in technology affect the look of mass media, in turn altering the nature and impact of presidential campaign communication. This chapter provides an overview of these changes over the course of American history. The chapter also provides a backdrop for the theme of this book, which is that we are in the midst of a "watershed period" in which the mass media landscape is shifting dramatically, with important implications for people's communication use in presidential campaigns and for democratic engagement.

THE DOMINANCE OF PRINT COMMUNICATION

The Founding Era

American democracy is a child of the printed word. Long before the thirteen colonies gained their independence from the Great Britain, Americans who resented the English Parliament's intrusions on their sovereignty shared and reproduced the printed words of John Locke's *Second Treatise concerning the True Original, Extent, and End of Civil-Government*. Locke wrote that "in the beginning, all the world was America" and that humans had a natural right to "life, liberty, and pursuit of property." The printed words that were so important to the colonists articulated both a dissent toward Britain and a justification for freedom and autonomy.

An example of the colonists' use of the printed word to defy British rule can be found in the Stamp Act of 1765, an act that sought to tax all formal documents. Because printers would be the ones paying the bulk of this new tax, colonial printers united in opposition to this effort. As part of the printers' organized opposition to the Stamp Act, the formerly apolitical colonial press "editorialized against the act and successfully defied it" (Davis, 1996, p. 19). The successful defiance of the Stamp Act offered revolutionary leaders a model for further colonial resistance to British authority, and it was a model that relied heavily on the written word.

The printed word continued to be important throughout the process of establishing American independence. In 1772, Samuel Adams institutionalized an intercolonial channel of communication that was designed to monitor imperial abuses of colonial liberty. These committees of correspondence "proved to be the most effective means yet discovered by the colonists for mobilizing public opinion" (Morgan, 1992, p. 56). Thanks, in large part, to their organizing influence, the First Continental Congress met in Philadelphia in 1774. Two years later, Thomas Paine made the case for American independence from Great Britain when he authored *Common Sense*, a pamphlet that sold an unprecedented 100,000 copies in just three months, helping shape public opinion in support in independence.

Later, when American independence was finally achieved and the fledgling nation struggled under the Articles of Confederation, newspapers provided the forums in which Federalists and Anti-Federalists presented their particular designs for American governance. The *Federalist Papers*, authored by James Madison, Alexander Hamilton, and John Jay under the pseudonym "Publius," provided a series of reasoned arguments for the adoption of the U.S. Constitution, in essence, making the case for a much stronger union than was possible under the Articles of Confederation, which vested almost all political power in individual states. The *Federalist Papers*, which were published in eighty-five installments in New York City newspapers and later distributed throughout the rest of New York and in Virginia, offered what is still one of the best examples of reasoned political discourse. They anticipated all serious objections of those who opposed the proposed Constitution and then systematically refuted them. In many ways, the campaign for the adoption of the Constitution represented America's first national political campaign. Ultimately, the Founding Fathers demonstrated their faith in the power of the print media to check government power by institutionalizing the freedom of the press as the First Amendment to the Constitution.

From the perspective of medium theory, print media was so important to the founding of the U.S. government that it functioned, in essence, as a *necessary* precondition for the conceptualization of democratic ideals. Postman (2001) writes that "the modern conception of democracy was tied to the printed word. . . . Locke, Madison, and Jefferson . . . assumed that political life would be conducted through print" (p. 144). In this way, the Founding Fathers illustrate Marshall McLuhan's (1967) notion that "societies have always been shaped more by the nature of the media by which men communicate than by the content of communication" (p. 8), that is, "the medium is the message" (McLuhan, 1995, pp. 236–237). Thus, from a medium theory viewpoint, the course of independence conceived of and realized by the Founding Fathers was both based on and determined by the reliance on the print medium. This is because, during this period, the print medium was the vehicle for much of the discourse that provided justification for separation from Great Britain and then the construction of a new government.

Print communication embodied the technology of the era. Postman (1993) argues that America's faith in its technology is more profound than its respect for cultural tradition. There are four reasons why this is the case: the American tendency to believe anything is possible, the genius of nineteenth-century inventors and capitalists who used technology to reap personal fortunes and in the process turn American into an industrial giant, the success of technology in its effort to provide convenience and comfort, and later the intellectual assault on tradition by the forces represented by postmodernity. America's faith in technology extends to its mechanisms for exchanging political information, and scholars have empirically demonstrated that politics is shaped by the nature of the communication forms or channels that people use to receive political information (Chaffee, 2001; Owen, 1991; Pfau, Cho, & Chong, 2001).

Just as the mass media influenced the American founding experience, so did the media impact the ways in which governance was accomplished after the birth of the American nation. In particular, the mass media influences the process by which America selects its president. "The medium of communication, interacting with historical and social pressures, influences what presidents say and how they say it" (Stuckey, 1991, p. 1). An exploration of the specific ways in which media and presidential politics interact begins in the 1828 presidential campaign.

Nineteenth-Century Mediated Campaigns

American constitutional governance was designed to accommodate faction. Indeed, the genius of the American experience is its capacity to accommodate yet control factions. During the debate over the adoption of the Constitution, James Madison, in *Federalist Papers 10* and *51*, had forcefully warned against the excesses of faction, arguing that political factions could unite one group of citizens against the interests of the whole (Rossiter, 1961). Following Washington's two terms as president, two competing political parties, the Federalists led by John Adams and the Democratic-Republicans led by Thomas Jefferson, vied for the presidency in the election of 1800. Soon political parties were the primary mechanism for organizing the national plebiscite.

These first political parties were controlled by political elites whose only means of communicating political information to their members was via the printed pages of partisan-subsidized newspapers (Davis, 1996). Only the very wealthy could afford subscriptions to the partisan organs, and only the highly educated could read them. By the 1828 election, however, intense competition developed between splinter groups within Jefferson's National-Republican

Party that would lead to intense competition between two new political parties: one, headed by John Quincy Adams and Henry Clay, became the National Republican (Whig) Party, and the other, led by Andrew Jackson, would become the Democratic Party. This realignment compelled a massive effort to involve the common man in American politics (Boyer et al., 1993). In the campaign of 1828, Jackson directed his appeal to "the common man," and both sides threatened opponents, prompting a vicious cycle of visceral charges and countercharges. Jamieson (1984) characterized 1828 as a "watershed year in presidential campaigns" because of the increased prominence of political parties and the tripling of the number of voters. Jackson's campaign, which had won the popular vote but not the electoral vote in 1824, swept the presidential election of 1828. With the growth in suffrage and the popular election of presidential electors, Jackson and his handpicked successor, Martin van Buren, implemented a system for organizing political activity that remained intact for more than a 120 years (Davis, 1996). Their tactics included the use of lurid accusations disseminated by partisan newspapers that had become more accessible to ordinary citizens, the establishment of grassroots political clubs throughout America, and the staging of mass rallies, bonfires, and processions. These innovative applications of mass media technology granted Jackson's nascent Democratic Party control of the presidency until 1840.

Throughout the first half of the nineteenth century, partisan newspapers continued to dominate the dissemination of political information. It was reputed that Jackson spent nearly $50,000 to begin and maintain partisan organs throughout America. In 1800, there were 200 newspapers in America. By 1830, there were over 1,200 (Davis, 1996). The Frenchman Alexis de Tocqueville proclaimed that America was a nation of newspapers. He observed that voluntary associations of like-minded people were the key to American democracy and that newspapers were crucial to the formation and maintenance of associations. As he observed, "Newspapers make associations, and associations make newspapers; and if it were true to say that associations must multiply as quickly as conditions become equal, it is equally certain that the number of papers increases in proportion as associations multiply" (in Mayer, 1969, p. 518). The Jacksonian era was the apex of the partisan press. During the last half of the nineteenth century, control over the flow of political information was gradually broken by the proliferation of newspapers during the era of the penny press.

The editorial independence of newspapers in the mid-nineteenth century was accelerated by the invention of the telegraph. According to Stephen Wayne (2001), the telegraph's efficiency and speed changed the very definition of news and professionalized the press. The ability to cheaply disseminate large amounts of information offered enterprising publishers a much larger market, but it was a market that could be earned only by increasing a publication's mass appeal. Instead of exploring ideas, newspaper content now increasingly focused on events, human-interest features, drama, and conflict. The emerging wire services also enabled the rise of a Washington press corps whereby reporters were given congressional office space and a previously unknown independence. Many national journalists sold their stories to myriad newspapers, thus avoiding partisan content so as not to offend potential consumers. However, while the mainstream press became more neutral and independent, the reform press was growing more extreme in both its tactics and its content.

Print communication played an instrumental role in events leading up to the Civil War. In the effort to end slavery, the abolitionist movement utilized books, newspapers, public speakers, political dialogue, demonstrations, and open confrontation in pursuit of their political agenda. In perhaps the most famous media event of the nineteenth century, Harriet Beecher Stowe's *Uncle Tom's Cabin*—published as a magazine serial in 1852—ignited a firestorm of public outrage against slavery. The novel sold 300,000 copies in 1852 and another 900,000 in 1853 (Boyer et al., 1993). The book was also made into a play that reached as many as 50 million Americans. Abolitionists responded to the success of the antislavery story by becoming more aggressively antisouthern, and at the same time a number of southern writers produced anti–Uncle Tom novels. By the time of the presidential election in 1860, Americans had become so polarized over slavery that no compromise seemed possible; America's Civil War was inevitable.

At the conclusion of the Civil War, journalists were more respected, and the press had become less partisan, as the war had made heroes out of journalists who risked life and limb to record the terrible carnage (Davis, 1996). For the first time, correspondents' names appeared on a byline with their news stories. Under Abraham Lincoln's administration, formal government subsidies of partisan newspapers were eliminated (Davis, 1996). Because of the antebellum dominance of the Republican Party, few Americans noticed the demise of the formally sanctioned partisan organ.

Late-Nineteenth- and Early-Twentieth-Century Changes

During the post–Civil War era, the newspaper business was growing, and America's economy was rapidly expanding, albeit cycles of boom and bust is a more apt description. Expanding literacy led to a dramatic expansion in newspaper and magazine readership, ushering in the era of the penny press. Public education spread throughout the nation during the late nineteenth century. Between 1970 and 1920, the number of high school graduates rose from a mere 16,000 to more than 300,000, and illiteracy was reduced by half (Jeffres, 1986). During the same period, newspaper circulation rose from just over 2.5 million to more than 15 million. By 1920, America published more than half of all of the newspapers in the world (Blum et al., 1968). In addition, mass circulation magazines, such as *Saturday Evening Post*, *Ladies Home Journal*, and many others, burst onto the scene. By the turn of the century, advertising revenues surpassed sales as the main source of revenues for both newspapers and magazines.

Unlike the narrow audiences of the partisan organs, the penny press had mass appeal. Less expensive materials, more efficient technology, improved marketing, and more advertising revenues gave the newspapers a new financial model that led to greater editorial independence (Wayne, 2001). Although some papers remained affiliated with political parties, their focus was no longer solely dedicated to the dissemination of partisan agendas. At this point, some papers occasionally criticized government officials within their own partisan affiliation, a radical departure from the years of the partisan press. Possessing little formal recourse to press criticism, politicians devised stratagems to bypass the penny press. For example, congressmen initiated the practice of franking their speeches directly to voters (Davis, 1996).

The effort to attract advertisers by boosting circulation led to the tactics of sensational ("yellow") journalism, with heavy emphasis on "sin, sex, and violence" (Jeffres, 1986, p. 36) and to "muckraking," or exposé, journalism, with feature stories against excesses of industrialization, such as low wages, deplorable working conditions, child labor, price fixing, and contaminated food and drugs, and against government corruption. "Newspaper men discovered that circulation could be greatly increased by making literature out of the News" (Park, 1975, p. 20), and more and more newspapers turned to exposés on various social evils to enhance readership.

In its pursuit of even larger audiences, the mass media championed a number of reform movements and became a crusading institution. The power of the press to set the national agenda was aptly demonstrated by William Randolph Hearst's publication of a series of inflammatory news stories that so mobilized American resentment against Spain following the sinking of the U.S. battleship *Maine* in Havana Harbor that Republicans, fearing a backlash from voters, declared war against that colonial power on April 11, 1898 (Conlin, 1990). It was during this atmosphere of an influential and crusading press that William McKinley was elected president in 1896 and again in 1900 with Theodore Roosevelt as his running mate. Roosevelt, governor of New York, who achieved national attention leading his "Rough Riders" up San Juan Hill during the Spanish-American War, assumed the presidency following McKinley's assassination and was elected on his own by a landslide in 1904.

Jeffrey Tulis (1987) argues that Roosevelt's presidency revolutionized both presidential communication as well as presidential leadership. He identifies three traditions of American presidential leadership: the Old Way, the Middle Way, and the New Way. Old Way presidential leadership limited executive authority and communication to those forms explicitly prescribed by the Constitution. The Constitution, however, did not assume the existence of a powerful, crusading national media. Roosevelt recognized the threat from socialistic leaders, such as Eugene Debs, who capitalized on people's growing discontentment with American industry's excesses. Roosevelt distinguished what to him were good and bad business practices (Conlin, 1990). After assuming the presidency following McKinley's death, he moved to enforce the Sherman Anti-Trust Act and personally assisted the United Coal Workers Union in their labor dispute with mine owners over safety and wages. While praising capitalism, he used his popularity to reform the railroads, enact the Pure Food and Drug Act, and conserve America's natural resources. Not only had Roosevelt broken with the ostensible platform of the probusiness Republican Party, he also broke with the constitutional tradition of presidential silence on domestic matters. Although a reformer indeed, Roosevelt claimed that he was at heart a conservative. He took on powerful interests, seeking to preserve capitalism by cushioning its excesses. Tulis (1987) argues that Roosevelt used demagoguery to fight demagoguery, he used popular rhetoric to fight popular rhetoric, and he formed a grudging alliance with the opposition to preserve the goals of his own party. Tulis (1987) calls Roosevelt's style of leadership the Middle Way.

Roosevelt also radically altered the relationship between presidents and the press. The press conference, the private interview, a White House briefing room, and the creation of a presidential press secretary can all be traced to his administration (Davis, 1996). By providing reporters with a reliable, predictable source of news, Roosevelt engaged the press in a symbiotic relationship. Until his cousin Franklin Roosevelt took office in 1933, no president would have such a mutually productive relationship with the press. Following Roosevelt's presidency and his successor's single term, Democrat Woodrow Wilson was elected to two terms and would use Roosevelt's presidency as a precedent from which to argue for a complete reconceptualization of presidential leadership.

Tulis (1987) calls Wilson the father of the second constitutional founding, or what he more frequently refers to as the New Way. Wilson believed that the president should have a national mandate to interpret and act on the people's will. Unlike Roosevelt however, Wilson did not have a good relationship with the press (Kernell, 1997). His chief rhetorical innovation was to deliver the State of the Union message live, directly to Congress. To facilitate its public impact and its chances of being reprinted, Wilson shortened the speech and limited its message to a single theme (Davis, 1996). Presidents since have similarly approached the State of the Union message. At the conclusion of World War I, Wilson's advocacy of the League of Nations was tragically frustrated by the sheer enormity of the task and by America's isolationist values, which were still powerfully entrenched and would remain so until after World War II. On an 8,000-mile speaking tour, he suffered a stroke and lost his struggle for the peace proposal. If Wilson had been president a mere forty years later, America might have willingly joined an international body mandated to preserve the peace. Although it was too early for him to reap its fruit, Wilson's ideal of presidential leadership would be his most important legacy. Tulis (1987) called it the New Way of presidential leadership.

The New Way was not foisted on Americans all at once. Like most transformations in America's style of political leadership and media use, the New Way's full implementation was the sum total of a several incremental events and actions (Kernell, 1997). Samuel Kernell has another name for the New Way. He calls it going public. When presidents go public, they bypass direct negotiations with other political elites and appeal directly to the people for support of their policies or propositions. Kernell contends that there are three reasons why this strategy has become America's dominant form of presidential leadership: the growth of huge constituencies tied to the modern welfare state, advances in communication and transportation, and the decline of political parties.

THE BROADCAST MEDIA EXPANDS POLITICAL REACH AND ALTERS POLITICAL DISCOURSE

Roosevelt's Fireside Chats

Radio burst onto the American scene in the 1920s and 1930s. After the creation in 1927 of the Federal Radio Commission (the forerunner to the Federal Communications Commission), which licensed radio frequencies, radio took off. "In 1924 there were 3 million radios in America; by 1935 ten times that number existed" (Jamieson, 1984, p. 19). Radio, which could transport audio messages simultaneously into millions of American homes, changed political campaign communication but less than changes in mass media that would come later, such as the proliferation of television sets in the 1950s or the availability of cable television during the 1980s.

During the 1928 presidential campaign, both the Republican and the Democratic candidates spent most of their publicity budgets on radio (Jamieson,

1984), but the strategy was thought to be ineffective (Davis, 1996). Franklin Delano Roosevelt (FDR) is largely credited with the first effective use of broadcast media in pursuit of presidential governance (Stuckey, 1991). Radio allowed FDR to speak directly with every American and in the comfort of his or her own home. His "Fireside Chats," which reached as many as 60 million listeners, quieted American nerves during the depths of the Great Depression.

Because of its reach and presence, radio was a powerful medium; however, it never completely replaced other communication forms in presidential campaign communication. As has largely been the case ever since, FDR's effective use of radio was part of a comprehensive communication strategy that met the professional needs of both Washington journalists and the president. No president before or since has had such a good relationship with the press (Kernell, 1997). According to Stuckey (1991), Americans were united through FDR's rhetoric, which defined, articulated, and focused the national character or mission. His most important legacy left Americans with the expectation that the president should lead public opinion and be the national agenda setter. Although radio waned as a political communication tool following the debut of television, it resurfaced as a vehicle for presidents to communicate with the American people during the Reagan administration.

Television's Debut

Television's debut ushered in a new era in presidential campaign communication. It burst onto the scene following World War II. In 1948, there were only seventeen stations, and they broadcast to only 102,000 television sets, two-thirds of which were located in New York City (Hearold, 1986). However, by 1960, more than 90 percent of American homes had a television set. Until the 1970s, television was little more than "radio with pictures," with news and advertisements featuring mostly talking heads, sometimes supplanted with pictures (Pfau & Parrot, 1993, p. 42). Slowly but surely, however, practitioners were learning how to exploit the visual nature of the medium, and by the 1970s television had developed a unique symbol system (Chesebro, 1984; Salomon, 1987) that Carpenter (1986, p. 353) maintained had ushered in "a new language" in American politics, one consisting more of images, emotions, and experiences (Jamieson, 1988; Meyrowitz, 1985; Pfau, 1990; Wright, 1974).

Television is the medium of choice in contemporary campaigns for all visible offices. Or, paraphrasing Richard Armstrong (1988, p. 29), today, for all intents and purposes, campaigns *happen* on television.

Dwight Eisenhower was the first to take advantage of television's capacity to personally reach out to Americans. According to Trent and Friedenberg

(2000), Eisenhower's twenty-eight political commercials revolutionized presidential campaigns by bringing "the techniques used in persuading Americans to buy commercial products to the front door of the White House" (p. 140). The first political advertisements were crude by contemporary standards. They featured candidates speaking directly to the camera, interacting with voters, or giving political speeches. The ads were created by Madison Avenue advertising giant Rosser Reeves, who had developed successful commercial advertising campaigns for Anacin, M&M's, and others. The "dean of the hammer-it-home school of advertising" (Moyers, 1984) believed that persuasion was about taking a simple theme, creating a catchy phrase, and repeating it over and over again.

Eventually, political commercials maximized their impact with the use of visual and aural effects as well as preconditioned, affect-laden symbols (Trent & Friedenberg, 2000, pp. 145–146). Another Madison Avenue adman, Tony Schwartz (1973), urged politicians to speak through the television as if they were speaking to just a few people in the comfort of their own living room. He argued that campaigns needed to use their audience like a workforce, meaning that the best commercials do not tell the voters anything but are like Rorschach patterns: "they surface the voter's feelings and provide a context for those feelings" (p. 93). Schwartz's famous "Daisy Girl" advertisement for Lyndon Johnson's 1964 presidential campaign against Barry Goldwater classically illustrated this principle in action. The laconic advertisement presented a peaceful child counting the petals of a daisy as a missile launch countdown proceeds in the background. The camera zooms in on the girl's eye, and the ad ends with the reflection of the conflagration of an atomic fire and an authoritative voice asking audience members to "Vote for President Johnson on November 3. The stakes are too high for you to stay home" (Schwartz, 1973, p. 142). Daisy Girl's powerful imagery surfaced its targeted audience's hope for a world free from threat of nuclear annihilation and its simultaneous fear of nuclear holocaust. It played on Barry Goldwater's expressed willingness to give military leaders more options in order to win the war in Vietnam, including the use of tactical nuclear weapons. Without ever stating his name, the ad implicated Goldwater, who many perceived as more likely to use nuclear weapons. Daisy Girl did not simply act on its audience; it interacted with it. It actually reached out to strike a responsive chord that was always already in people's minds. Great political campaigns are spearheaded by great messages such as the Daisy Girl commercial, but their appeal is very different than the print-based arguments that shaped earlier political appeals.

Neil Postman (1985) argues that the television commercial has become America's "chief instrument in creating the modern methods of presenting political ideas" (p. 129). Kaid, Chanslor, and Hovind (1992) argue that political advertising is ubiquitous because it reaches "large numbers of voters, requires limited information-seeking behavior on the part of the voter, and provides the candidate with complete control of the message" (p. 303). Roberts and McCombs (1994) demonstrated that political advertising is second only to newspaper coverage in its power to set the news agenda. In the presence of television's power to directly mobilize the plebiscite, political parties have become substantially less influential players in presidential politics.

The decline of parties began in earnest with Dwight Eisenhower's 1952 election. Not only did Eisenhower subvert the nominating process by seizing delegates at the last moment, he operated his entire campaign outside the formal Republican Party structure, and every successful presidential candidate since has managed his campaign independent of but usually parallel to his party's formal campaign structure (Lowi, 1985). By 1972, the political parties reformed the presidential nominating process to more accurately reflect the direct will of the people. Thomas Patterson (2002) reports that the adoption of a primary-centered nominating system forced presidential candidates to more aggressively court public opinion than ever before. The result has been that successful candidates of this era often are better campaigners than policymakers, as campaigning is exactly the skill needed to conduct presidential politics according to the demands of "going public" (Kernell, 1997). Politics is now candidate centered, and the main qualification for office is the ability to use the media to sell oneself to voters. "Going public" characterizes a process in which presidential leadership equates to a permanent communication campaign.

This is not to suggest that party identification has lost its position as the most important predictor of voting. It is still powerful, "still dominant in many people's decisions on how to vote and . . . still one of the few factors transcending immediate elections" (Shively, 1980, p. 236). What we are arguing is simply that candidates increasingly appeal to public opinion directly, independent of the political party apparatus. Successful candidates in a television age must be effective communicators, although the criteria for effective communication today are strikingly different than in an earlier era.

The irony of contemporary American political culture is that we celebrate the memory and birthday of presidents who are, for all practical purposes, unelectable by the standards of today's multimediated political culture (Jamieson, 1988). The great presidents of the nineteenth century were expected to keep a low profile, rarely engage in oratory, and generally float above political fray (Tulis, 1987). Thomas Jefferson and James Madison were writers of great acumen, but today's presidents are not expected to be great public speakers, writers, or even thinkers. Today's popular presidents are expected to be great public presenters (Stuckey, 1991). The emphasis on president as presenter has become so manifest that the public no longer cares that presidents write very few, if any, of their own speeches (Meyrowitz, 1992). The advent of the populist presidency (Tulis, 1987), the demise of national political parties (Lowi, 1985), and the rise of the independent electronic media (Owen, 1991) have transformed the presidency and presidential communication (Stuckey, 1991). Liebes (2001) argues that the requirement of politicians to interact with the public via television has invaded the soul of the political process. Presidents must speak more frequently and intimately not only to the nation as a whole but also to each individual American (Jamieson, 1988; Meyrowitz, 1992; Nimmo, 1974). The television age ushered in a new type of presidential campaign. Surprisingly perhaps, it was Richard Nixon, the candidate who had previously lost a presidential campaign to John F. Kennedy, some say because of the power of television, who played an important role in moving presidential campaigns into a new era.

THE SELLING OF THE PRESIDENT

In 1968, the era of the modern political campaign was born during the presidential campaign between Republican Richard Nixon and Democrat Hubert Humphrey (McGinniss, 1969). The Nixon–Humphrey campaign was the first time in which both political campaigns were managed by advertising agencies for the purpose of packaging the candidates in much the same way as marketers would package a commercial product, such as laundry detergent, and the packaging of the candidates in 1968 was accomplished primarily through television. The advertisers working on the Nixon campaign argued that voters were not highly interested in issues but were more swayed in their voting decisions by the image of the candidates (McGinniss, 1969). Although this notion may be common sense now, it was a radical revision of the way in which campaigns and politics were understood in 1968. Ultimately, the Nixon campaign was more successful in packaging an appealing candidate, as is evidenced by the fact that Nixon won the election.

Nixon's success in the 1968 election was in many ways the result of his campaign's understanding of the importance and power of the medium of television (McGinniss, 1969). In 1968, Nixon was a veteran of presidential campaigns who had learned an important lesson about candidate image and television during the 1960 presidential election, when Nixon, looking thin and pale—partly because he was worn down by the travel demands of the campaign and partly because he opted not to take full advantage of makeup—struck television viewers as looking no more presidential than the less experienced, young, and handsome John F. Kennedy during the first televised presidential debate (Berry, 1987; Reinsch, 1998). The lesson Nixon learned from the 1960 debate was that constructing the proper image was an essential part of communicating effectively on television.

Beyond offering the opportunity to package oneself in a manner that is appealing to the public, Nixon also believed that television offered the opportunity to take his message directly to the people (Stuckey, 1991). This direct route to the public sidestepped both the interests and the desires of the political party, which had historically played an important part in constructing candidate messages, while also sidestepping the analysis and judgments of the printed press, which Nixon perceived to be antagonistic to his cause (Stuckey, 1991).

The 1968 Nixon campaign took place toward the end of a decade in which network television news had eclipsed newspapers as the primary source of candidate and campaign information for Americans (Roper Organization, 1981). The growing popularity of television as a source of information about presidential candidates impacted presidential politics by requiring candidates to possess a quality of humanness that was very different from the requirements of candidates running in presidential campaigns in a previous era (Stuckey, 1991). Presidential candidates construct images that connect with citizens—images that suggest that candidates are, in many respects, just like normal citizens. The Nixon campaign constructed an image of Nixon as an emotional being via the controlled use of television appearances and advertising spots that stressed visual, emotional representations of America and effectively sold this construction to the electorate (McGinniss, 1969). In addition to the requirement that candidates in the television age project themselves as "regular" people, it has been traditionally understood by political scholars that candidates must also possess a quality of sophistication that at some levels sets them apart from the average citizen. As Stuckey (1991) explains, presidents "must appear to be mass and at the same time above it" (p. 96).

It should be noted also that throughout the 1968 Nixon–Humphrey campaign and in the 1972 Nixon–McGovern race, Nixon also used radio to supplement the primary use of television as a means for communicating political messages (Jamieson, 1996). In 1968 and 1972, Nixon used radio as an inexpensive way of reaching his very important rural constituency, and this approach was also utilized by the candidates in the Carter–Ford contest in 1976. So, while the 1968 Nixon campaign is noted for its impact on transitioning presidential politics into an era of televised political marketing, this effort did not mean abandoning all other communication media; in particular, radio offered a specific utility, one that would eventually be exploited during a "new media" revolution that took place almost a quarter of a century later.

When Gerald Ford assumed the American presidency following the resignation of Nixon after the Watergate scandal in 1974, the American electorate had reached a point in which the prestige of the office of president had fallen so precipitously and television had made Americans so comfortable with the "humanness" of presidents that it had now become acceptable to laugh at or make fun of sitting presidents (Stuckey, 1991). Ford attempted to capitalize on this political reality by making fun of himself on entertainment television shows such as *Saturday Night Live*. This appearance was a political maneuver and, following on the heels of Nixon's appearance on *Laugh In* during the 1968 campaign, institutionalized the expectation that presidential candidates appear on entertainment television programs.

During the 1976 campaign between Republican Gerald Ford and Democrat Jimmy Carter, Carter portrayed himself as a Washington outsider, someone who was different from the corruption that had plagued politics since Watergate (Jamieson, 1996). This packaging was successful in getting Carter elected, but he eventually served a presidency that ended in deep dissatisfaction with his performance among the American people. While Ford and Carter's failings as presidents could easily be analyzed by political scientists in order to provide policy reasons for their unpopularity, Stuckey (1991) argues that the failings of both of these candidates were attributable to the fact that neither of these individuals was successful at offering good versions of their presidency on television. She writes that "as good television becomes ever more important to—perhaps synonymous with—good governance, successful presidents will be presidents who produce good television" (p. 113). Thus, as the 1970s came to an end, the politics of the American presidency entered a time in which making good television was essential to successful politics, and no candidate proved this relationship better or took greater advantage of it than Ronald Reagan.

Hollywood Comes to Washington

In 1980, Ronald Reagan, a former Hollywood actor, assumed the American presidency by defeating incumbent Jimmy Carter. Reagan was "the first American president to have truly mastered television," a feat that was accomplished by Reagan's use of "short, sharp, and thematic" rhetoric (Stuckey, 1991, p. 115). Reagan was a master of the new style of televised, political discourse, communicating through the medium with an intimate and conversational nature (Hellweg, Pfau, & Brydon, 1992). While Reagan's rhetoric was perfect for television, he also possessed the interpersonal skills required of any successful Hollywood actor, skills that are favored by the medium of television (Atkinson, 1984; Hellweg et al., 1992; Pfau, 1990).

In addition to his mastery of television, Reagan also utilized the medium of radio throughout his 1980 campaign. Reagan thought that listeners would believe what a speaker was saying on the radio more than they believed content disseminated on other media, and he also appreciated the ability to speak at a much greater length on radio than was possible on television (Jamieson, 1996). Thus, Reagan resumed Nixon's successful use of radio and likely set the stage for radio to be a tool in the Republican political arsenal that would lead to the eventual explosion of talk radio in the late 1980s and early 1990s.

George H. W. Bush succeeded Reagan as president following the 1988 campaign by using the power of television, not so much to facilitate his own image but to destroy the image of his opponent, Democrat Michael Dukakis (Jamieson, 1992). Lacking the mastery of television possessed by his predecessor, Bush eventually won a campaign in which he initially trailed by framing his opponent as soft on crime. However, ultimately the Bush campaign and presidency was transitory in that it filled a gap between one phase of mediated politics and another. Just as Nixon began a new phase of politics by conducting a marketed, fully televised campaign, only to be followed by a period of presidents—Ford and Carter—who were unable to capitalize and harness the changing media landscape, so was Reagan, the master of television, followed by a president who was also unable to capitalize on the current political realities by offering good television. Thus, Bush's inability to truly harness the power of television or any other communication form during his presidency made way for the birth of "new media" that took place during the 1992 presidential election.

THE GROWING INFLUENCE OF NEW MEDIA

New media, which includes communication genres or forms such as political talk radio and entertainment television, evolved during the 1980s, and most of the new communication forms—with the exception of the Internet—were exerting an influence as early as the 1992 presidential campaign between Republican George H. W. Bush, Democrat Bill Clinton, and Independent Ross Perot (Davis & Owen, 1998). More extensive use of new media during the 1992 presidential campaign was a strategy relied on more by challengers Clinton and Perot than by incumbent Bush. For example, Ross Perot publicly announced his candidacy for the presidency on *Larry King Live*, a televised political talk show (Bimber & Davis, 2003). In 1992, televised talks shows were a new form of media, "a modern variant of the old afternoon blue collar tabloid, a hybrid of entertainment and journalism, public affairs and primal scream" (Rosenstiel, 1993, p. 168). Televised talk shows constituted a relatively new communication form in presidential campaigns. They had been used prior to the 1992 campaign but never this extensively.

Clinton also embraced various forms of new media during the 1992 campaign, appearing on Arsenio Hall's late-night talk show, the newsmagazine *60 Minutes*, and the music video station MTV (Bimber & Davis, 2003). Clinton's appearance on these new media communication forms was an overt campaign communication strategy, part of a "Manhattan project" assembled by Clinton's media staff (Rosenstiel, 1993). Clinton's media consultant, Mandy Grunwald, was responsible for the strategy of utilizing new media and explained the impetus for appearing on such communication forms with the admission that "we know that moments of passion, personal reflection and humor (available in these popular culture programs) do more for us than any six-second soundbite on the network news or for that matter any thirty-second television commercial" (in Rosenstiel, 1993, p. 174).

Thus, the glimpses into the humanity of political candidates that began with campaigns such as Nixon in 1968 had by 1992 advanced to the point where successful candidates had to display a convincing range of emotion to the electorate and reach out to the marginally attentive prospective voter who, with the explosion of cable programming options, had become harder to reach through traditional venues. One of the best ways to emotionally connect with viewers—and simultaneously reach out to less-involved, marginally attentive citizens—was through appearances on quasi-entertainment communication venues as opposed to traditional network news or even political advertising. These new communication forms are able to convey the personal side of a candidate. Stuckey (1991) explains that "with the rise of television and passive participation that television encourages, the audience is expecting what they normally receive from both entertainment and public affairs television: emotion played out on the screen, emotions they can share in from the comfort and safety of their couches and living rooms" (p. 106). In 1992, then, political campaigns began using television in new ways, allowing candidates to generate emotion and thereby connect with the electorate in ways that were much different than had been seen previously in the history of presidential campaigns.

In addition to the use of new television communication forms, the 1992 presidential campaign coincided with the rise of political talk radio, a new use of an old communication medium. Political talk radio had become a largely politically conservative communication modality (Moy & Pfau, 2000), one that has been characterized as containing discourse that is negative, unsupported, and "shrill" (Kurtz, 1996). The typical format for political talk radio involves a host-based show where the host provides commentary and analysis on a variety of political and social issues. Political talk radio also affords listeners with an opportunity to call in to the host, offering their opinions on current topics. The content on radio differs from that of television in that radio is a hot medium (McLuhan, 1964), meaning that it favors confrontation. Beyond the characteristics of the medium, conflict on political talk radio works for the format because such conflict is entertaining, and talk radio, like all modern communication forms, is based on a revenue model where the goal is selling advertising, and entertaining conflict attracts listeners (Davis & Owen, 1998). The popularity of political talk radio continued to grow beyond the 1992 election. By the midterm elections of 1994, perhaps the apex of conservative talk radio, there were more than 900 different political talk radio shows aired in the United States (Trent & Friedenberg, 2000).

Thus, the 1992 presidential campaign marks the beginning of a transition to using new forms of media in presidential campaigns. In subsequent campaigns, use of the entertainment television and political talk radio continued, plus the newest of new media—the Internet—gained in popularity as a campaign venue. By the 2000 election, the Internet had become a standard campaign tool (Trent & Friedenberg, 2000). However, while the presidential campaigns of Democrat Al Gore and Republican George W. Bush actively used the Internet as a tool to reach prospective voters in 2000, the usefulness and impact of the new media is still debated by political analysts and academics. For example, Dick Morris (1999), former strategist for Bill Clinton, argues that the Internet allows citizens to deal with political information directly, sidestepping the mediating influence of political operatives and the traditional news media. Conversely, Sunstein (2001) believes that the Internet reduces political dialogue and debate by encouraging users to pursue information that exclusively aligns with predetermined views and, as such, fragments the audience of users.

We are in the initial stages of the emergence of this new communication technology, and it is unclear what the future holds. So far, however, the Internet has changed politics more at the margins. Its impact, thus far, has mainly been on activist publics, those who are more involved and partisan than most people (Norris, 2000). The Internet has proven to be a revolutionary tool for raising campaign contributions and mobilizing volunteers, as both the 2000 McCain and 2004 Dean campaigns illustrate. However, it hasn't yet developed into a communication tool capable of reaching the general public. The number of people who seek political information online is relatively small. For example, the Pew Research Center for the People and the Press reported that, in the 2000 presidential campaign, about twice as many people relied on radio than on the Internet as their primary source of campaign news (Norris, 2002a). The number of prospective voters who visit campaign websites is even less. The reason that the Internet is not effective in reaching the broader public is that seeking out political content online requires effort, but most people are not politically involved. As Davis (1999) put it, "The Internet does not cause people to suddenly become politically active or even interested" (p. 172). Thus, the Internet doesn't now—and may never—"compete with television—the medium that goes out and 'pulls' often reluctant citizens into contact with candidates" (Kamarack, 1999, p. 121).

THE CHANGING COMMUNICATION LANDSCAPE

As has been outlined here, the way in which Americans receive their news about presidential candidates has changed dramatically several times since presidential campaigns began in the United States. Often, it seems that changes in media technology influence who wins a presidential contest, such as when the image of John F. Kennedy came across as more presidential than Richard Nixon on the medium of television during an early televised presidential debate. At other times in history, specific presidential candidates come along who understand the changing media and are able to exploit these changes, increasing not only their own popularity but also the importance of the new media in American culture. An example of this relationship is Bill Clinton's specific efforts to utilize nontraditional television programs to convey an image of an emotional, caring candidate to the American public in 1992.

Thus, the relationship between presidential candidates and media is often a question of the chicken and the egg. That is, determining which comes first, the media technology or the candidate, is often difficult to discern. However, what does seem clear is that the political process is shaped by the communication forms or channels that citizens rely on to receive political information (Chaffee, 2001; Geer & Lau, 1998; McLeod, Kosicki, & McLeod, 1994; Owen, 1991; Pfau et al., 2001). Therefore, the reality that the political media landscape has changed—and presently is in the midst of what seems to be a radical change—has implications both for the practice of political communication and for the American electorate as a whole.

As has been illustrated here, the American media landscape has shifted from a century in which Americans relied on traditional "mass" media venues for information about campaigns and candidates to the current period in which use of these venues is declining. Where Americans once relied primarily on traditional media—newspapers, newsmagazines, radio news, and network television news—use of such media has fallen sharply. For example, at the end of the twentieth century, only half the American population reported reading newspapers, a trend of declining readership that will likely continue, as readership has fallen most precipitously among younger people (Hoenisch, 1991; Norris, 2000). In addition, while network television news was the primary source of political information for Americans between the 1960s and 1980s, attracting about 70 percent of the viewing audience (Roper Organization, 1981), in recent years network television news viewership has declined to less than 40 percent, a trend that, if anything, is accelerating (Norris, 1999, 2000). The Pew Research Center for the People and the Press indicates that the proportion of Americans who say that they "regularly" watch network news has declined by half from 1994 and 2000 (in Pennington, 2002), a loss that Norris (1999) describes as "a dramatic hemorrhage" of viewers (p. 77). The decline in network television news use stems from the proliferation of television channels, now averaging over one hundred for a typical American household and growing ("The Small Screen . . .," 2003).

Traditional sources of political information, then, are declining just as—and perhaps as a result of—various forms of new media continue to make gains in popularity. The Internet, cable television, and talk radio provide alternative sources of information to the traditional media, but these new communication forms are more than simply different locations for finding the same information that would otherwise be provided via traditional media sources. The content of these new communication forms is often markedly different than content disseminated by traditional media, and because of these differences, audiences are gaining their political knowledge via communication venues that harbor very different motivations.

For example, citizens with high levels of political involvement—that is, partisans—are increasingly inclined toward political information sources in today's new media environment that reflect their own political disposition. This can be seen in the case of political talk radio, a communication form that provides a bounty of politically conservative talk shows and, as a result, draws a listenership that is predominantly Republican (Moy & Pfau, 2000). Thus, in this case, politically conservative partisans seek out political information on talk radio because it agrees or supports their political worldview. Furthermore, political information is continually available for those who are highly involved in politics. Cable news sources such as the Cable News Network (CNN) and the Fox News Channel, plus a multitude of websites on the Internet, allow individuals with high levels of political involvement to access political content at any minute of any given day. In the twentieth century, most Americans used traditional communication forms, such as radio news, newspapers, and later television as primary sources of political information so that political partisans in the middle of that century were still participating in a "mass" mediated political discourse. Use of a "mass" media no longer characterizes the media use of many of today's partisans, who rely more and more on specialized communication forms, such political talk radio and the Internet. These communication forms draw more committed partisans who are exposed, primarily, to information that is compatible with their political and social ideology.

The proliferation of communication options is unmistakable and will undoubtedly accelerate in the years ahead (Turrow, 1997). The communication environment of today and, even more so, of tomorrow is much more "individual" than it is "mass." The individual is in control of the communication one is exposed to. The explosion of communication options balkanizes people's political communication use (Norris, 1999). It permits citizens of differing interest in politics to go their own ways. Webster (2005) points to the "worrisome prospect" that the mass media audience is splintering into "many small, relatively exclusive communities of interest that never encounter dissident voices or different points of view" (p. 366).

More involved political partisans, who manifest high levels of political involvement, are able to "exercise greater selectivity to avoid discordant views" (Comstock & Scharrer, 2005, p. 84). In this new communication era, political partisans are able to cherry-pick more ideologically homogeneous news sources, insulating them from exposure to counterattitudinal political opinions. Barry Schwartz (2004), projecting ahead to a furthering splintering of what once was a "mass audience," cautioned that "in a decade or so, . . . when folks gather around the watercooler to discuss last night's big TV events, no two of them will have watched the same shows" (p. 18). He lamented lost "shared TV experience," expressing concern over the likely prospect of 250 million "separate islands" (p. 18).

The new media landscape also carries implications for citizens who belong to the group that Russell Neuman (1986) characterizes as "the marginally-attentive public" (p. 170). This group is comprised of individuals who often vote but are not cognitively engaged in politics and public affairs. They "rationally minimize the time and effort required to monitor the political environment" (p. 172). When they form political judgments, usually they are the product of what Popkin (1991) generously calls "low-information rationality," which consists of various decision-making shortcuts: retrospective judgments of the past performance of a candidate or his/her party, the opinions of other people who they trust, or holistic assessments of candidate character (pp. 7, 213). The marginally attentive public usually tunes out political content except to the extent that they "inadvertently" encounter such content when using media they have chosen because of their primary motivation—to be diverted or entertained (Blumler, 1999). As Moy and Pfau (2000) explain, "Individuals who do not regularly watch the evening news can turn to *The Late Show with David Letterman* or *The Tonight Show* and still get a sense of what has transpired recently in Washington" (p. 135). In today's evolving media landscape, political content is available in many unusual locations so that viewers who are simply using media to have a few laughs at the end of a long day may encounter political content in David Letterman's monologue that, quite simply, becomes that person's sole knowledge about candidates or issues.

The idea that a late-night talk show could replace newspapers as the primary source of political information for some Americans is a radical shift from how communication forms were used for most of the past century. Furthermore, the reality that some citizens may utilize only media that reflect their own worldview as opposed to consuming some measure of "mass" political media illustrates that a shift in media usage is currently taking place. In fact, the reality of the current transformation in media use in the United States suggests that nothing short of a "sea change" is under way as to the ways that American citizens receive their political information. Kern, Just, and Crigler (1997) offered this characterization nearly a decade ago to capture the shift in prospective voters' use of traditional communication sources, such as newspapers and network television news, to newer web-based venues.

However, this sea change in media use isn't about the debut of any one technology, such as the Internet. Rather, it is the inevitable result of the "demassification" of all media. The greatest change wrought by the Internet is to have sped up something that was already in progress: the fragmenting of what once was a mass audience into a myriad of smaller, more homogeneous entities and the resulting advent of narrowcasting technologies that can target these superspecialized audience segments (Chaffee & Metzger, 2001; Hill & Hughes, 1998; Norris, 2000). In the short term, we are fast approaching a "500-channel universe" (Wilkinson, 2002); in the intermediate term, we are headed toward a communication environment with seemingly infinite choices and complete user control expressed in the mantra "anything you want to see, any time, on any device" (Levy, 2005, p. 50).

The sea change in media use carries enormous ramifications for political communication, which is the focus of this book. We examine prospective voters' communication use during the 2004 presidential campaign, focusing on the influence of people's communication use on their perceptions of George W. Bush and John Kerry and on the implications of communication use for American democracy. The reality of today's diversified media landscape is that "politically-relevant information can take many forms . . . , emanate from many sources, . . . and have many different impacts" (Delli Carpini, 2004, p. 423). This book is steeped in this reality and desires to examine specifically "what *all* the media have to say" (Page, 1996, p. 7).

Chapter Two

Communicating along Party Lines

> He who knows nothing is nearer to truth than he whose mind is filled with falsehoods and errors.
>
> —Thomas Jefferson, author of the Declaration of Independence and former president, letter to John Norvell, June 11, 1807

> The greatest threat to civility—and ultimately to civilization—is an excess of certitude.
>
> —George Will (2005), syndicated columnist (p. 84)

The news media serve many roles, but perhaps their most important function is to provide relatively neutral, substantive content to Americans about matters important to their communities, nation, and world, content that can become the basis for subsequent interaction. In the context of U.S. presidential campaigns, such content should focus on candidates' qualifications for office and their positions on important issues.

The notion that news can fuel political interaction is unmistakable. In two classic campaign studies during the 1940s, Lazarsfeld and colleagues (Berelson, Lazarsfeld, & McPhee, 1954; Lazarsfeld, Berelson, & Gaudet, 1948) uncovered a "two-step flow" to mass media influence in which the mass media reach some people, those designated as "opinion leaders" who are more interested in the content domain (in this case, politics), and they, in turn, interact with others, thus boosting the media's reach.

In this scenario, mass media news, particularly network television news and print venues (newspapers and newsmagazines), provide content that all Americans, both left and right, can discuss. It provides the core content—the meat—of subsequent interpersonal political discourse. Moy, Xenos, and Hess

(2005) maintain that political content disseminated through media news provides "grist" for political conversation (p. 115), and past research indicates that mass media news does, in fact, spur political talk (Kim, Wyatt, & Katz, 1999; McLeod, Scheufele, & Moy, 1999) and that political talk is related to other forms of political participation (Beck, 2002; Scheufele, 2002).

The evidence indicating that news coverage of politics in past campaigns is able to trigger political interaction is impressive, especially given the glaring deficiencies in the media's coverage of politics. In a nutshell, both the nature of political coverage and the quantity of coverage, particularly in television news, have been criticized. Television news has been chastised for excessive attention to the strategy and tactics of campaigns (Cappella & Jamieson, 1997), or what's called "the horse race" (Patterson, 1993). The emphasis of media news is on who is ahead or on the implications of major candidate pronouncements for who will gain or lose. As a result, candidates' words, which should be the heart and soul of political discourse, have declined precipitously over the years, and those that do appear in news are cheapened by a frame that reduces them to little more than mere strategy. Moreover, the horse race fixation has shifted the emphasis in political campaign coverage from newsmakers (candidates) to the people who report the news (journalists).

There is ample evidence of this shift. Daniel Hallin (1992) has studied the length of newsmakers' words in network television news. He reported that the average length of segments (what are called "sound bites") containing candidate words fell from sixty seconds per segment in 1968 to less than ten seconds by 1988. In the 1992, 1996, 2000, and 2004 campaigns, the average segment containing candidate words ranged from seven to eight seconds. In addition, the quantity of serious political coverage has declined. The number of general election campaign stories in network television news in recent election cycles fell from 728 in 1992 to 483 in 1996 and 462 in 2000 (Patterson, 2002). The decline was even more precipitous for local television news coverage of state and local political campaigns (Hunt, 2002).

The case for the failings of the news media in covering politics has been made before and does not need to be belabored here. Our point is that, even with inadequacies in the news media's political campaign coverage, news stories still function as a catalyst to political interaction, and political talk, in turn, triggers participatory behaviors.

The key to this process is political talk. We maintain that it is imperative that citizens, no matter their political disposition, are able to talk to one another about politics and public affairs. A system of shared media news use makes this possible. As Bennett (1986) argues, "Mass media news remains our only broadly shared window on reality. Turning our backs on this window isolates us from the only commonly experienced reality we have as a people" (p. xiii).

Are we "turning our backs on this window"? We maintain that we are in the midst of a fundamental change in media use that carries serious implications for American democracy. As noted previously, there has been a proliferation of media forms during the past two decades that has resulted in a dramatic shift in the ways Americans acquire political information. The changes in technology have fueled the proliferation of media choices, producing an increasing splintering of what once was a "mass" audience into a myriad of smaller, homogeneous entities. In essence, the "common carrier" model of mass communication, in which most people rely on a limited number of national venues for information about politics and public affairs, had characterized American democracy for nearly a century, is being replaced by a system of specialized media use.

Once more involved partisans, both Democrats and Republicans, and even less involved marginally attentives relied pretty much on the same communication forms for their political information. The main differences in patterns of political communication use were subtle: more involved partisans of both parties relied on newspapers more than network television news, and they supplemented newspapers and network television news with other communication forms, such as books and newsmagazines. Overall, however, Democratic and Republican partisans and marginally attentives shared a common set of facts that functioned as the grist for political engagement.

Today, by contrast, we anticipate that changes in the media landscape have made it much easier for Democratic and Republican partisans and the marginally attentive to go their own separate ways. The downside for political discourse is that Democratic and Republican partisans have become more rabid as they rely increasingly on partisan-charged media venues, whereas nonpartisans are tuning out political content altogether but absorb some content in the form of political ads aired during their favorite television shows or in the form of politics as entertainment, such as *The Tonight Show* or *Saturday Night Live*.

What this means for political communication is that there are *no more captive audiences* for political content. Comstock and Scharrer (2005) maintain that proliferating media choices increase the likelihood that the audience for political content will further fragment as people choose options that reflect their predilections. This development has impacted people's choice of communication forms for information about candidates and campaigns and portends serious implications for democratic dialogue.

Where will Americans acquire information about candidates and campaigns in this new communication environment? It depends, in large part, on people's interest in political content. Citizens who are more interested in political content, generally, are highly partisan. The rest of the adult population, the "marginally attentive," usually are not cognitively engaged in politics and public affairs (Neuman, 1986).

COMMUNICATION USE FOR PARTISANS

America is experiencing a resurgence of partisan identification. Between 1960 and 1984, party identification weakened (Wattenberg, 1986), evidenced by significant growth of the unaffiliated ranks (a combination of politically apathetic and independent) to as much as one-third of the electorate and increases in crossover voting (Republican identifiers who cast votes for Democratic candidates and vice versa) (Axelrod, 1986; Campbell, Munro, Alford, & Campbell, 1986; Wattenberg, 1986). However, even in the mid-1980s, at the peak of concern over the decline in people's attachments to political parties, party identification was still considered to be the single best predictor of voting behavior (Abramson, 1983).

However, in recent years, the trend toward a weakening of party identification has reversed itself. The past decade has seen a marked increase in party identification and in the strength of people's partisan affiliation. Hetherington (2001) documents that "elite polarization" has resulted in an "impressive increase in party-centric thinking on the mass level" (p. 619). He concludes that "parties . . . are far more important today than in the 1970s and 1980s" (p. 619).

This is a much more partisan era. It is this development, coupled with changes in the communication landscape—a unique combination of inclination and opportunity—that, for partisans, is responsible for an increasing bimodal pattern of political communication use. Overholser and Jamieson (2005) note that "increasingly, . . . the public is choosing its news medium based on ideological preference" (p. 436).

For partisan Americans, the proliferation of communication options provides an opportunity to select from a growing number of political communication venues that tend to mirror their predispositions. There is a natural tendency in people that was documented early in communication research: we are drawn to communication that reinforces existing opinions, and we tend to avoid communication that is discordant. These tendencies were subsequently labeled "selective exposure" and "selective avoidance," and they functioned as key axioms in the limited-effects view of mass communication (Klapper, 1960), which posited that mass communication was mainly response reinforcing and, therefore, that media influence was limited. The underlying rationale for both selective exposure and selective avoidance are intuitively appealing, although subsequent research during the 1960s was somewhat equivocal, especially concerning selective avoidance (Freedman & Sears, 1965; Sears & Freedman, 1967). Apparently, people can tolerate discordant views, at least to some degree.

However, the explanation for partisans being drawn increasingly to reinforcing communication venues lies deeper than simple selectivity. We suspect that the motivation stems from growing distrust of mainline news media as politically biased. This view has become prevalent not only on the part of conservatives, who have railed against network news bias for decades, but also with people of the political right, left, and center. Survey research indicates that the proportion of Americans of all partisan stripes who believe the national news media, particularly television, is biased has escalated since the 1970s and now stands at more than 60 percent (Smith, Lichter, & Harris, 1997). The Pew Research Center for the People and the Press (2004b) reports that from 2000 to 2004, Republicans in particular became "more distrustful of virtually all major media outlets," and overall Republicans are half as likely as Democrats to rate as "credible" such news outlets as ABC, CBS, NBC, NPR, PBS, *Newsweek*, *Time*, and *U.S. News & World Report*.

Since media news programs can't be simultaneously biased against *all* points of view, there is something else at work than the content of these programs. Furthermore, the best evidence of national news media objectivity in presidential campaigns suggests minimal bias. Allen and D'Alissio (2000) conducted a meta-analysis (a study synthesizing results of extant research) featuring fifty-nine content analyses conducted to examine the tone of national news media coverage of presidential election campaigns since 1948. They found scant evidence of bias in news coverage.

We suggest that the notion of hostile media perception (Vallone, Ross, & Lepper, 1985) is the most plausible explanation for partisan perceptions of bias. This perspective is based on the premise that partisans of both left and right perceive identical news report as biased against their particular point of view (Gunther, Christen, Liebhart, & Chia, 2001; Perloff, 1989). If, for example, Democrat and Republican partisans viewed the same television news report on John Kerry's Vietnam service or George W. Bush's Air Guard service, both would perceive it to be biased against their preferred candidate. The point is that, whether national media news is biased or not, partisans perceive that it is, and this, above all, has driven them to seek out more concordant news venues, which are more readily available in today's fragmented mass media environment.

Based on recent trends in communication use during campaigns, this investigation anticipated that political party identifiers are making much heavier use of more partisan communication forms. For Democrats and Republicans, we expected greater use of the Internet, including candidate websites, ideologically oriented blogs, and online news. For Democrats, uniquely, we expected heavy use of movies/DVDs, which burst onto the American scene as a source of overt political communication in 2004, plus television newsmagazines and prime-time television political drama, primarily *The West Wing*, which offers an insider's perch from which to view a Democratic presidential administration. For Republicans, we anticipated a unique and heavy reliance on political talk radio and television.

These expectations were based on a combination of anecdotal and empirical evidence from recent campaigns. Committed Democratic and Republican partisans have been relying ever more heavily on partisan-charged communication forms in recent elections. Both of them have been drawn increasingly to the Internet, particularly to online sites that tend to mirror respective political dispositions. As we observed in chapter 1, the Internet is a site for strong partisans, and hence it is not a venue for influence as much as it is a source for reinforcement, mobilization, and fund-raising. Stephen Carter (1998) terms the "online world" as "the place to eliminate dissonance" because we surround ourselves with others who reassure us that our "most unlikely fantasies are the reality" (p. 201). Carter maintains that this is troubling because it precludes genuine discussion. Instead, "[people] can deny the truth of anything from outside [their] circle that may contradict what [they] already believe" (p. 201). Unfortunately, many sites are partisan in the extreme. Former NBC News anchor Tom Brokaw, who surfed the Web during the 2004 campaign, located and analyzed 527 "assaults" on Bush and Kerry. He characterized many partisan websites as "a kind of political jihad" and termed them "outrageous" (in Hajela, 2004).

Of course, more committed Republicans have been tuning in to political talk radio in large numbers for nearly two decades. They have found Rush Limbaugh, G. Gordon Liddy, Oliver North, and other conservative talk radio hosts as ideologically therapeutic. In Republican primaries and for Republicans in general election campaigns, political talk radio consistently is one of the most influential communication forms (Pfau, Cho, & Chong, 2001; Pfau et al., 1997). More committed Republicans also have found a myriad of television talk venues, particularly on Fox, including *Hannity and Colmes*, *The Beltway Boys*, *The O'Reilly Factor*, and others.

Democrats have turned to their own preferred communication venues to reinforce their political views, including movies/DVDs, such as *Fahrenheit 911*, Michael Moore's scathing attack on the Bush administration's handling of the war on terror in the wake of 9-11; television newsmagazines, such as *60 Minutes* and *20/20*, which routinely expose political and corporate abuse;

and prime-time television political dramatic programming, such as *The West Wing*, a drama depicting how a fictional Democratic president and his inner circle battle ongoing trials and tribulations that confront the nation.

This study investigated partisans' communication use during the 2004 general election campaign, anticipating that political party identifiers relied most heavily on the specific communication venues described previously. Pearson *r* correlations were computed to examine associations involving communication use and political party identification, strength of party identification, and political interest. These data are displayed in tables 2.1 and 2.2.

Media Use for Party Identifiers

The results offered partial support for these expectations, particularly with regard to radio and television communication forms. The study's expectations for Internet use, however, were not supported.

Compared to other communication forms, the Web proved not to be a significant venue during the general election campaign. It was not significantly used by either Democrat or Republican party identifiers during either phase 1 or phase 2 of the general election campaign. Contrary to expectations, partisans didn't rely heavily on the Internet as a source of information about candidates or the campaign, at least *not relative to other communication forms*.

This is the second consecutive study of macrocommunication use during U.S. presidential campaigns that revealed limited use of the Internet (Pfau et al., 2001). The Internet may be a safe place where partisans can surround themselves with other people who share their unique view of the political world, as Carter (1998) maintains, but these results suggest that it still remains more of a niche tool (Norris, 1999, 2002a): a venue for activists, well suited for raising campaign funds and for mobilizing volunteers and, thus, relevant during primary campaigns but less important as a main source of information in general election campaigns (Norris, 2002a). These results tend to support the position of Howard and Rainie (2000), who maintain that "the Internet and related technologies are making a difference inside campaigns, but they are having a minimal effect in the way citizens interact with campaigns and each other" (p. 1).

During phases 1 and 2, Democratic Party identification was positively associated with use of movies/DVDs and television newsmagazines, as was anticipated. In addition, at both phases, Democratic Party identification was positively related to use of local television news and television entertainment talk shows, neither of which was expected. Furthermore, at phase 1 only, Democratic identification was positively associated with use of television political drama, which was predicted, but this finding didn't extend to phase 2.

Finally, during phase 2, Democrats were marginally drawn to comedic television shows.

For Republican identifiers, a very different pattern emerged. During phases 1 and 2, Republican identification was positively associated with use of political talk radio, as expected, and with greater uses of radio news and political advertising. During phase 1, Republicans were looking ahead positively to the candidate debates, but after the debates had occurred, at phase 2, debates no longer served as a significant source of information for Republicans. Finally, Republican identifiers made heavy use of newspapers during phase 2, an association that was virtually absent at phase 1.

The uneven role of political advertising in the 2004 campaign, as an important source of political information for Republicans but not for Democrats, points to the success of Republican 527 advertising efforts. Campaign finance laws allow outside groups to air issue advertising during campaigns, although such efforts are supposed to operate independent of candidates, and the major parties and ads are not supposed to explicitly advocate the election or defeat of individual candidates. Spending on such advertising has skyrocketed in recent campaigns. More than $500 million was spent in the 2000 presidential election (Annenberg Public Policy Center, 2004c), and spending during the 2004 presidential campaign was on track to eclipse that amount.

Early in the 2004 campaign, Democratic groups, such as MoveOn.org, employed television advertising to inflict damage on Bush. However, by late August, Swift Boat Veterans for Truth ads dominated the campaign with messages that continued to resonate throughout the fall. Initially, the Swift Boat ads attacked Kerry's war record, specifically the combat decorations that he earned while serving in Vietnam; later in the campaign, the Swift Boat ads turned their attention to Kerry's outspoken opposition to the war following his military service. The Global Language Monitor's PQ (political-sensitivity quotient) tracked persistence of media themes during the course of the campaign. They found that Kerry's campaign messages were "swamped" by Republican themes, particularly Swift Boats and "flip-flop" (Global Language Monitor, 2004). By contrast, the influence of *Fahrenheit 911* peaked during the summer, although it continued to exert some impact throughout the fall.

Of equal interest were the results highlighting the communication forms that strong party identifiers shunned. Not surprisingly, Democrats exhibited avoidance of political talk radio during phases 1 and 2. As we indicated previously, political talk radio is a primary communication venue for Republicans. Republicans, in turn, shunned a number of communication forms that Democrats were inclined to use. During both phases, they avoided movies/DVDs and television newsmagazines. At phase 1, they also avoided television comedic shows, and at phase 2, they avoided television entertainment talk shows, television prime-time political drama, and, to a lesser degree, television comedic programs. In short, the communication forms that partisans were drawn to and avoided were virtually reverse images for Democrats and Republicans.

The expectations of researchers were largely confirmed. This investigation assumed that the proliferation of mass media options has made it much easier for Democratic and Republican partisans to go their own separate ways. The results indicate that they have. Democratic and Republican partisans increasingly are drawn to their own unique communication venues for information about candidates and the campaign, and they tend to avoid those forms used by partisans of the opposing party.

This pattern of results indicates that Democratic and Republican partisans are, in fact, abandoning more traditional communication forms, such as newspapers and television network news, in favor of more partisan-charged communication venues (the exception would be the use of televised presidential debates, which is treated later in this book). Network television news, newspapers, and newsmagazines did not emerge as significant communication options for partisans during the 2004 presidential campaign. Instead, "new media" were more prevalent but not the Internet. Democrats turned to movies/DVDs, television newsmagazines, local television news, television entertainment talk shows, and, to a lesser degree, television political drama and avoided political talk radio. By contrast, Republicans relied primarily on political talk radio, radio news, and political advertising and, with the exception of local television news, avoided all communication forms that were popular among Democrats.

This pattern of results confirms our expectation that "people are increasingly picking their media on the basis of partisanship" (Samuelson, 2004, p. 37). The results are consistent with a 2004 survey by the Pew Research Center for the People and the Press (2004b) that found that national audiences for Rush Limbaugh's syndicated radio show and Bill O'Reilly's Fox television show are "overwhelmingly conservative and Republican," whereas the remaining audiences for NPR's *The NewsHour* and traditional television network news programs (e.g., CNN and CBS) tend to be more "liberal and Democratic but not nearly to the same degree."

Stronger Party Identifiers

This investigation anticipated that communication use patterns reported here would be more pronounced among stronger party identifiers. During both phases of the campaign, respondents' strength of party identification was positively associated with their uses of political talk radio, political talk television shows, radio news, campaign advertising, televised presidential debates, and printed materials. In addition, during phase 2, strength of party identification also was related to political conversations. This pattern of results indicates that strength of party identification is most closely associated with those communication forms used more heavily by Republicans, which may reflect the fact that Republicans tended to be more committed to their partisan allegiance than Democrats or at least that they were more committed than Democrats in the context of the 2004 presidential campaign, which featured a besieged incumbent Republican president.

IMPLICATIONS OF PARTISAN MEDIA USE

We believe that the pattern of results reported in this chapter carries significant implications for democratic dialogue. What the results clearly indicate is that Democrat and Republican partisans no longer drink from a common pool of information. Instead, they are increasingly drawn to alternative communication forms that reflect their partisan predispositions. This is what our data reveal. In this section, we explore the implications of this development. Although our analysis of the implications is based on our findings, it is admittedly more speculative in nature, an attempt to provide reasoned explanations for what these data mean for democratic discourse.

The results suggest that genuine political discourse across the partisan divide is less and less possible. It is less possible because, in this bimodal communication environment, there are fewer shared facts. Shared facts are those that are not contested. Instead, they are accepted at face value, and they can form the building blocks for reasoned compromise between partisan discussants.

Partisan media and traditional media differ dramatically in the tenor and tone of their political rhetoric. Partisan media provide a steady diet of unproven claims, many of which border on the outrageous. Traditional media news outlets once functioned as gatekeepers, screening noncandidate political claims for veracity before printing or airing them. With the decline of traditional news venues, all claims see the light of day. Partisan charges of all types are treated as facts, no matter their veracity. In some venues, for example, such as talk radio or movies/DVDs, baseless claims are aired without qualifier or rebuttal. In other forums that feature heated exchanges between left and right, they are aired, and political surrogates are permitted to comment (Patterson & Sieb, 2005). As a result, high-visibility campaigns, such as for president, are less about what the candidates say and more about gross assertions (usually about character) that originate with extreme partisans and are spread through the media by partisan talking heads spewing their talking points.

The classic example during the 2004 presidential campaign is the role of 527 attacks on Kerry's Vietnam service and on Bush's Air Guard service. When the attacks were aired in 527 television ads, respective partisan venues made the charges the primary focus on their campaign coverage, and in time, because of the intense scrutiny, even the traditional news outlets joined the fray, "balancing" their coverage by having campaign surrogates comment on the charges. This irresponsible, charge/countercharge political climate is the antithesis of responsible political dialogue. Partisan spokespersons seem compelled to spin all information no matter how benign. They have perfected an ability in mediated forums to look at the truth straight on and, often with a dismissive tone and sometimes even with a soft-spoken demeanor, unflinchingly deny it. They operate from the maxim "Never give an inch," no matter the facts of the matter.

When dueling partisans do appear on the same radio or television programs, the exchanges border on the absurd: they constitute little more than supervised "shouting matches, as on CNN's *Crossfire*, MSNBC's *Hardball*, or countless Fox TV programs," and during the 2004 presidential campaign the "highly-charged clash of opposing party spin lines . . . helped to polarize the country" (Kellner, 2005, p. 179). Today's political communication climate has become inhospitable to responsible political dialogue, which starts with shared facts.

Shared facts are essential to democratic dialogue. As Hannah Arendt (1961) observes, "Freedom of opinion is a farce unless factual information is guaranteed and the facts themselves are not in dispute" (p. 238). We are not suggesting that shared facts necessarily produce agreement between political adversaries. Rather, we insist on the critical distinction between interpreting facts from your perspective and inventing facts. Adversaries would be expected to interpret the facts in accordance with their rhetorical position but not to treat facts as rhetorical inventions. Arendt (1961) helps us understand this crucial distinction. She insists that people have a right to interpret the facts from their perspective, but "we don't admit the right to touch the factual matter itself" (p. 239). She adds, "Facts are beyond agreement and consent . . . unwelcome facts pose an infuriating stubbornness that nothing can move except plain lies" (p. 241). A liar operates from the premise that he "is free to fashion his own 'facts'" (p. 251), which, in the context of politics, provides a significant rhetorical advantage because the liar is unconstrained by the inconvenience of facts that contradict his or her position. It permits advocates to appear to be certain in the face of the many nuances that characterize most issue disputes.

Advocates justify their tainting of the truth on the basis of their perception that they occupy the high moral ground: that they are absolutely certain about the correctness of their position. Cynthia Crossen (1994) provides numerous examples of "inaccurate and corrupt information," much of which comes from people who seek to influence others, fervently believe in their cause, and have deluded themselves into believing that the end justifies any means (p. 16). The appearance of certainty and ideological purity tend to go hand in hand. In the wake of the American Civil War, the ideological excesses of people who acted as if they were certain prompted jurist Oliver Wendell Holmes (2001) to declare, "I detest a man who knows that he knows" (p. 62). Holmes was convinced that political certainty leads inevitably to a mind-set that it is right, even imperative, to impose one's views on other people. In the context of our own era, syndicated columnist George Will (2005) warned that "the greatest threat to civility—and ultimately to civilization—is an excess of certitude" (p. 84).

In a partisan-charged political communication environment, such as the one America faces at the outset of the twenty-first century, all facts are disputed. The implications of this scenario for democratic dialogue are telling. One journalist wondered, "What happens in a society in which the facts are no longer 'stubborn things,' as John Adams called them, but plastic toys that can be stretched and shaped for any purpose" (Alter, 2005, p. 39). Increasingly, American's media use during political campaigns allows people "to believe what we want to believe, . . . no matter what the facts are" (Mauldin, 2004, pp. 2–3). People trust only those facts presented via venues that mirror their partisan prejudices (Alter, 2005). Carter (1998) maintains that this is troubling because it precludes genuine political debate. Instead, "[people] can deny the truth of anything from outside [their] circle that may contradict what [they] already believe" (p. 201). In the wake of revelations about the identity of "Deep Throat," columnist Jonathan Alter posed the hypothetical "if Watergate happened now." He concluded that, in this partisan-charged communication environment, more partisan Republicans would have vehemently denied the facts of the case, conservative media outlets such as "Fox, talk radio, and a bunch of noisy partisans on the Internet and the best-sellers list who almost never admit their side does anything wrong" would have buttressed the Nixon White House, and a partisan-ridden Congress, on a straight party-line vote, would have prevented hearings from ever taking place (Alter, 2005, p. 33).

Genuine political dialogue also is less possible today because the present media environment and partisans' inclinations to insulate themselves from exposure to opposing views mean that there is little political talk across partisan lines. Instead, partisans try to avoid political discussion with those of the opposing party; or, if they do interact, the exchanges take on the flavor of shouting matches in which each side makes claims, and when they offer support, the evidence usually takes the form of tainted facts obtained from partisan media. This is what political debate has come to in twenty-first-century America.

A healthy and robust democratic process depends on civil political discourse between interested citizens. Yet genuine political dialogue requires that people listen to what opposing advocates have to say, attempting to understand opposing perspectives. Carter (1998) insists that "democracy ... requires debate" (p. 282), but debate is possible only if the political climate facilitates civil public engagement to resolve differences of opinion. Unfortunately, the present media environment has made it all too easy for partisans to do what comes naturally: to effectively insulate themselves from opposing political views.

Many political communication theorists have argued that exposure to discordant views is an essential precondition to a healthy public sphere (Calhoun, 1988; Habermas, 1989; Mill, 1859). More recently, Mutz and Martin (2001) argue that "communication across lines of political difference is essential to the social psychological basis of a pluralist society and is integral to the democratic process" (p. 109). Their investigation synthesized survey data from U.S. and British campaigns during the 1990s (1992 and 1996) assessing a variety of different communication forms for the proclivity to expose people to discordant political views. They found that people's exposure to newspapers, television news, and newsmagazines was most likely to produce exposure to discordant political views. In addition, they found greater support in Britain than in the United States for selective exposure but acknowledged that "when people have a choice, they tend to use it to reduce their exposure to cross-cutting political views" (Mutz & Martin, 2001, p. 109). Their data support our position that traditional communication forms are more likely to provide a common pool of information, which is important to political discourse. As for the finding that there is less selective exposure in U.S. versus British communication use, the most plausible explanation is the time frame of their data collection, which occurred more toward the beginning of the changes in media use that we documented during the 2004 campaign.

Our argument is that the media landscape is rapidly changing, providing more opportunities for partisans to opt for those communication forms that tend to mirror their predispositions. It is a combination of greater opportunity and inclination. In addition to greater opportunity for selective communication use, partisans are more inclined to use the media in this way. We argue that these tendencies have rapidly accelerated in the past ten years. In a subsequent study, Mutz (2002) coupled a 1996 survey with an experiment to examine the effect of exposure to dissimilar political views. Her survey data revealed that exposure to "cross-cutting views" familiarizes people with opposing viewpoints (p. 118), and her experimental results indicated that people who scored higher in perspective taking were more tolerant when exposed to dissonant political views. She concluded that "these findings . . . lend supporting evidence to arguments about the benefits of cross-cutting networks of political communication" (p. 123).

Democratic discourse requires that people listen to others who disagree with them, understand opposing positions, and respect those who advocate them. In this way, a person can engage the ideas of another, which admittedly is more difficult to do than to attack their character.

America's Founding Fathers understood the need for civil public engagement, but contemporary changes in media use may be making this less and less likely. Hunter (1991) makes the case that "the newer communication technologies provide an environment that predisposes actors to rhetorical excess" (p. 320). Instead of turning to news sources that ensure shared facts, partisans are drawn to communication forms where like-minded people gather, where there is no true "dialectic" and, therefore, "no mechanism for ensuring accountability" (p. 320).

The pattern of results of this investigation confirms an increasingly partisan divide in communication use during presidential campaigns, which carries serious implications for American democracy. What the results suggest is what Fiorina, Abrams, and Pope (2005) call "*partisan* polarization," which is not the same as "*popular* polarization" (p. 25). The results indicate simply that partisans are relying on increasingly homophilious communication venues. This does not necessarily signal increasing polarization across the electorate. What it does mean is that the nature of political discourse is changing—and not for the better.

If Democratic and Republican partisans are increasingly drawn to more partisan-charged communication venues, then genuine political dialogue across partisan lines is less likely because there are no shared facts and little understanding of opposing points of view. Partisans are able "to believe what they want to believe, . . . no matter what the facts are" (Mauldin, 2004, pp. 2–3), in essence denying the validity of anything that contradicts their preconceived views (Carter, 1998). When Thomas Jefferson (1807) declared that "he who knows nothing is nearer to truth than he whose mind is filled with falsehoods and errors," he could well have been referring to today's partisan communication environment, where things people think that they know bear only scant resemblance to "truth" and where ideological intransigence, grounded in "falsehood and error," renders political debate across partisan lines more and more difficult. Without shared facts and respect for opponents, genuine debate is nearly impossible because there can be no give-and-take.

Instead, discourse between people who are of different partisan dispositions resembles ships passing in the night; as Hunter (1991) puts it, "discourse is polarized and people tend to talk past one other" (p. 159). If political partisans draw information from their own communication forms, which twist facts to mirror users' ideological predispositions, then discourse is possible only among people who tend to be like-minded (Powers, 2005). Healthy democracy demands civil, intelligent exchanges across partisan lines to address differences of opinion (Carter, 1998). Civil, intelligent engagement involves a "dialectic" in which a political advocate's positions are "challenged directly by rebuttal, counterpropositions, cross-examination, and, inevitably, the presentation of evidence" (Hunter, 1991, p. 320).

Increasing partisan reliance on ideological pure communication forms undermines this prospect. Turrow (1997) laments that "a strong collective media" is being replaced by an increasingly "hyper-segmented" communication environment that, in time, may render political dialogue less likely because "people . . . may be unwilling to connect in debates with people outside their circles" (p. 199).

Instead, partisans are disposed to rhetorical excess. Genuine engagement is "replaced by name calling, denunciation, and even outright intolerance" (Hunter, 1991, p. 136). Kellner (2005) refers to partisan "extremists" who "are impervious to argument, ignore facts and analysis, and demonize" opponents (p. 180). All claims are exaggerated to the extreme, which results in a political climate characterized by "fear, mistrust, and resentment" (p. 152). Even tamer partisan exchanges on political television programs such as *Hardball*, *The McLaughlin Group*, *Crossfire*, and others "are set in a kind of duel-to-the-death scenario" (Garry, 2003–2004).

LESS ENGAGED CITIZENS

What about less engaged marginally attentive citizens? They do acquire political information but usually inadvertently. The proliferation of media has made it easier for people with little interest in public affairs to avoid political content altogether. Blumler (1999) argues that the emergence of "a more abundant and fragmented [media] system" means "more opportunities for audiences to ignore [political messages] in favor of sheerly enjoyable fare" (p. 241). Still, they consume some political content. Marginally attentives inadvertently consume political content. We expect that they acquire it from television entertainment programming, which happens to contain political information; from televised political ads, which are aired during entertainment programming; and from televised debates, which they are drawn to because they are genuine "media events" (Dayman & Katz, 1992).

There has been very little research about the use and influence of communication forms that specifically focuses on the marginally attentive. Furthermore, patterns of communication use are disguised by the fact that more politically involved people make greater use of virtually all communication forms. This study probed communication use on the part of prospective voters with less political interest.

The results at phases 1 and 2 revealed no significant inverse associations of communication use and political interest. Indeed, the only relationship that even came close was people's use of television comedic shows during phase 1 of the campaign. It revealed a negative relationship to both political interest and strength of party identification but attained statistical significance on only the latter variable. The pattern of results shown in tables 2.1 and 2.2 indicated that people with more political interest and partisan disposition tend to make greater use of virtually all communication forms.

The results of this study indicate simply that the marginally attentive rely less on all communication forms, even what might be considered more entertainment-oriented sources of political content. Of course, people who manifest less political interest consume some political content, but an absence of negative associations between political interest and specific communication forms suggests that there were no unique venues employed mainly by the marginally attentive to derive information about presidential candidates and the campaign.

This result is disappointing, but, given our approach, it is not surprising. We employed surveys, and we assessed the results using data analysis techniques that are designed to reveal associations. The shortcoming of the method lies in the nature of the questions asked about people's communication use. We asked, "What is the extent that you use"—and "how much attention do you pay to"—specific communication forms "as a source of information about the presidential candidates or the presidential campaign?" People who are uninterested in politics probably do make considerable use of various entertainment-based communication forms featured in this study but, for diversionary purposes, not as a source of information about the 2004 presidential candidates or the campaign. Thus, even though their use may have been extensive, they would have answered the questions posed in such a way as to suggest minimal use. The questions were appropriate for comparing people's use of traditional and nontraditional, entertainment-based communication venues as sources of political content. But the wording was unable to accurately gauge use for marginally attentive viewers, who would have been drawn to such programs for their entertainment value and not their political content but who may well have inadvertently absorbed political content. The shortcoming of the data analysis approach is that more involved partisans make greater use of virtually all communication forms as sources of information about candidates and the campaign, even so-called soft venues, which are primarily diversionary. Hence, associations involving partisans' uses of communication forms would dominate.

Table 2.1. Phase 1 Correlations of Communication Use and Political Party Identification, Strength of Identification, and Political Interest

Communication Use	Democrat (n = 405)	Republican (n = 405)	Strength of Party Identification (n = 264)	Political Interest (n = 406)
Network television news	.09+	−.06	−.00	.24*
Local television news	.13**	−.04	.03	.16**
Newspaper	.09+	.00	.06	.22*
Magazines	.07	−.055	.03	.15**
Political talk radio	−.19*	.315*	.14**	.29*
Radio news	.01	.10**	.08+	.26*
Television talk	−.01	.08**	.09+	.35*
Television entertainment talk	.12**	−.09+	−.02	.07
Television political drama	.17**	−.05	.04	.08
Television comedic shows	.03	−.10**	−.10**	−.07
Television newsmagazines	.18*	−.11**	−.00	.21*
Movies/DVDs	.22*	−.21*	−.025	.00
Web	.01	.06	.07	.13**
Candidate debates (anticipation of)	.005	.15**	.22*	.48*
Candidate ads	.01	.09**	.12**	.23*
Conversations	.02	−.01	.07	.37*
Printed materials	.05	.05	.10**	.23*

Note. Political party identification was assessed as Democrat, Republican, Independent, or no affiliation. In phase 1, there were 111 Democrats, 153 Republicans, 65 independents, and 72 unaffiliated (5 failed to respond to this item). However, prior to data analyses, dummy variables for Democratic and Republican affiliation were computed, resulting in the n's above. The results using dummy coding are consistent with results based on just the 264 respondents who identified with one of the two major parties. Strength of party identification was assessed on the 264 people who identified with a political party. It was scored on a scale from 0 (no affiliation) to 7 (strong affiliation). Political interest was scored from 1 to 7, with higher scores indicating greater political interest.
* Significant at $p < .01$.
** Significant at $p < .05$.
+ Significant at $p < .10$.

Table 2.2. Phase 2 Correlations of Communication Use and Political Party Identification, Strength of Identification, and Political Interest

Communication Use	Democrat (n = 405)	Republican (n = 405)	Strength of Party Identification (n = 264)	Political Interest (n = 406)
Network television news	.075	−.03	.12+	.27*
Local television news	.09+	−.07	.10	.09+
Newspaper	.07	.115**	.10	.18*
Magazines	.05	−.08	.07	.19*
Political talk radio	−.21*	.34*	.14**	.19*
Radio news	−.06	.11**	.12**	.25*
Television talk	.025	.025	.13**	.25*
Television entertainment talk	.14**	−.11**	.13**	.13**
Television political drama	.06	−.105**	.09	.12**
Television comedic shows	.095+	−.09+	.11+	.07
Television newsmagazines	.12**	−.13**	.07	.21*
Movies/DVDs	.16**	−.20*	.08	.08
Web	−.07	.06	.07	.09+
Candidate debates	.07	.155	.19**	.44*
Candidate ads	−.07	.11**	.12**	.27*
Conversations	−.05	.07	.17*	.23*
Printed materials	.00	.05	.15**	.12**

Note. Political party identification was assessed as Democrat, Republican, Independent, or no affiliation. In phase 2, there were 119 Democrats, 144 Republicans, 61 independents, and 73 unaffiliated (5 failed to respond to this item). However, prior to data analyses, dummy variables for Democratic and Republican affiliation were computed, resulting in the n's above. The results using dummy coding are consistent with results based on just the 263 respondents who identified with one of the two major parties. Strength of party identification was assessed on the 263 people who identified with a political party. It was scored on a scale from 0 (no affiliation) to 7 (strong affiliation). Political interest was scored from 1 to 7, with higher scores indicating greater political interest.
* Significant at $p < .01$.
** Significant at $p < .05$.
+ Significant at $p < .10$.

Chapter Three

Political Communication, Emotions, and the Intellect

> The role of . . . affective mechanisms in political decision-making has rarely been investigated.
>
> —Victor C. Ottati, Department of Political Science, State University of New York at Stony Brook, and Robert S. Wyer Jr., Department of Psychology, University of Illinois (1993, p. 296)

> In nearly all cases . . . feeling is not free of thought, nor is thought free of feelings . . . thoughts enter feelings at various stages of the affective sequence, and the converse is true for cognitions.
>
> —Robert B. Zajonc, Department of Psychology, University of Michigan (1980, p. 154)

An important media-effects question concerns the nature of the responses elicited in users by different communication forms. Specifically, what needs answering is the question, How do communication forms vary in terms of their relative capacity to elicit emotional or cognitive impacts on users? For example, does an individual who relies heavily on newspapers or newsmagazines for his or her information about politics respond more cognitively than a person who gains information about politics from the Internet? Or does an individual who is exposed to an issue via film have a more emotionally laden attitude on the issue than a person who secures content about the issue from viewing television news? Specific to the domain of political communication is the question investigated in this chapter: Do some communication forms elicit more affective or cognitive responses to political candidates? Further, if the results indicate that communication forms vary in terms of their cognitive and affective influence, what implications does this portend for political communication?

Answering these questions will provide a more nuanced understanding of the emotional and cognitive impact of using different communication forms, and this knowledge is an essential consideration in how political candidate evaluations are formed in relation to communication use. Previous research addressing the influence of communication forms has tended to examine their impact on attitudes generally, not seeking to distinguish between the affective and cognitive components of an attitude, or the research has employed nonevaluative measures, such as political learning.

Measuring only cognitive impacts, such as political learning, or assessing candidate evaluations overall without attention to the separate affective and cognitive components of an attitude ignores the role and impact of emotion in political communication. This omission is unfortunate because emotions are "often present across . . . campaigns"; however, political scholars and practitioners are "unattuned" to the emotions of audiences, producing "an *emotional deficit* in contemporary political communication" (Richards, 2004, pp. 342, 347). Ottati and Wyer (1993) observe, "The role of . . . affective mechanisms in political decision-making has rarely been investigated" (p. 296). Therefore, this study seeks to understand the way that different communication forms impact users' thoughts and feelings about political candidates.

Before examining the data collected during this project—which involves a simultaneous assessment of the cognitive and affective impact of multiple communication forms—it is helpful to first understand what is known about the role and influence of cognition and affect and apply this knowledge to expectations about how communication forms vary in their tendencies to elicit more cognitive or affective emphasis in people's assessments of political candidates.

THE TENSION BETWEEN REASON AND EMOTION IN POLITICAL DECISION MAKING

Scholars studying political behavior have long conceived of prospective voters' decision process as primarily cognitive, and because of this emphasis on cognition, researchers largely ignored the role and impact of emotions in political decision making. In the few instances when emotion was examined in political decision making, it was viewed as exerting a minor impact. For example, emotion played an indirect, even destabilizing, role in the psychological theory of voting, which grew out of the national election studies conducted in 1952 and 1956 at the University of Michigan (Campbell, Converse, Miller, & Stokes, 1960; Campbell, Gurin, & Miller, 1954). The theory posited that people's party identification exerted dominant influence of voting decisions so that the partisan-based "normal vote" was somewhat habitual. Emotion functioned as what Marcus, Neuman, and MacKuen (2000) termed "an intransigence pathology" in that it contributed to stronger partisan allegiances, rendering people more resistant to the persuasive influence of campaign communication (p. 22). Occasionally, however, this theory posited that short-term forces are able to intervene in vote decisions. Short-term factors, such as issues or candidate image, are capable of exerting "psychological cross-pressures," causing people to vote contrary to partisan allegiance. In this case, emotion was viewed as destabilizing in that it functioned as a somewhat "cursory reaction to current political symbols and personalities," what Marcus and colleagues (2000) call an "alternative" to rational judgment grounded more in ideology (p. 22). In either case, emotion's role in voting decisions was considered, in most instances, to be insignificant, and in those occasional circumstances in which it might influence voting, it was thought to be pejorative. Therefore, the psychological theory relegated emotion and, for that matter, communication to relatively minor roles in elections, and as a result, Survey Research Center questionnaires devoted few items to them (Chaffee & Hockheimer, 1985). In time, the psychological theory of voting gave way to rational choice theories (RCT) of electoral behavior, a theory that places an emphasis on self-interest as the key to driving voting decisions.

Rational choice theories have proved to be the most popular theoretical paradigms used to explain mass political behavior during the past few decades (Lohmann, 1995). Rational choice theory attempts to understand *why* people behave the way they do. Although there are numerous variations of RCT, all RCT variants revolve around the idea that individuals make decisions by determining which option—out of all options—will most benefit their personal interests (Green & Shapiro, 1994). So, to take a political example, according to RCT individuals will vote for the presidential candidate whose election is perceived to produce the greatest benefit to the personal interests of each individual voter. The *rationality* inherent to RCT is the cognitive process of weighing all options and selecting that option that will most benefit the individual. As Simon (1995) explains, "A decision is only rational if it is supported by the best reasons and achieves the best possible outcome in terms of all goals" (p. 48).

Therefore, according to the RCT model of behavior, political decisions—such as which candidate to support, whether to contribute time and/or money to a political cause, and so on—are all decisions that are made as a result of a strictly cognitive process. Cognition is essential to the functioning of RCT because the theory requires that when an individual makes a political decision, he or she must first scan the environment for all possible options, decide how each option will impact his or her personal interests, and then select the option that provides the greatest benefit. However, such cognitive models of behavior as explanations of political decision making trouble many political scientists (Green & Shapiro, 1994; Kuklinski & Quirk, 2000; Lodge & Taber, 2000; Lupia, McCubbins, & Popkin, 2000; Popkin, 1994). Cognitive models are questioned on several levels, but the most criticism centers on the fact that Americans tend to exhibit low levels of political knowledge (Kinder, 1983; Sniderman, 1983), and low levels of political knowledge are insufficient or incompatible with the assumption of cognitive models that people use the "best reason" in arriving at political decisions.

Thus, the criticism that RCT is impractical because it is based solely on the cognitive mechanisms of decision making has led researchers to explore other ways in which individuals make political decisions. Modifications of or alternatives to RCT attempt to understand how people make political decisions when they lack the knowledge or motivation to weigh all options (Green & Shapiro, 1994; Kuklinski & Quirk, 2000; Lodge & Taber, 2000; Lupia et al., 2000). One way people may arrive at decisions about which candidate to support when they are unable or unwilling to process a decision-making task cognitively is by using various heuristic cues that are found in their environment (Iyengar & Valentino, 2000; Kuklinski & Quirk, 2000; Popkin, 1994; Sniderman, Brody, & Tetlock, 1991). Heuristics are shortcuts used to understand something when the full range of information about that object is not possessed by an individual. One of the most useful political decision heuristics is political party. By simply knowing the political affiliation of a candidate, voters are able to glean information about the candidate and their positions on the issues without possessing personal knowledge about either. Thus, relying on heuristics, individuals are able to make decisions without the cognitive processing specified by RCT. Popkin (1994) discusses other heuristic cues used in political decision making, such as using perceptions about a candidate's character to develop an overall impression of the candidate or the cue of using information about the sociodemographic makeup of a candidate's supporters as a rationale for supporting or opposing a candidate.

In addition to the use of heuristics for decision making, other researchers argue that emotion is essential to understanding the process by which individuals make political decisions (Lodge & Taber, 2000; Rahn, 2000). Indeed, Lodge and Taber (2000) argue not only that emotion is relevant to political decision making but also that "all social concepts are affect laden; all social information is affectively charged" (p. 183). Antonio Damasio (2003), a neuroscientist, agrees, writing that "by the time we are old enough to read books, few if any objects in the world are emotionally neutral" (p. 56). Therefore, according to this perspective, how an individual feels about many things—such as one's own life, the state of the nation, the way a candidate presents him- or herself, or any other emotional trigger—can influence the political decision-making process. Beyond influencing the judgment of active processing of stimuli, emotion is also tied to the way information is stored in long-term memory, providing another way in which emotion can impact human decision making. Ultimately, "emotion and reasoning are inseparable, unitized in memory, and therefore next to impossible to disentangle in the everyday process of information processing" (Lodge & Taber, 2000, p. 185). Or, as Zajonc (1980) observes, "In nearly all cases . . . feeling is not free of thought, nor is thought free of feelings. . . . [T]houghts enter feelings at various stages of the affective sequence, and the converse is true for cognitions" (p. 154). This means that attempting to understand the political decision-making process absent consideration of affect, that is, by using only a cognitive model, ignores an integral, inherent aspect of human decision making.

Therefore, an accurate understanding of the political decision-making process should incorporate the role of affect in decision making. Ultimately, it should not be a surprise to those studying human behavior that emotion plays a critical role in attitude formation and behavior. This premise has its roots in the work of Aristotle (1991), who thought of the human self as a tripartite being with an affective center. The affective center of the human functions as the point where desires and drives emanate, elements of the self that are strong enough to impact the actions and beliefs of the individual.

Following Aristotle's lead, contemporary social psychologists have continued to focus on the importance of affect. For example, Zajonc (1980) argues that affect precedes cognition and thus ultimately guides an individual's attitude and actions, while Lazarus (1982, 1984) disagrees with Zajonc's (1980) causal analysis, believing that cognition and affect co-occur. The debate regarding the primacy of affect and cognition is beyond the scope of the work here, but what can be taken from this debate is the understanding that decision processes leading to attitude formation and behavior utilize both affect and cognition in varying combinations, likely depending on the circumstances, such as the receiver's involvement in the topic, as is specified in the Elaboration Likelihood Model (Petty & Cacioppo, 1979) or the Heuristic-Systematic Model (Chaiken, 1980).

Additional evidence of interplay of cognition and affect in the process of forming evaluations can be found in contemporary attitude theory, which generally considers attitudes to be comprised of both an affective and a cognitive component (Cacioppo, Petty, & Green, 1989; Eagly & Chaiken, 1993; Rosenburg & Hovland, 1960). The affective component of evaluation is the emotion or feeling associated with an attitude object, whereas the cognitive component consists of beliefs about an attitude object (Crites, Farbrigar, & Petty, 1994).

Since the processes of political decision making is based on a combination of cognition and affect, it stands to reason that communication forms vary in terms of the capacity to elevate thinking or feeling. Communication form is relevant to this discussion because it is the vehicle for the dissemination of campaign communication.

Previous research has overlooked the specific nuances unique to communication forms. Political communication forms undoubtedly embody both reason and emotion (Ryfe, 2003); indeed, Richards refers to the relationship between the two as "one of deep interconnection and complementarity" (Richards, 2004, p. 340)—therefore, it is essential that research about the influence of communication forms examine both cognitive and affective impact. It is plausible that, in the course of affecting people's perceptions of candidates, some communication forms rely more heavily on cognition, some rely more heavily on affect, and some embody a relatively even mix of cognition and affect.

Although macrostudies of people's communication use during election campaigns have not placed much emphasis on differentiating the cognitive and affective bases of people's perceptions of candidates, microevidence on the workings of particular communication forms in isolation provides a basis for some expectations. The evidence of previous micromodality studies helps form expectations about the way in which communication modality use will impact users' evaluations about political candidates. The next section explores the results of research investigating the impact of individual communication forms on the cognitive and affective bases of individual attitudes about presidential candidates. Exploring these results will help develop a rationale for expectations of this study.

THE COGNITIVE AND EMOTIONAL
BIASES OF COMMUNICATION FORMS

The purpose of this chapter is to provide a more nuanced understanding about the way that communication forms impact both cognitive and affective components of users' attitudes about political candidates. This section focuses on the different communication forms featured in this research. We examine previous research on each communication form as we seek to provide a rationale for expectations about the ways in which the communication form impacts user attitudes—that is, will the impact be primarily cognitive, affective, or both? Then we present the findings of our study on cognitive and affective bias and explore the implications of the findings for democratic discourse.[1]

However, before the influence of communication forms is explored, we examine the role and influence of various sociodemographic variables on respondents' thoughts and feelings about presidential candidates. This information provides a baseline on how personal differences impact thinking and feeling about candidates and how the results, in turn, function as controls for the influence of communication forms. In other words, we first extract the influence of variables such as party identification and education on thinking and feeling about candidates and then, after parsing the impact of all relevant sociodemographic variables, examine the influence of communication forms.

Sociodemographic Variables

Certain sociodemographic variables were measured in this research in order to determine how individual qualities, such as level of education or income, were related to feeling or thinking about the 2004 presidential candidates. The specific sociodemographic variables accounted for in this research were gender, age, education level, income, party identification, and level of political expertise. Overall, the combined sociodemographic variables measured here accounted for more of the difference in respondents' reports of feeling and thinking about presidential candidates than did the varying levels of communication form used.[2]

Analysis of the relationships between sociodemographic variables and respondents' thoughts and feelings about the 2004 presidential candidates revealed that, in the first phase of the campaign, in September, two sociodemographic variables were related to cognitive and affective perceptions of George W. Bush: level of education and political party identification (see table 3.1). Specifically, respondents' education level was negatively related to feelings of contentment toward and cognition about Bush and was positively associated with feelings of anger toward Bush. In other words, people with higher levels of education reported fewer thoughts and more negative feelings about Bush: specifically, less contentment and more anger.

Political party identification was also related to cognitive and affective perceptions about Bush during the first phase of this study. Not surprisingly, Republican respondents exhibited more contentment and less anger toward Bush and possessed more thoughts about Bush than did Democratic respondents. The other sociodemographic variables tracked in this research—gender, age, income, and political expertise—were not related to differences in feelings or thoughts about Bush.

Two sociodemographic variables impacted thoughts and feelings about John Kerry during the first phase of the campaign (see table 3.2). Gender played a role in the amount of cognition about Kerry that was reported by respondents in that males possessed more thoughts about Kerry than did females. In addition to gender, political party identification also played a role in the cognition and emotion associated with Kerry. Specifically, respondents who identified themselves as Democrats reported greater feelings of contentment, less feeling of anger, and more thoughts about Kerry than did Republican respondents. The other sociodemographic variables—age, education, income, and political expertise—were not related to emotional or cognitive perceptions of Kerry.

At the second phase of the study, which took place during the last two weeks before the election, three of the sociodemographic variables impacted thoughts and feelings about Bush (see table 3.3). Respondents' level of education was positively associated with feelings of anger about Bush. Although this association was somewhat weak, it suggests that respondents with higher levels of education felt more anger toward Bush. In addition, respondent education was negatively related to thoughts about Bush, indicating that those respondents with more education possessed fewer cognitive thoughts about Bush.

During the second phase of the study, level of political expertise also impacted feelings about Bush. Although this was a weak association, those with higher levels of political expertise generally felt more contentment toward Bush than did respondents with low levels of political expertise. Finally, just as in the first phase of the study, Republican respondents manifested more positive feelings toward Bush, greater feeling of contentment, and less anger, and they revealed more thoughts about Bush than did Democratic respondents. Political party identification was also influential in determining thoughts and feelings about Kerry during the second phase of this study, with Democratic respondents reporting more feelings of contentment, less feelings of anger, and more thoughts about Kerry than did Republican respondents.

Overall, then, only a few demographic variables impacted respondents' thoughts and feelings about both candidates. Education level impacted thoughts and feelings about Bush during both phases of the campaign. Gender played a slight role in thoughts about Kerry during the first phase of the campaign, and levels of political expertise were weakly related to positive feelings about Bush during the latter phase of the campaign.

The sociodemographic variable that was consistently related to thoughts and feelings about the candidates was political party identification. Not only was party identification the most powerful predictor of thoughts and feelings about candidates during both phases of the campaign, but it was predictable in that Republicans and Democrats exhibited more cognition and greater levels of positive feelings and lower levels of negative feelings about their respective candidates. The role and impact of party identification on thinking and affect was not surprising. Ultimately, the 2004 presidential campaign was a tightly contested battle for the presidency, with both parties drawing partisan lines, and, according to the analysis of the data collected in these studies, those affiliated with parties toed the party line so that Republicans felt good and thought a lot about Bush, while Democrats had the same reaction to Kerry.

Beyond the relationships between sociodemographic variables and thoughts and feelings about political candidates are the issues that lay at the heart of this part of the project, that is, how do different communication modalities impact respondents' thoughts and feelings about presidential candidates? To answer this question, we begin with an analysis of the impact of political advertising and television news.

Political Advertising and Television News

Research on political advertising and television news hints at a blending of cognitive and affective influences on candidate perception. Exposure to political advertising has been shown to exert both cognitive and affective influence. Studies indicate that people's exposure to political ads contributes to knowledge both about candidates (Graber, 1976; Kaid, 1982; West, 1994) and candidates' positions on issues (Atkin & Heald, 1976; Benoit, Hansen, & Holbert, 2004; Brians & Wattenberg, 1996; Kahn & Kenney, 2000; Kaid & Sanders, 1978; Martinelli & Chaffee, 1995; Patterson & McClure, 1974; Zhao & Bleske, 1995). These findings suggest that political advertising impacts people's cognitions. However, political advertising is not likely entirely cognitive in its impact. Research also indicates that emotional appeals in political ads are more frequent than more rational or logical appeals (Kaid & Johnston, 2001). Television political advertising has also been shown to exert an affective impact on viewers. Rahn and Hirshorn (1999) found that negative political advertisements lead to temporary mood changes in children. In addition, Hitchon and Chang (1995) reported that televised political attack ads produce negatively valenced thoughts.

People's exposure to television news, similarly, has been shown to exert both cognitive and affective impact. Studies show that exposure to television news enhances political learning, which is a cognitive impact (Chaffee, Zhao, & Leshner, 1994; Martinelli & Chaffee, 1995; Weaver & Drew, 1995; Zhao & Chaffee, 1995), with some studies revealing effects comparable to newspapers (Graber, 2001; Neuman, Just, & Crigler, 1992; Norris & Sanders, 2003; Stauffer, Frost, & Rybolt, 1981; Zhao & Chaffee, 1995). However, television is a cool medium, associated with less user involvement (Meyrowitz, 1985). In such circumstances, exposure to television generally and television news in particular is ideally suited to convey feelings about candidate persona

(Graber, 2001; Pfau, 1990). This tendency should have increased in recent years because television news is devoting less time to campaign coverage, a reduction that has occurred on both network news (Patterson, 2002) and local television news (Hunt, 2002). The proclivity of television news toward visual images, in conjunction with sharp reductions in campaign coverage, suggests a trending toward more affective and less cognitive impact.

Contrary to the cognitively and affectively balanced effects hinted at by previous media research, analysis of data collected during this investigation revealed that political advertising and television news exerted very little impact on respondents' thoughts or feelings for either presidential candidate. Specifically, at phase 1, viewing of television news was not associated with either cognitive or affective perceptions of Bush (see table 3.1). At the same time, use of political advertising was positively associated with feelings of contentment toward Bush and nearly with cognition about Bush. Toward the end of the campaign, viewing of television news made a positive impact on thoughts about Bush but still lacked any association with feeling about the candidate, whereas political advertising exhibited no impact on thoughts or feelings about Bush (see table 3.3).

Viewing television news and using political advertising exerted even less of an impact on respondents' affective or cognitive perceptions of Kerry. Whereas use of both forms led to some impact on the thoughts and feelings about Bush, in both phases of the campaign neither television news nor campaign advertising was significantly related to cognitive or affective perceptions of Kerry (see tables 3.2 and 3.4).

Therefore, the results of our data illustrate no support for the expectation that viewing television news and political advertising would impact respondents' thoughts and feelings about the 2004 presidential candidates. The expectation that television news and political advertising use would exert a dual impact on respondents—that is, impact both thoughts and feelings—was the product of examining previous research that had investigated the use of television news and political advertising. A possible explanation for the discrepant finding here is that most of the previous research investigating the effects of these two communication forms on users was the product of projects examining these communication forms in isolation from the entire media environment, whereas this investigation measured the use of multiple communication forms in conjunction with respondents' thoughts and feelings about the presidential candidates. Therefore, it is possible that, when examined in isolation, viewing of television news impacts individuals' thoughts and feelings about a political candidate in different or stronger ways than occurs in the natural environment, where a respondent typically uses a variety of media. It is the possibility of this distinction—that the multimedia environment influences perceptions in ways that are much different than can be found in investigations of single-media experiments—that not only justifies but also encourages researchers to examine the content and influence of *all* media, not just individual communication forms.

Print Media (Newspapers and Newsmagazines) and the Internet

Previous research on people's use of print media (newspapers and magazines) and the Internet presents a pattern of effects that are more cognitive than affective, as print media and the Internet require users to actively seek out political content and also assume more elaboration of message content (Davis & Owen, 1998; Norris, 2000; Scheufele & Nisbet, 2002), factors that should lead to a high cognitive impact. Previous research on the impact of print media use on users supports this claim. For example, research indicates that a strong positive association exists between newspaper use and political knowledge (Becker & Dunwoody, 1982; Berkowitz & Pritchard, 1989; Chaffee & Tims, 1982; Chaffee et al., 1994; Hansen, 2004; Lichter & Noyes, 1995; Patterson, 1980; Patterson & McClure, 1974), therefore suggesting a cognitive impact in that the more people utilize newspapers, the more they know about political content. Although the role and influence of newsmagazines in presidential campaigns has been largely overlooked, newsmagazine readership also requires individual effort to seek out and process political content, which should result in greater cognitive impact than affective impact.

Studies also suggest that use of the Internet for the purpose of acquiring political content compares favorably with traditional print sources in enhancing political knowledge (Eveland & Dunwoody, 2002; Eveland, Marton, & Seo, 2004; Eveland, Seo, & Marton, 2002), again suggesting greater cognitive impact. Thus, on the basis of previous research that has investigated the impact of newspapers, newsmagazines, and the Internet on individuals, it is likely that use of these communication forms exerts greater impact on thoughts than feelings about presidential candidates.

Contrary to expectations, the results indicated that the Internet exerted no impact on thoughts or feelings about either candidate at either phase of the campaign. However, for the print modalities examined here, the expected pattern of influence did occur, but only for one of the candidates: Kerry. For Bush, during both phases of the campaign, use of newspapers or newsmagazines was not related to any cognitive or affective outcomes (see tables 3.1 and 3.3). Thus, whereas our expectation was that print communication forms would influence thoughts more than feelings about candidates, the results for Bush were that communication use impacted neither.

For Kerry, however, some influence was found. During the second phase of the campaign, use of newspapers and newsmagazines was positively associated with more thoughts about Kerry (see table 3.4). This pattern did not appear at phase 1, however. Early in the campaign, use of newspapers and newsmagazines was related only to more positive feelings about Kerry (see table 3.2). Overall, for Kerry, early print media use positively impacted feelings of Kerry, whereas later in the campaign, print communication use exerted cognitive influence, which was anticipated.

Political Conversations

Bennett, Flickinger, and Rhine (2000) argue that "ignoring political discussions risks overlooking an important facet of the ways in which citizens interact with one another in the public arena" (p. 118). Scholars generally agree that mass media use contributes to political talk (Kim, Wyatt, & Katz, 1999; McLeod, Scheufele, & Moy, 1999) and that political conversation is positively associated with political participation (Beck, 2002; Kennamer, 1990; Scheufele, 2000, 2002).

Research consistently indicates that political conversations are associated with enhanced political cognition (Bennett et al., 2000; Eveland, 2004; Kennamer, 1990; Scheufele, 2000, 2002). Robinson and Levy (1986) reported effects that rivaled those of the news media. Taking a cue from Lazarsfeld's two-step flow model (Berelson, Lazarsfeld, & McPhee, 1954; Lazarsfeld, Berelson, & Gaudet, 1948), Lenart (1994) argues that political conversations mediate the cognitive influence of media. Eveland (2004) goes further, revealing that political conversations contribute to cognitive elaboration about information present via other media about candidates, national issues, and foreign policy.

Information that circulates in the marketplace of political ideas is most often antecedent to some other form of mediated exposure (Lippman, 1922). Given America's size, population, and diversity, citizens rarely have direct experience with national political candidates or the issues that require an informed action on Election Day. Most people acquire information about candidates and campaigns through the communication media (Owen, 1991). Further, media content is the substance of conversations. Lenart (1994) argues that "the media play a key role because the content of most politically relevant information, as well as of conversation about politics, is dependent on information obtained from the media" (p. 4).

Most empirical studies of the relationship between political conversations and cognition assume antecedent media exposure as an important moderating influence (Eveland, 2004; Lenart, 1994; Scheufele, 2000, 2002). *The People's*

Choice study found that "ideas often flow from radio and print to the opinion leaders and from them to the less active sections of the population" (Lazarsfeld et al., 1948, p. 151). Scheufele (2000) compared two distinct forms of talk to their participant's antecedent media use: political talk, which consists of national politics, local politics, and neighborhood affairs, and conversational talk, which consists of personal issues, work-related issues, and/or leisure. Scheufele found that people who relied more on "hard news" (e.g., international, national, and local news as well as editorials) were much more likely to engage in political talk than were those who relied more on "entertainment" (e.g., human-interest news stories, crime and action adventure dramas, as well as sitcoms). He reported that "entertainment" users also possessed less political knowledge than "hard news" consumers.

Lenart (1994) found that political conversation was associated with enhanced retention of objective political information that originated in exposure to traditional news media. Eveland (2004) demonstrated similar results but rejected the premise that "individuals glean information from their discussion partner in much the same way that they would gain information from the news media directly" (p. 179). Instead, this author offered two alternative theoretical explanations for the link between conversations and knowledge. Eveland's anticipatory elaboration explanation suggests that "the expectation of impending discussion is an internal motivation that then increases cognitive elaboration on news content" (p. 180). This explanation draws from Petty and Cacioppo's (1986) Elaboration Likelihood Model, which has empirically demonstrated an association between cognitive elaboration and enduring beliefs. Eveland (2004) also posed a discussion-generated explanation for the persistent link between conversation and knowledge that "suggests that the act of engaging in discussion forces meaningful information processing . . . and thus increases learning due to an influence of information processing *during* discussion" (p. 180). Eveland demonstrated that cognitive elaboration of political information offered the most substantial explanation for the link between conversation and knowledge, meaning that merely being exposed to information within a conversational context was insufficient to enhance knowledge retention.

In spite of multiple distinct operational and conceptual definitions of political cognition, as well as the application of stringent controls, empirical tests of the association between political conversation and political knowledge have consistently demonstrated a significant connection. Kennamer (1990) argues that political discussion is a form of political cognition, and he defined cognition as "the ability to name important issues in the campaign and to express political opinions" (p. 349). While controlling for exposure to multiple communication forms, Kennamer found that political knowledge was an important concomitant of political knowledge. Eliosoph (1998) found that political discussion is a "necessary condition for people to make sense of the large amount of political information they have to deal with on a daily basis" (p. 730). Scheufele (2002) confirmed that "talking about certain issues with other citizens will help people to understand these issues in all their complexity, tying them to other, preexisting knowledge, and consequently meaningfully participating in political life" (p. 47). The most striking results were demonstrated by Bennett et al. (2000), who, in spite of stringent controls for demographics and media exposure, found a consistent relationship between public affairs talk and political knowledge in multiple British and American data sets that spanned three decades and "a period of substantial political change in both countries" (p. 117).

Given the consistent findings confirmed under myriad circumstances, it is expected that political conversations would generate a greater cognitive impact on candidate perceptions when compared to the affective impact on these same perceptions. Unfortunately, the data from both phases of this research failed to confirm the association between political cognition and political conversations. The results indicated that political conversations were not related to any cognitive or affective outcome for either Bush or Kerry (see tables 3.1, 3.2, 3.3, and 3.4).

In light of past findings, these outcomes are very surprising. The best explanation for these results concerns our measure of political cognition. While we measured cognition with recognition assessments of broad political opinions, most of the studies that we cited in our literature review equated political cognition with objective political knowledge. Scheufele (2002) measured political knowledge by testing respondents' civic and current affairs knowledge, and Eveland (2004) assessed knowledge as familiarity with prominent political figures, recall of particular candidates, and the ideological placement of two parties, all measures of objective knowledge. Kennamer (1990), on the other hand, used a combination of objective and subjective measures, namely, the number of candidate issue positions that people could identify as well as the number of political opinions one was able to recall. Our measures used recognition-style measures of broad political opinions. By reducing all political knowledge to only a few simply worded statements, it seems reasonable that our measures may have failed to capture the kind of nuanced political opinions that those who engage in frequent political conversations are likely to hold. In other words, where a fine instrument may have been needed, we used a blunt one. Future investigations of the relationship between political talk and cognitions should use measures more specifically tailored to the audience's political knowledge as well as opinions.

Televised Debates

The role of thinking and feeling in televised presidential debates is a bit more intricate, although on the basis of previous research, it is likely that debates exert more of a cognitive than an affective impact. The question is difficult in the context of debates because they are carried via television. Hellweg, Pfau, and Brydon (1992) argue that because debates are televised events, they stress nonverbal over verbal messages and, hence, elevate relational communication over substantive content. Indeed, one study has definitively found that relational messages exert a significant influence in presidential debates (Pfau & Kang, 1991). However, issue content is the focus of most verbal exchanges in debates (Benoit et al., 2002; Joslyn, 1990; Sears & Chaffee, 1979), and, consequently, the preponderance of research demonstrates that televised debates enhance viewers' issue knowledge (The Racine Group, 2002), provide an extensive narrative review (Benoit, Hansen, & Verser, 2003), and offer a meta-analytic review of the learning effects of debates.

Campaign debates are subject to the context in which they occur (Hellweg et al., 1992). In particular, the nature of presidential general election debates as televised events constrains their form and content in important ways. American political discourse may have reached its zenith in the seven senatorial debates between Abraham Lincoln and Stephen Douglas in the election season of 1858. Postman (1985) argues that the Lincoln–Douglas debates "illustrate the power of typography to control the character of discourse" (p. 48). Like the written word itself, those debates were characterized by "semantic, paraphrasable, propositional content" (p. 49). Jamieson (1988) argued that television requires a "new eloquence." Pfau and Kang (1991) postulated that television penalizes the traditional strengths of public speaking (i.e., well-crafted prose and well-reasoned arguments) and rewards the strengths of interpersonal communication (i.e., facial cues, warmth, and immediacy cues). In an experimental study of undergraduate students who were exposed to the first 1988 debate between George H. W. Bush and Michael Dukakis, these authors demonstrated that general attitude, voting intention, and viewer perception were partially accounted for by the candidates' communication of cooperative attitude, warmth, interest, similarity, friendliness, sincerity, and honesty. While these findings suggest that the influence of debates is more complicated than conventionally assumed, they have never been replicated. Sears and Chaffee (1979) reported that there was no statistically significant difference between the reactions of people who watched the televised Carter–Ford debates and those who listened to them. The vast majority of political communication research regarding presidential debates focuses on their superiority "to other communication forms in that they offer an opportunity for candidates to advocate the relative superiority of their positions via a communication venue that facilitates clash, depth, and unfiltered access" (Pfau, 2002, p. 251).

Myriad analyses of presidential debate content, in opposition to other contemporary communication forms, demonstrate their focus on substantive policy issues. The questions posed to candidates by debate moderators are overwhelmingly focused on issue content (Benoit et al., 2002; Joslyn, 1990; Sears & Chaffee, 1979). Sears and Chafee (1979), in their comprehensive summation of 1976 presidential and vice-presidential general election debate research, found that 77 to 80 percent of candidate speaking time was devoted to issue content. According to Hellweg et al. (1992), "Virtually all studies concur that presidential debates increase the manifest information available to the public" (p. 105). Joslyn (1990) adds that "the presidential debates held during the general elections of 1960, 1976, 1980, and 1988 were much more policy oriented than either the news coverage or spot advertisements" (p. 108). Finally, a consortium of political communication scholars concluded that "issue content is the principal focus of the questions posed by moderators and panelists and, therefore, of candidates' responses" (The Racine Group, 2002, p. 207).

Voters reward the presidential debate's issue focus with their rapt attention and some of the highest ratings on television. As the organizing role of political parties in campaigns has diminished, so too has their heuristic utility (Sears & Chaffee, 1979). Within the context of rational choice theory, voters require issue information to weigh their options when selecting the candidate who will most benefit their individual and material interests. Debates provide that information. In a desert of media coverage focused on the "horse race" (Joslyn, 1990), voters find refuge in the issue information provided by general election presidential debates. The "most common reason voters gave for watching debates was to seek issue information" (Sears & Chaffee, 1979, p. 228). Patterson (2002) reports that general election presidential debates rank among the Olympics and the Super Bowl as the three most watched events on television. The advantages to attentive watchers have been clearly demonstrated by the vast preponderance of political campaign communication research (Pfau, 2002).

Empirical evidence has consistently supported the proposition that viewing presidential debates is associated with greater levels of voter learning (Hellweg et al., 1992). Voters often expect that debates will teach them something important about the candidate's substantive policy positions on issues that they perceive as relevant to their interests (Sears & Chaffee, 1979; The Racine Group, 2002). Within the context of Eveland's (2004) anticipatory elaboration explanation (as was explained in the section "Political Conversations" in this chapter), it makes sense that attentive voters will perform more cognitive elaboration on material that may be of later use in situations, for example, such as casting one's vote on Election Day. In a study of media effects, Shrum (2001) stimulated deeper levels of cognitive processing among subjects who believed that their performance had personal relevance. Joslyn (1990) reported that, in spite of hostile formats that limit lengthy statements and lively exchanges, attentive "viewers of the 1960 and 1976 presidential general election debates formed more accurate perceptions of the candidate's positions" (p. 114). The Racine Group (2002) conveyed that "there is strong empirical support for the contribution of television debates to viewer learning. Studies of intra-party and inter-party presidential debates in 1960, 1984, 1992, and 1996 indicate that televised debates enhance learning" (p. 207).

Given the relevance of presidential debate viewing to the voter's decision-making process and debate viewing's consistent association with issue learning, it is expected that people's use of televised presidential debates will be associated with more cognitive than affective perceptions of candidates.

The results offered mixed support for this expectation. During phase 1, the anticipation of debates and at phase 2 the actual viewing of debates were associated with thinking about Bush and Kerry but in contrary patterns: debate use was negatively related to thinking about Bush (see tables 3.1 and 3.3), but it was positively associated with thinking about Kerry (see tables 3.2 and 3.4). Thus, debates seemed to exert contrary influences on cognitive perceptions. Neither the anticipation of debates early in the campaign nor actual debate viewing later exerted an influence on affective perceptions of Kerry. However, for Bush, actual debate viewing was associated with less contentment and more anger. Thus, the pattern of results suggests that debate viewing exerts both cognitive and affective impact on viewers. If anything, the results confirm the position that it is hard to disentangle cognitive and affective elements of political influence (Lazarus, 1982, 1984; Lodge & Taber, 2000; Zajonc, 1980) and that the verbal content of debates contributes to cognition, whereas their televised form may elevate affect.

Political Talk Radio

Political talk radio has become "a powerful source of communication for conservative causes and candidates" (Pfau, Cho, & Chong, 2001, p. 97) and exerts significant influence on prospective voters' perceptions of candidates (Hollander, 1994, 1996; Lee & Cappella, 2001; Moy & Pfau, 2000; Owen, 1997; Pfau et al., 1997, 1999, 2001). Political talk radio users report that a desire for information is a primary motivation for listening (Hofstetter et al., 1994; Owen, 1995), a motivation that hints at a cognitive function of talk radio. However, political talk radio does carry a strong affective bias. For example, most listeners are partisan (Hollander, 1996; Lee & Cappella, 2001), and their use of political talk radio enables them to "experience and vent a wide range of emotions while considering political actors, issues, and events" (Owen, 1997, p. 337). Furthermore, contemporary political talk radio revolves around a host who presents views and opinions on social issues in a manner that is passionate, animated, and provocative (Davis & Owen, 1998), using his or her persona to entertain listeners, thus compelling the audience to pay attention. The most popular hosts working in today's talk radio landscape boast a politically conservative disposition and convey a sense of anger regarding many political and social issues, and it is this projection of anger or "lashing out" that makes such programs so popular. Ultimately, political talk radio is a communication form that, quite simply, exudes emotion (Herbst, 1995; Pfau et al., 1999). Because previous research indicates that political talk radio is more of an emotional communication form, we anticipated that talk radio would exert more impact on users' feelings than thoughts about political candidates.

An examination of our data, however, indicated that use of talk radio impacted *both* the cognitive and the affective perceptions of each candidate. For example, during both phases of this project, use of talk radio was positively associated with thoughts about and positive feelings of contentment toward Bush, and during the first phase of the study, talk radio use was negatively associated with anger toward Bush (see tables 3.1 and 3.3). Use of political talk radio also impacted thoughts and feelings about Kerry, though in an opposite pattern than the one found for Bush. That is, during both phases of the study, use of talk radio led to higher levels of reported anger felt toward Kerry and led to fewer thoughts about Kerry, though this second association was a weak one during phase 1 (see tables 3.2 and 3.4). In addition, early in the campaign, use of political talk radio led to less feelings of contentment toward Kerry, though this relationship was weak.

Overall, then, the use of political talk radio exhibited both affective and cognitive impact on listeners. Admittedly, people claim they are drawn to political talk radio for information (Hofstetter et al., 1994; Owen, 1995), but listeners are heavily partisan (Hollander, 1996; Lee & Cappella, 2001), and listening exudes emotion (Herbst, 1995; Owen, 1997; Pfau et al., 1999). Thus, political talk radio has been shown to exhibit both cognitive and affective influence on listeners. This dual impact can be explained by the possibility that while it is the affective component that entertains listeners and thus motivates listeners to attend to the programs, the content disseminated on political talk radio—which is often focused on political and social issues—is still cognitively processed by listeners, even those who use the modality to serve an emotional need. In this way, talk radio can impact both listeners' thoughts and feelings about political candidates. In retrospect, results of this study showing a balance of cognitive and affective perceptions are not all that surprising.

Movies/DVDs

Movies/DVDs are, perhaps, the most powerful communication form in eliciting emotion in users (Blair, 1996; Forgas & Moylan, 1987). Research of viewer responses to politically charged films, such as *Roots* (Surlin, 1978) and *JFK* (Butler, Koopman, & Zimbardo, 1995), revealed significant elevation in a number of viewer emotions. Indeed, researchers of mood and affect have employed film clips for the explicit purpose of eliciting specific emotions (Gross & Levinson, 1995). During the 2004 presidential campaign, the movie (and later DVD) *Fahrenheit 9/11*, which critiqued President Bush's response to 9/11 and his decision to invade Iraq, seemed to function as a partisan lightning rod, enthusiastically embraced by Democrats and reviled by Republicans (Annenberg Public Policy Center, 2004b).

The 2004 presidential election campaign marked the first time that an overtly partisan movie was released for the primary purpose of directly influencing prospective voters. Kathleen Hall Jamieson called *Fahrenheit 9/11* a "remarkable" political spectacle (in Farhi, 2004), but the Michael Moore film was hardly the only cinematic attempt to influence the presidential contest. Other politically motivated documentary-style films released during the 2004 campaign included *Outfoxed*, *The Faith of George W. Bush*, *Bush's Brain*, *The World according to Bush*, *Control Room*, and *Fear and the Selling of American Empire*, to name just a few.

Hollywood's recent and direct attempt to enter the 2004 political campaign should not obfuscate the cinema's role in American political history. At least since W. D. Griffith's *The Birth of a Nation*, movies have made political statements and, as such, have affected the cultural landscape on which politics are conducted. According to Robins and Post (1997), Griffith's film (originally titled *The Clansmen*) was widely credited with sparking a resurgence of the Ku Klux Klan, and it also established a cinematic pattern characterized by naturalizing stories with filmic and aural techniques, advocating strong moral messages; telling simple, definitive, and one-sided stories; manifesting forces of good and evil in people; injecting heroes who represent the audience; and conveying a powerful emotional tone. Robins and Post (1997) maintain that movies represent powerful "cultural, intellectual, and political influences. Research suggests that films, such as the antinuclear *The Day After*, the anti-Soviet *Amerika*, *Holocaust*, and the multigenerational saga of a black family, *Roots*," exerted some influence on beliefs and feelings (p. 3).

Filmmakers' ability to use this medium's structure to stimulate emotion has grown in recent years. Schwartz (1973) observes that the electronic media have cultivated a store of standardized experiences that persuaders can invoke in order to strike a "subjective" responsive chord among their target audiences. Through a process of classical conditioning, inherent in decades of electronic media consumption, audiences have come to treat particular stimuli as an "objective correlatives" for the feelings with which they have been persistently associated (Williamson, 1978). Blair (1996) observed that conventionalized visual images (e.g., colors, people in uniform, landscapes, and animals) can be used to "cause feelings and attitudes and to evoke responses" (p. 13). More specifically, Blair argues that movies "can bring us as close to actual experiential knowledge as it is possible get, short of living the experience . . . movies can bring us to the experience the panoply of emotions—impatience, fear, disappointment, joy, rage, frustration, contentment" (p. 61). Feelings produce a sense of ownership that is impossible to achieve with a cold, detached cognitive experience (Williamson, 1978; Zajonc, 1980). Movies dramatically engage their target audiences and in the process assemble their several disparate beliefs, feelings, and components of self-image under one narrative umbrella. *Fahrenheit 9/11*, as only one example, embodies these powerful cinematic levers.

Fahrenheit 9/11, which was created by and stars Michael Moore, employs a powerful and affectively resonant narrative structure. Moore presents himself as a common-man heroic figure. Moore's argument is that Bush is a tyrant who sees the economic elite as his base, advances business interests through continuous war (e.g., the oil and military production industries), and uses undercover informants to infiltrate the peaceful organizations of his enemies. Moore makes his argument with an ambitious array of visual images. For example, he uses a split screen to depict President Bush stubbornly reading *My Pet Goat* to an elementary school classroom while jumbo jets are shown crashing into the World Trade Centers. O'Brien (2004) makes the case that "simply by making the recent past visible—by bringing these little pieces of reality into the movie theatre—Moore unleashes a reservoir of feeling. It's almost like the symbolic breaking of a spell: we can begin to remember everything we started to forget" (p. 21).

Of course, the "we" that *Fahrenheit 9/11* speaks to is not a broad, general audience. The National Annenberg Election Survey (Annenberg Public Policy Center, 2004b) found that the overwhelming majority of the film's attendees already agreed with its partisan positions. The film was not so much a piece of political propaganda as it was a piece of political therapy for Democrats who felt deeply betrayed by the 2000 election, the war in Iraq, and many other policies of the Bush administration. Much like television commercials, the emotionally laden visual content of this movie seeks to connect more with the audience's self-image than to intellectually engage viewers (Williamson, 1978). Blair (1996) explains that movies exploit "unconscious, unexamined identifications" (p. 44). Like television commercials, movies can easily use the "overt, surface, verbal argumentation of the spoken script to mask the manipulation of feelings by the music, the drama, and the visuals" (p. 43).

Research indicates that movies instill affect in their audiences. Studies have shown that even the subliminal or mere exposure to pictures of affect-laden faces is associated with brain activity, skin conductivity (Morris, Ohman, & Dolan, 1998), and parallel facial motor activity as evidenced by electromyographic (EMG) reactions (Dimberg, Thunberg, & Elmehed, 2000). Huston and colleagues (1992) report the findings of several studies associating filmed images of loving activity, humor, violence, and horror with physiological reactions. Gross and Levenson (1995) used subjective reports to reveal that sixteen film clips reliably produce eight distinct emotions (i.e., amusement, anger, contentment, disgust, fear, neutral, sadness, and surprise). Rottenberg, Ray, and Gross (in press) report that about one-third of women who viewed their sadness clip actually cried.

On the basis of evidence suggesting the potential for movies/DVDs to instill emotion, we anticipated that more use of this communication form would elicit more affective than cognitive perceptions of candidates. The pattern of results revealed that, both early and late in the 2004 campaign, movie/DVD use was associated with more affective than cognitive perceptions. Perhaps a slightly more accurate assessment of the relevant results is that this communication form elicited a combination of cognitive and affective perceptions. During both phases, use of movies/DVDs was associated with feelings of contentment toward Kerry and more thoughts about Kerry (see tables 3.2 and 3.4). In addition, at phase 2, use of movies/DVDs was associated with fewer feelings of contentment with Bush, less anger toward Kerry, and fewer thoughts about Bush (see tables 3.3 and 3.4).

Movies are intrinsically affective instruments of influence (Forgas & Moylan, 1987), but our measures were not designed to distinguish time order of the emotional and cognitive effects on respondents. Lazarus (1982, 1984) and Zajonc (1980) agree that emotion and cognition are often intimately connected, but Zajonc contends that emotion serially precedes cognitions. He argues that "most of the time, information collected about alternatives serves less for making a decision than for justifying it afterward" (p. 155). Thus, Zajonc (1984) argues for the primacy of affect. It is possible that some movies/DVDs, such as *Fahrenheit 9/11*, instill a set of emotions so powerful that they subsequently impact respondents' cognitive perceptions. To further study this possibility, researchers need to examine the influence of political films under experimental conditions in order to distinguish the time order of cognitive and affective impacts.

Radio and Printed Materials

Many communication forms have not been studied as to their cognitive or affective influence on political perception. There is no consistent rationale to base clear expectations about the cognitive or affective bias of communication forms such as printed materials (e.g., direct mail, flyers, and yard signs) or radio news. These and other communication forms (e.g., newsmagazines) have been "neglected" in political communication research (Chaffee et al., 1994, p. 309).

Before it was supplanted by television, radio was an important source of political news (Davis, 1996). What little radio news still exists is now confined largely to superficial hourly reports and publicly funded programming, such as National Public Radio (NPR). Patterson (2002) reports that sophisticated news consumers, frustrated by the commercial network's emphasis on soft news coverage, have flocked to public radio. In recent years, over two-thirds of public radio programming earned higher ratings, and NPR has experienced a 300 percent increase in audience share since the early 1990s. This resurgence of interest in radio news is worthy of attention, but there is so little systematic evidence that we are unable to offer a meaningful expectation about how this communication form will impact users' thoughts or feelings about political candidates. On the one hand, audio's influence has been traced to its cognitive content (Pfau, 1990); on the other hand, auditory mediums have actually been shown to frustrate their audience's capacity to comprehend complicated arguments (Chaiken & Eagly, 1976). Schwartz (1973) contends that the voices conveyed by radio speak to their audiences in an intimately personal space and that they are perceived as more real than actual face-to-face interaction. Given the lack of available evidence to reasonably support either a cognitive or an affective bias, we simply probed whether people's use of the radio news during the 2004 presidential campaign generated more cognitive or affective (or perhaps mixed) perceptions of candidates.

With respect to their influence on cognition or affect, printed materials are an even less understood mechanism of political campaign communication. In a test of the mere exposure hypothesis, Harrison (1977) reported that the posting of campaign flyers for a fictitious candidate across a large college campus was associated with positive affect and votes for the nonexistent person. On the other hand, ample evidence demonstrates that printed subject matter is associated with greater levels of cognition, more elaborate processing, and substantive judgments (Chaiken & Eagly, 1976; Pfau, 1990; Postman, 1985).

Nevertheless, we are unaware of any empirical data on the cognitive impact of direct mail in particular. Direct mail is targeted to particular audience segments as part of a broader campaign of political influence. Meyrowitz (1992) maintains that when mediated personas communicate through multiple venues (e.g., direct mail and televised advertising), they are perceived as real. There is scant evidence on the influence of printed matter in campaigns, let alone about the cognitive and affective bias of this communication form. Thus, we simply probed the relationship of people's use of printed materials during the 2004 campaign absent specific expectations for cognitive and affective bias.

The pattern of results revealed that radio news exerted a mix of cognitive and affective influence, while printed material failed to register any significant influence. Given the paucity of empirical evidence regarding radio news (Chaffee et al., 1994), our findings are important. Radio news' impact was felt later in the campaign. People who relied more on radio news experienced less contentment with Bush, and they manifested more negative thoughts about the incumbent president (see table 3.3). At the same time, those who used radio news during phase 2 revealed less anger toward Kerry (see table 3.4).

Other Televised Forms

The remaining communication forms involve television, but here the logic for cognitive or affective bias runs both ways. There is some evidence that television entertainment talk shows and political comedy exert cognitive influence. On the other hand, because television inherently prizes visual over verbal content (Meyrowitz, 1985), it elevates the role and impact of source considerations in influence (e.g., Chaiken & Eagly, 1983; Graber, 1976; Meyrowitz, 1985; Pfau, 1990; Worchel, Andreoli, & Eason, 1975), particularly the influence of positive relational cues (Chesebro, 1984; Chesebro & Bertelsen, 1996; Pfau & Kang, 1991). As Delli Carpini and Williams (1998) explain, "Television consciously mimics the elements of immediate personal exchange" (p. 151). This suggests the potential for an affective bias on the part of more entertainment-oriented television forms. Richards (2004) supports this position, arguing that "the incursion of political experience of the values of popular culture means that we now seek certain kinds of emotionalized experience from politics that we have not done in the past" (p. 340).

Postmodernism has been credited with blurring the line that separates entertainment and information in contemporary political culture (Richards, 2004). The fuzziness of the line between entertainment and information was made evident in the 1992 presidential election when the three presidential candidates appeared on *Larry King Live* a total of thirteen times, and Bill

Clinton made his famous "boxers over briefs" comment on *MTV* (Davis & Owen, 1998). Scholars call these communication forums "new media" or "nontraditional media." Moy and Pfau (2000) observe that new media are "non-traditional . . . because their goal is not to disseminate public information, yet they provide a large portion of Americans with information about current affairs" (p. 180). Davis and Owen (1998) report that "entertainment is critical to the new media's ability to retain and increase their audience" (p. 18). Delli Carpini and Williams (1998) add that "understanding the impact of television on the construction of public opinion requires expanding the definition of politically relevant television to include both fictional and non-fictional programming" (p. 155). In an analysis of how focus group participants integrated media into their discussion of environmental pollution, Delli Carpini and Williams (1998) found that nearly half of media citations included references to fictional media (e.g., *The Simpsons* and *The Day After*) and/or entertainment personalities (e.g., Cyndi Lauper and Captain Planet). Pfau and colleagues (2001) observed that "the 2000 presidential election may be remembered . . . for once and for all trampling the boundaries that once separated serious campaign discourse and parody" (p. 89).

Empirical research provides strong support for the new media's cognitive influence as measured by greater political knowledge. The National Annenberg Election Survey (2004) revealed that viewers of late-night entertainment talk shows (*The Tonight Show* and *Late Night with David Letterman*) and late-night comedy shows (*The Daily Show with Jon Stewart*) were more likely than nonviewers to know information about candidates and their positions on issues. These results are consistent with Chaffee et al.'s (1994) finding that television is the equal of newspapers in the conventionalized sense, as it conveys live speeches and events, provides information about the candidates as both policymakers and persons, and correlates with greater retention of candidate issue information. Delli Carpini and Williams (1998) found that entertaining political content, even if partially fictionalized, could elicit political conversations. Political talk's association with enhanced political cognitions and knowledge has been well documented (Bennett et al., 2000; Eveland, 2004; Kennamer, 1990; Scheufele, 2000, 2002).

On the other hand, the new media also seem intrinsically oriented toward affect. Moy and Pfau (2000) argued that the goal of the new media is not to teach. Pfau (2003) calls viewers of these communication forms the politically marginally attentive. They turn to these programs for diversionary entertainment. Under such conditions, any political information that is retained should be viewed as merely incidental. Krugman (1977) has convincingly argued that television is a right-brain medium, and the right brain has been shown to represent the brain's emotional functions. As a result, Krugman

(1971) insists that television is a low-involvement medium and thus is hostile to traditional learning (Petty & Cacioppo, 1979). Chaiken and Eagly (1976) found that television inhibited the comprehension of complicated messages. Worchel et al. (1975) demonstrated that television elevated the interpersonal content of a persuasive message. Pfau (1990) found that persuasion via "the relational dimension accounts for more variance in television communication, whereas content is responsible for more variance in radio, print, and public address communication" (p. 208). Pfau and Kang (1991) demonstrated that the relational dimension of similarity/depth accounted for a significant amount of attitude formation among subjects who watched the first 1988 presidential debate.

The impact of these recently politicized televised communication forms is mixed with experimental and theoretical evidence supporting their affective impact and survey evidence supporting their cognitive impact. For the purposes of this discussion, we understand the new televised communication forms to include television talk shows (*Donahue* and *Larry King Live*), television entertainment talk shows (*The Tonight Show* and *The Daily Show*), television news magazines (*60 Minutes* and *48 Hours*), television political drama (*K Street* and *The West Wing*), and television comedic shows (*Saturday Night Live* and *Mad TV*). Given the lack of consensus regarding the cognitive influence of the previously mentioned forms, this investigation simply probed whether people's use of television talk shows, television entertainment talk shows, television newsmagazines, television political drama, and televised comedic shows during the 2004 presidential campaign generated cognitive, affective, or mixed perceptions.

The results were interesting. Late-night television entertainment talk was associated with feelings about both Bush and Kerry during both phases of the campaign (see tables 3.1, 3.2, 3.3, and 3.4). During both phases of the campaign, television entertainment talk show use was associated with feelings of contentment toward Bush, although this relationship was weak. However, the valence changed over time: early on it was negative, but later it was positive. In addition, use of television entertainment talk shows was associated with less anger toward Kerry during phase 1, although this effect dissipated by phase 2. Use of this communication form revealed no cognitive effects. The pattern of results suggests that television entertainment talk is a communication form that is exclusively associated with emotional perceptions of presidential candidates.

Consistent with Delli Carpini and Williams's (1998) finding that fictional television programming affects political attitudes, our results revealed significant relationships between people's use of television political drama and their anger toward both candidates during phase 1: the valence was positive for Bush and negative for Kerry, meaning that use was associated with greater anger toward Bush and less anger toward Kerry. However, there were no significant effects at phase 2. The results are interesting in that it seems as if televised political dramas, such as *The West Wing* and *K Street*, may elicit comparisons of real politicians to the fictionalized ones presented on television. The nature of these comparisons warrants further inquiry since their implications for presidential campaign influence may be important.

Further evidence of the affective bias of these televised communication forms is found in the paucity of relationships involving these venues and thoughts about either of the candidates. Television newsmagazines registered the only cognitive impact, later in the campaign for Bush, but it was only marginally significant.

Conclusion

This investigation sought to understand the ways in which different communication forms impact both the cognitive and the affective components of individual attitudes. If, as Ryfe (2003) argues, communication forms embody both cognition and emotion and if attitudes are comprised of both an affective and a cognitive component (Cacioppo et al., 1989; Eagly & Chaiken, 1993; Rosenburg & Hovland, 1960), then it is likely that communication forms will be associated with varying affective and cognitive perceptions, such that some communication forms manifest more cognitive than affective perceptions, others more affective than cognitive perceptions, and still others a relatively even mix of both.

Previous research in the area of media effects has provided some evidence to support the claim of different cognitive and affective influence among various communication forms. For example, research on the effects of using print modalities has illustrated a pattern of cognitive impact on users (Becker & Dunwoody, 1982; Berkowitz & Pritchard, 1989; Chaffee & Tims, 1982; Chaffee et al., 1994; Hansen, 2004; Lichter & Noyes, 1995; Patterson, 1980; Patterson & McClure, 1976). Therefore, with regard to print media, previous research indicates that using these communication forms would impact the cognitive components of an individual's attitude more than the affective aspects of that attitude. Conversely, the communication form of movies/DVDs exudes more emotion than, perhaps, any other communication form in this study (Blair, 1996; Forgas & Moylan, 1987). Therefore, it seems logical that use of movies/DVDs would impact users' feelings about an attitude object more than it would thoughts about an object.

Although some of the patterns of differentiated cognitive and affective bias suggested by previous media research were supported by the results of this investigation, overall, the use of most communication forms seemed to elicit both affective and cognitive perceptions. Perhaps the position of Zajonc (1980), Ryfe (2003), and Richards (2004) is right: most communication elicits both reason and emotion, and seldom does communication generate one without the other. This position is consistent with theory and research on emotion, which posits that reason and emotion are inextricably intertwined (Lazarus & Lazarus, 1994; Zajonc, 1980) and that affect depends on reasoning. Or, in the words of Lazarus and Lazarus (1994), reasoning is "the heart of the emotion process" (p. 143). These results are also consistent with recent political communication scholarship indicating that negative emotions, such as anger, stimulate thinking, which can result in a reassessment of political preferences. Thus, emotion and thought are "essentially complementary" processes (Marcus et al., 2000, p. 140).

Most communication forms were associated with a blending of cognitive and affective perceptions about candidates, suggesting a complementary pattern. Ultimately, then, if most communication forms, even those that might appear on the surface to be more affective in nature, elicit both cognitive and affective perceptions about candidates, this is an outcome that we view as more positive for American democracy than if the results had indicated that many widely used forms are associated with largely affective responses. Graber echoes this position. Relying on recent research by Rahn (2000) and others, Graber (2004) maintains that emotion, in combination with "cognitive resources," "is an essential element" in "well-reasoned" political judgments (p. 557). Damasio (2003) agrees that emotion is complimentary to the decision-making process and states that "the emotional signal is not a substitute for proper reasoning. It has an auxiliary role, increasing the efficiency of the reasoning process and making it speedier" (p. 148). Thus, the presence of emotion and cognition indicates a more complete decision-making process, a position that is reinforced by our results. Overall, most communication forms were related to a blending of cognitive and emotional perceptions about candidates, suggesting that communication use is part of a complex media landscape that, at least with regard to cognitive and affective influence, may be providing prospective voters with a broad range of tools that are needed to make political decisions.

NOTES

1. Hierarchical regression analyses were employed to assess hypotheses and research questions about expectations related to communication use and affective and cognitive perceptions of the candidates during the 2004 presidential election. The full

regression equations for the phase 1 survey, conducted during mid- and late September, were significant for all dependent variables—for Bush: feelings of contentment, $F(24, 380) = 6.76, p < .001$; anger, $F(24, 380) = 7.475, p < .001$; and cognitive perceptions, $F(24, 380) = 16.52, p < .001$; and for Kerry: contentment, $F(24, 380) = 6.40, p < .001$; anger, $F(24, 380) = 4.32, p < .001$; and cognitive perceptions, $F(24, 380) = 13.74, p < .001$.

The full regression equations for the phase 2 survey, which were administered during the last two weeks of the 2004 campaign, were significant for all dependent variables—for Bush: feelings of contentment, $F(24, 380) = 10.97, p < .001$; anger, $F(24, 380) = 7.24, p < .001$; and cognitive perceptions, $F(24, 380) = 19.31, p < .001$; and for Kerry: contentment, $F(24, 380) = 6.40, p < .001$; anger, $F(24, 380) = 6.645, p < .001$; and cognitive perceptions, $F(24, 380) = 15.57, p < .001$.

2. Overall, sociodemographic variables dwarfed communication variables in the total variance accounted for on affective and cognitive perceptions of the candidates at phase 1. The combined sociodemographic variables accounted for 26 percent and communication use 4 percent of the variance in feelings of contentment with Bush, 27 and 7 percent of variance in feelings of anger toward Bush, and 45 and 6 percent of variance in cognitive perceptions of Bush. Sociodemographic variables were responsible for 22 percent and communication use 7 percent of the variance in feelings of contentment with Kerry, 15.5 and 6 percent of variance in feelings of anger toward Kerry, and 39 and 7 percent of variance in cognitive perceptions of Kerry.

Again at phase 2, sociodemographic variables exerted much greater influence than communication variables in affective and cognitive perceptions of candidates. Sociodemographic variables accounted for 34 percent and communication use 7 percent of the variance in feelings of contentment with Bush, 27 and 5 percent of the variance in feelings of anger toward Bush, and 48 and 8 percent of the variance in cognitive perceptions of Bush. Sociodemographic variables were responsible for 22 percent and communication use 7 percent of the variance in feelings of contentment with Kerry, 21 and 9 percent of the variance in feelings of anger toward Kerry, and 40 and 10 percent of the variance in cognitive perceptions of Kerry.

Table 3.1. Phase 1 Media Use and Feelings and Thinking about George Bush

	Feel Contentment	Feel Anger	Thinking
Control variables			
Gender (male)	−.05	.04	−.02
Age	.03	−.01	.01
Education	−.11**	.115**	−.08**
Income	.02	.07	.02
Party identification (Democrat)	−.26*	.16*	−.32*
Party identification (Republican)	.25*	−.32*	.36*
Political expertise	.02	.06	−.01
R^2	.26*	.27*	.45*
Communication use			
Network television news	.01	−.085	.07
Local television news	−.02	.02	−.02
Newspapers	−.04	−.07	−.06
Magazines	.02	−.05	−.05
Political talk radio	.13**	−.13**	.16*
Radio news	−.015	−.02	.01
Television talk	.00	.02	−.02
Television entertainment talk	−.10+	−.05	−.045
Television political drama	−.035	.11**	−.035
Television comedic shows	.01	.03	−.07
Television newsmagazines	.00	.04	.00
Movies/DVDs	.05	.10+	−.07
Web	−.07	−.03	−.02
Candidate debates	−.09	.03	−.105**
Candidate ads	.14**	−.03	.09+
Conversations	−.05	−.01	−.02
Printed materials	.04	−.025	.045
Incremental R^2	.04	.07**	.06*
Model F(24, 380)	6.76*	7.475*	16.52*

Note. Entries are standardized coefficients from ordinary-least-squares regression.
* Significant at $p < .01$.
** Significant at $p < .05$.
+ Significant at $p < .10$.

Table 3.2. Phase 1 Media Use and Feelings and Thinking about John Kerry

	Feel Contentment	Feel Anger	Thinking
Control variables			
Gender (male)	−.07	−.01	.09**
Age	−.01	.05	−.06
Education	.00	−.015	−.02
Income	−.01	−.04	.02
Party identification (Democrat)	.24*	−.19*	.32*
Party identification (Republican)	−.21*	.17*	−.28*
Political expertise	−.08	.01	−.065
R^2	.22*	.155*	.39*
Communication use			
Network television news	−.02	.05	−.01
Local television news	.03	.00	.01
Newspapers	.04	−.01	.06
Magazines	.11**	−.01	.03
Political talk radio	−.10+	.14**	−.09+
Radio news	.00	.06	−.08
Television talk	.02	.00	−.01
Television entertainment talk	.00	−.11+	−.06
Television political drama	−.06	−.12**	−.05
Television comedic shows	−.02	.04	.03
Television newsmagazines	.05	−.08	.065
Movies/DVDs	.16*	.10	.13*
Web	−.03	−.075	−.085+
Candidate debates	.08	−.09	.135*
Candidate ads	.00	.05	−.07
Conversations	−.01	−.03	.00
Printed materials	.07	.07	.02
Incremental R^2	.07*	.06**	.07*
Model F(24, 380)	6.40*	4.32*	13.74*

Note. Entries are standardized coefficients from ordinary-least-squares regression.
* Significant at $p < .01$.
** Significant at $p < .05$.
+ Significant at $p < .10$.

Table 3.3. Phase 2 Media Use and Feelings and Thinking about George Bush

	Feel Contentment	Feel Anger	Thinking
Control variables			
Gender (male)	−.04	−.03	.04
Age	.065	−.01	.03
Education	−.06	.09+	−.11*
Income	.00	−.06	.06
Party identification (Democrat)	−.31*	.14*	−.345*
Party identification (Republican)	.26*	−.36*	.32*
Political expertise	.09+	−.02	.065
R^2	.34*	.27*	.48*
Communication use			
Network television news	.03	−.015	.10**
Local television news	.04	.085	.015
Newspapers	−.03	.075	−.02
Magazines	−.04	.00	−.02
Political talk radio	.19*	−.075	.19*
Radio news	−.13**	.04	−.11*
Television talk	−.08	−.04	−.01
Television entertainment talk	.11+	−.06	.06
Television political drama	.00	.06	.03
Television comedic shows	.01	.06	−.02
Television newsmagazines	.00	.06	−.09+
Movies/DVDs	−.16*	.09	−.19*
Web	.03	.01	.01
Candidate debates	−.15*	.11**	−.145*
Candidate ads	.08	−.04	−.05
Conversations	.02	−.05	.06
Printed materials	.03	.07	−.02
Incremental R^2	.07*	.05+	.08*
Model F(24, 380)	10.97*	7.24*	19.31*

Note. Entries are standardized coefficients from ordinary-least-squares regression.
* Significant at $p < .01$.
** Significant at $p < .05$.
+ Significant at $p < .10$.

Table 3.4. Phase 2 Media Use and Feelings and Thinking about John Kerry

	Feel Contentment	Feel Anger	Thinking
Control variables			
Gender (male)	−.06	.09	.04
Age	.05	.07	.03
Education	−.01	−.07	.065
Income	.02	.04	−.04
Party identification (Democrat)	.22*	−.25*	.24*
Party identification (Republican)	−.245*	.10+	−.33*
Political expertise	.03	.05	−.055
R^2	.22*	.21*	.40*
Communication use			
Network television news	−.05	.09	.02
Local television news	.105+	−.09	.005
Newspapers	.04	.00	.09**
Magazines	.04	−.06	.10**
Political talk radio	−.07	.21*	−.15*
Radio news	.045	−.09+	.015
Television talk	.00	−.025	.01
Television entertainment talk	−.10	−.07	.02
Television political drama	.04	.06	.03
Television comedic shows	.06	.04	.03
Television newsmagazines	.025	−.07	.04
Movies/DVDs	.16*	−.18*	.14*
Web	−.01	.05	−.02
Candidate debates	.03	−.06	.11**
Candidate ads	.03	.06	−.06
Conversations	−.07	.07	−.06
Printed materials	.03	−.04	.01
Incremental R^2	.07*	.09*	.10*
Model F(24, 380)	6.40*	6.645*	15.57*

Note. Entries are standardized coefficients from ordinary-least-squares regression.
* Significant at $p < .01$.
** Significant at $p < .05$.
+ Significant at $p < .10$.

Chapter Four

Perceiving Presidential Candidates

> The election of 2004 . . . revealed that we live in a new media environment.
>
> —Cathy Young, *Boston Globe* columnist
> (MIT Communications Forum, 2005, p. 1)

Media effects research addresses how the use of media impacts an individual. The *impact* of interest to media effects researchers is most often conceptualized in terms of one of two types of effects: how media use impacts a user's attitudes, which consist of some combination of thoughts and feelings, or how media use affects a user's behaviors. The attitudinal impact of media use often involves the way that media usage and attitudes interconnect. For example, an exploration of the relationship between media use and attitudes may ask a question such as, How do attitudes about a current military conflict differ for those who watch network television news compared to those who read newsmagazines? This type of question seeks to understand whether an attitude changes as media use changes. As discussed in the previous chapter, attitudes consist of affective and cognitive elements, so thoughts or feelings about an attitude object may be affected by media use, but it is ultimately attitude that is the preoccupation of most media effects research.

The question of how media usage impacts users' behavior is much more difficult because behavior is an active process that must be observed in order to be measured precisely. Because of the difficulty of observing people performing specific actions, behavior is often measured by having people report the likelihood with which they will engage in whatever behavior is being studied. Thus, examples of media effects questions about behavior might be, Will viewers of healthy-lifestyle information contained in a television news program or in an entertainment program be more likely to adopt the healthy behavior recommended? Or, more specific to this study, Will viewers of presidential debates or some other communication form alter the likelihood of voting for a particular candidate? These types of questions get at how media usage impacts behavior. The response to questions that seek to understand media–behavior relationships involve an indication of how likely it is that a person intends to perform the behavior in question.

As noted previously, the term "media" is broad, encompassing within its bounds many discrete communication forms, from traditional news venues such as newspapers and network television news to entertainment-based forms such as comedy and prime-time drama. Hence, we prefer the term "communication forms," which includes the complete multiplicity of mass media venues plus nonmedia forms, such as political conversations.

However, this phase of the investigation follows the media effects tradition in that it seeks to understand the relationship between people's communication use and their perceptions of the presidential candidates during the 2004 general election campaign. While the specific procedures and methodology for this project are explained thoroughly in the appendix, it is worth noting that the respondents' *perceptions* of presidential candidates in this investigation include both the attitudinal and the behavioral components typically found in most media effects research. Ultimately, three separate measures were utilized to measure respondents' perceptions of the 2004 presidential candidates: the respondents' overall attitude about candidates, the perception of the candidate's character, and the likelihood of voting for candidates.

Determining what communication forms people rely on for information about candidates and campaigns, coupled with the knowledge about how people perceive candidates, allows us to understand how communication use affects political perceptions. For example, this investigation explored whether users of political talk radio manifested perceptions of George W. Bush that are markedly different than the attitudes that are held by users of other communication forms, such as network television news, newspapers, or newsmagazines. Or, to use another example, the study probed whether respondents who consume large amounts of television comedic shows revealed different perceptions of John Kerry than users of television talks shows or other communication forms.

The current generation of studies investigating the effects of communication form use—the family of studies to which this investigation belongs—employs survey data to examine the relative influence of communication on people's perceptions of candidates. This approach assumes that the campaign communication environment is increasingly "interwoven" (Owen, 1991) in that campaign communication that is initiated in one venue then matriculates into other forms, and these secondary communication venues include both traditional media and some "new media." As noted in the appendix, this increasingly "fragmented" political communication environment produces "measurement and conceptual problems . . . in disentangling the impact of various sources of information" (West, 2000, p. 155). An appropriate approach to account for this multimedia environment is to measure the impact of all relevant forms simultaneously, parsing the influence of any one form while controlling for the influence of all other forms. That was the approach taken in this investigation, which featured surveys of respondents at two points during the 2004 presidential election campaign. The study examined what communication people use and how they perceive presidential candidates. The results reveal the influence of relevant sociodemographic variables on people's perceptions of candidates, the net impact of specific communication forms on perceptions of candidates, and how these influences varied across the 2004 general election campaign. It is this last question that is addressed first.

AS THE CAMPAIGN UNFOLDS

Overall, analysis of the data collected for this project suggests that the impact of people's communication use on their perceptions of candidates is modest[1] but increases as an election nears.[2] The pattern of results clearly revealed that the influence of communication on people's perceptions of candidates increased as the campaign unfolded. During phase 1 of this project, during September of the election year, combined communication forms were responsible for 5, 6, and 4 percent of variances, respectively, in dependent measures for incumbent Bush (perception of character, overall attitude, and likelihood of voting for) and 8 percent of variances on all dependent measures for challenger Kerry. By phase 2, from mid-October right up until the eve of the general election, combined communication forms accounted for 7, 8, and 7 percent of variances, respectively, in dependent measures for Bush and 9, 8, and 10 percent of variances, respectively, in dependent measures for Kerry.

The pattern of results indicates that the influence of people's communication use on their perceptions of presidential candidates increases, albeit modesty, as the election draws nearer. This suggests that communication use begets even more communication use as a presidential campaign unfolds (Chaffee, 1986; Holbert, 2005). Ultimately, Barber (2003) is right in asserting that "communication is at the heart of democracy" (p. xiv), and as Election Day nears, communication increasingly affects people's perceptions of candidates and the likelihood of voting for them.

SPECIFIC INFLUENCES ON PEOPLE'S PERCEPTIONS

This investigation examined the influence of sociodemographic variables (which involve the characteristics of respondents) and then, controlling for their impact, examined the influence of communication forms. We anticipated that both affect people's perceptions of candidates but that sociodemographics, especially party identification, exert the greatest impact.

Sociodemographic Variables

Overall, the sociodemographic variables measured in this project accounted for more of the difference in respondents' perceptions of presidential candidates than did different levels of communication form use. This is not surprising given the proven power of party identification as a predictor of perceptions of candidates. Party identification has been the dominant explanation of voting behavior ever since Campbell and colleagues (see Campbell, Converse, Miller, & Stokes, 1960; Campbell, Gurin, & Miller, 1954) articulated a psychological theory of voting in the 1950s. This perspective posits that, absent psychological cross pressures in the form of short-term considerations in the form of candidate image or issues that are unique to individual elections, people's party identification is the most significant predictor of their attitudes toward and choice of presidential candidates.

The results of this study support the expectation that political party identification exerts considerable impact on presidential candidate perceptions. Specifically, during phase 1 in September, being a Republican was associated with a positive attitude toward Bush, favorable perceptions of Bush's character, and likelihood of voting for Bush (see table 4.1). Conversely, respondents in this project who reported being a Democrat were associated with a negative overall attitude toward Bush, unfavorable perceptions of Bush's character, and less likelihood of voting for Bush as president.

For Kerry during phase 1 of this project, political party identification imparted a similar impact as was found for Bush, although because Kerry was the Democratic candidate, the pattern was reversed (see table 4.2). This means that in Kerry's case, Republican respondents reported negative overall attitudes about Kerry, unfavorable evaluations of Kerry's character, and less likelihood of voting for Kerry. Conversely, Democratic respondents reported having a positive overall attitude about Kerry, positively perceived Kerry's character, and were much more likely to vote for Kerry.

During phase 2 of this project in mid- and late October and early November, political party identification was also associated with attitudes about, character evaluations of, and likelihood to vote for both candidates (see tables

4.3 and 4.4). Republican identifiers reported both positive overall attitudes about Bush and positive evaluations of Bush's character, along with likelihood of voting for Bush for president, while Democrats reported this same pattern of positive perceptions about Kerry. This pattern of results reaffirms that, even though ideological constraints imposed on political party allegiance may have weakened in recent years, thus causing many more centrist Americans to identify themselves as independents (Rauch, 2005), political party identification is still the single most powerful predictor of how people respond to political candidates.

Beyond political party identification, a few other sociodemographic variables were related to perceptions of the presidential candidates in this project. During phase 1, respondents' education level was negatively related to overall attitude toward Bush, so that respondents with higher levels of education reported a more negative attitude about Bush than did respondents with lower levels of education. During phase 2 of this study, respondent education level exerted an even greater impact on perceptions of Bush, with education level negatively associated not only with overall candidate attitude but also with perception of character and likelihood of voting for Bush. Also during phase 2, respondent income was positively associated with overall attitude about Bush and evaluation of Bush's character, though both of these relationships were weak. Also at phase 2, respondents with high levels of political expertise were more likely to vote for Bush and reported a more positive overall attitude about Bush, though the latter association was weak. Finally, during phase 2, older respondents reported a more favorable evaluation of Bush's character than did younger respondents, but this relationship was weak. Gender was not related to perceptions of Bush during phase 2 of this project.

Sociodemographic variables exerted less influence on perceptions of Kerry. During phase 1, respondent political expertise was negatively related to overall attitude about Kerry and intention to vote for Kerry, though both of these relationships were weak. In phase 2, the only sociodemographic variable besides political party identification that exerted an influence on perceptions of Kerry was education level: respondents with higher levels of education reported a greater likelihood of voting for Kerry, a more positive overall attitude about Kerry, and a more positive evaluation of Kerry's character, though the latter association was weak. Gender, age, and income were not related to perceptions of Kerry during phase 2 of this project.

Traditional Communication Venues

This investigation began with the assumption that traditional communication forms—newspapers, network television news, televised debates, and televised political ads—would exert considerable influence on people's perceptions of presidential candidates. Previous media effects research suggests that traditional communication forms often affect candidate perception, at least in campaigns in which attitudes are fluid (Becker & Kraus, 1978). For example, research investigating the impact of viewing network television news or reading print news has found considerable impact on people's perceptions of presidential candidates (e.g., Drew & Weaver, 1990; Fan & Tims, 1989; Iyengar & Kinder, 1987; Jordan, 1983; McLeod & McDonald, 1985; Neuman, Just, & Crigler, 1992; Patterson, 1980; Ranney, 1983; Roberts, 1979). In addition, research investigating the impact of televised debates (e.g., Benoit, Hansen, & Verser, 2003; Holbrook, 1996; Shaw, 1999; The Racine Group, 2002) and televised campaign advertising (e.g., Ansolabehere & Iyengar, 1995; Atkin, 1980; Christ, Thorson, & Caywood, 1994; Faber, Tims, & Schmitt, 1993; Freedman, Frantz, & Goldstein, 2004; Just et al., 1996; Kaid, 1997; Newhagen & Reeves, 1991; Owen, 1991) also has found that greater use of these communication forms during presidential campaigns impacts users' perceptions of candidates. Thus, we expected that respondent use of newspapers, television network news, newsmagazines, televised debates, and televised political advertising during an election cycle would exert considerable impact on their perceptions of presidential candidates. Analysis of the data collected for this project largely supported these expectations.

For Bush, people's use of newspapers and newsmagazines were not related to any dependent measures. However, use of television network news was positively associated with perceptions of Bush's character at phase 1 (see table 4.1) and manifested a weak positive relationship with overall attitude toward Bush at phase 2 (see table 4.2). People's anticipation of debates during phase 1 was negatively related to perceptions of Bush's character, overall attitude toward Bush, and likelihood of voting for Bush. The actual viewing of debates during phase 2 was negatively associated with overall attitude toward Bush and likelihood of voting for Bush. Finally, use of televised advertising displayed a weak positive relationship with the likelihood of voting for Bush at phase 1 and with overall attitude toward Bush during phase 2. Viewing television advertising was also positively associated with people's perceptions of Bush's character at phase 2. Thus, for Bush, people's uses of television network news, televised debates, and political ads exerted significant influence on people's perceptions, although respondents' uses of newspapers and newsmagazines revealed no effects.

With Kerry, print media exerted modest impacts. People's use of newspapers during phase 2 showed a weak positive relationship with overall attitude toward Kerry and was positively associated with perceptions of Kerry's character (see table 4.4). Use of newsmagazines at phase 2 manifested a weak positive relationship with attitudes toward Kerry. Use of television network news exerted no influence on perceptions of Kerry, and use of televised ads at phase 2 showed a weak negative association with likelihood of voting for Kerry. Anticipation of televised debates during phase 1 was positively associated with perceptions of Kerry's character, overall attitudes toward Kerry, and likelihood of voting for Kerry (see table 4.2). People's viewing of debates during phase 2 showed a weak positive association with overall attitudes toward Kerry, and use of debates was positively related to perceptions of Kerry's character and likelihood of voting for Kerry. Thus, for Kerry, uses of newspapers and debates exerted considerable impact on people's perceptions. Uses of newsmagazines and televised ads manifested relatively weak influence on perceptions of Kerry, and network television news exerted no influence.

Overall, then, for both candidates, people's anticipation of debates at phase 1 and their actual viewing of debates at phase 2 proved to be a significant source of influence. Presidential debate use was negatively associated with perceptions of Bush and was positively related to all measures of perception about Kerry during both phases of the investigation. The only other communication form that influenced people's perceptions of both candidates was televised advertising, but it impacted mainly perceptions of Bush, negatively impacting only the likelihood of voting for Kerry, and doing so only slightly.

Other more traditional communication forms exerted unique influence on either Bush or Kerry but not both. People's use of network television news was positively associated with perceptions of Bush, but it exerted no influence on perceptions of Kerry. Use of newspapers and newsmagazines was uniquely influential with Kerry in that these communication forms were positively associated with perceptions of Kerry but exerted no impact on perceptions of Bush.

Thus, more traditional communication forms did exert impact on people's perceptions of candidates: at the least, some traditional forms exerted an influence on some candidates. The results affirm the clout of presidential debates. Various syntheses of results of studies dating to 1960 indicate that presidential debates have proven an informative, influential communication source in past campaigns (Benoit et al., 2003; Holbrook, 2002; The Racine Group, 2002). Despite increased competition from other viewing options, televised presidential debates still draw sizable audiences, far more than any other campaign event (Patterson, 2002). The reason is that in contested elections, debates are "media events" (Dayman & Katz, 1992, p. 1). They provide compelling spectacle, or what Schroeder (2000) characterizes as "human drama at its rawest" (p. 201).

The influence of print news and television network news is more selective. Despite declining use,[3] the results of this study reveal that network television news use exerted modest impact on the incumbent but no influence on the challenger. By contrast, newspaper and, to a lesser degree, newsmagazine use exerted modest influence on the challenger, but only during the latter days of the campaign. These print findings are understandable in part. Clearly, attitudes in the 2004 campaign were more fluid about challenger Kerry than incumbent Bush, portending the potential for greater influence on Kerry (Becker & Kraus, 1978). However, there is no theoretical explanation for the positive valence of the influence of print news on Kerry.

The positive impact of television news on people's perceptions of Bush is explainable in that the incumbent has more opportunities to appear in television network news, a communication modality that, by its nature, communicates more through visual images than words (Meyrowitz, 1985), and this characteristic elevates the role and impact of source considerations (Chaiken & Eagly, 1983; Graber, 1976; Pfau, 1990; Worchel, Andreoli, & Eason, 1975), particularly positive relational cues (Chesebro, 1984; Chesebro & Bertelsen, 1996; Delli Carpini & Williams, 1998; Pfau & Kang, 1991). Therefore, images of the incumbent president are more likely to carry positive valence, which we suspect is responsible for the finding that television news use was positively associated with viewers' perceptions of Bush.

Nontraditional Communication Venues

Recent national elections demonstrate that the line between traditional media and nontraditional media has blurred (Davis & Owen, 1998). This diversification of the political communication environment represents what Kern, Just, and Crigler (1997) have called a "sea change" in media use and influence. Norris (2000) argues that "the new information environment has greatly expanded the opportunities to learn about public affairs from a wider variety of channels, programs, formats, and levels" (p. 13). Communication scholars and national surveys, including the Pew Research Center for the People and the Press (2004b) and the National Election Studies (2000), confirm that media consumers increasingly partake of options in this new communication environment (Benoit & Hansen, 2004). With few exceptions, however, the question of the new media's influence on user's perceptions of political candidates remains unexplored (Davis & Owen, 1998; Moy & Pfau, 2000; Norris, 2000; Pfau, 2002; Pfau & Eveland, 1996). In an attempt to fill the gap in the empirical literature, we believe that the extant evidence justifies the claim that several new communication forms, within the constellation of the broader new media, displayed significant effects on users' perception of the 2004 presidential candidates.

The nontraditional, or new, media have been variously conceived. Hollander (1995) conceptualized new media as focusing on entertainment over information, providing candidates with easy questions by officious hosts, offering direct access to average listeners via telephone or perhaps e-mail, and displaying explicit interaction between the public and the candidate. Moy and Pfau (2000) contend that the "non-traditional sources of political news are non-traditional . . . because their goal is not to disseminate political information, yet they provide a large portion of Americans with information about current affairs" (p. 180). Davis and Owen (1998) offer a number of conceptual distinctions between nontraditional and traditional media. In particular, they note that the new media are not monolithic and that some of their most salient features are that they rely on a broad and less politically interested audience, emphasize populist themes, personalize political news, more frequently employ ad hominem attacks, pursue an explicit bias, maintain a distant and adversarial relationship toward government, and, most important for political candidates and officeholders, provide an open and unimpeded forum to speak to the public directly. Ultimately, Davis and Owen (1998) conclude the new media's most salient feature is their dual interest in entertainment and profit procurement. In their broad study of the new media's influence, these authors agree that one or more of these conceptual traits are manifest in the following communication forms: political talk radio, television talk, electronic town meetings, television newsmagazines, MTV, and print as well as television tabloids. Regardless of the particular conceptualization or operationalization, however, what remains clear is that there has been a substantial blurring of the line between traditional and nontraditional sources of political information.

Kurtz (1996) observes that "politics and pop culture seem to have merged" (p. 12). Richards (2004) credits postmodernism with blurring the line between entertainment and information in contemporary political culture. Ultimately, some scholars credit a hostile media and political opportunism with the recent emphasis on alternative formats. Patterson (2002) reports that after Vietnam and Watergate, journalists adopted a more interpretive style of journalism that replaced the emphasis of the news on newsmakers with an emphasis on reporters. This approach has angered politicians who dislike this new style of journalism because their own voice is drowned out by the drumbeat of reporters providing primarily their own analyses and criticism. But it is not just politicians who are critical of the modern press; new consumers are also dissatisfied with American press performance. Evidence of news consumers' frustration with the mainstream press is evidenced by the fact that over half distrust mass media news organizations (Pew Research Center for the People and the Press, 2004b). More specifically, Kurtz (1996) observes that the "public has grown tired of the prosecutorial media culture" (p. 99). As a result of this new interpretive style of journalism, Jamieson and Waldman (2003) report that, "in 1992, candidates began to look beyond the traditional news media for places they could appear that would allow them relatively unfiltered access to the voters" (p. 69).

Some of the new media venues that politicians turned to were television talk shows and other popular entertainment outlets. The explosion of campaign use of new media commenced in 1988 when Democratic presidential candidate Michael Dukakis appeared on *Larry King Live* to counter charges that he was insensitive to the plight of those victimized by violent crime. During the 1992 presidential election season, the three presidential candidates appeared on King's show a total of thirteen times (Davis & Owen, 1998). In that same year, Bill Clinton appeared on MTV to announce that he did not inhale and that he prefers boxers to briefs. Davis and Owen (1998) observe that "the four years following the 1992 campaign demonstrated that the new media were not a fad and that they had become entrenched in the political world" (p. 5). In 1996, Bob Dole unofficially declared his candidacy on *Late Night with David Letterman*, and Texas billionaire Ross Perot announced the creation of a third party on *Larry King Live* (Kurtz, 1996). Jamieson and Waldman (2003) note that in the 2000 presidential election, the major party presidential candidates made appearances across the nontraditional media landscape. For instance, Al Gore appeared on MTV; Bush was on *Live with Regis and Kathy Lee*; both contenders spent time on air with Oprah Winfrey, Letterman, and Jay Leno; and the candidates even appeared together on *Saturday Night Live*. When Bush was interviewed by Letterman, he received more airtime in that one segment than he did in an entire year from the *CBS Nightly News* (Patterson, 2002). Whereas the collusion between politics and the popular media began as a reaction to journalistic standards, it has now become an institutionalized feature of contemporary political communication.

Contrary to conventional wisdom, the most attentive and knowledgeable voters have come to expect that they will receive a sizable proportion of their information about politics and political candidates from new media outlets. Davis and Owen (1998) found that 63 percent of Americans follow governmental activities "most or some of the time." This compares to 76 percent of talk radio users, 73 percent of newsmagazine viewers, and 68 percent of online media users (p. 181). Pew Research (2004a) found that 31 percent of Americans "highly attend" to hard news sources, and of those consumers, anywhere from just below one-third to just above one-half also pay attention to new media sources (e.g., political talk radio, television newsmagazines, entertainment news shows, and television talk shows). Pew Research also found that *Larry King Live* viewers are as knowledgeable as those who get political information from literary magazines such as *The Atlantic* and *The New Yorker*. Both Pew Research (2004b) and the National Annenberg Election

Survey (2004) confirm that those who watch the Peabody Award–winning *Daily Show with Jon Stewart* are more knowledgeable than *The O'Reilly Factor* audiences. Pew Research (2004b) also demonstrated that *Daily Show* viewers know more about politics than those who watch PBS's *Newshour with Jim Lehrer*, listen to talk radio, or watch the Sunday morning news shows. Norris (2000) argues that a "more educated and literate public is capable of using the more complex range of news sources and party messages to find the information they need to make political choices" (p. 17).

On the other hand, Benoit and Hansen (2004) observe that "many voters are not 'political junkies' who avidly seek out information about the candidates; they learn about the campaign from whatever information they happen to encounter before Election Day" (p. 165). With the use of National Election Studies data, these authors conclude that media users from 1952 to 2000 have gradually increased their reliance on nontraditional sources for information about presidential candidates and campaigns. Pew Research (2004b) found that 56 percent of Americans pay only moderate attention to hard news sources and that around 13 percent report never following or seeking out hard news. That means nearly 70 percent of the public acquires political information only incidentally. For the 13 percent who never pursue hard news, entertainment communication venues may be their only source of political information. Regarding the 2000 presidential election, Pew Research surveys revealed that 28 percent of Americans got their information about the campaign primarily from television entertainment talk shows, while another 6 percent got their information from television comedy shows, and these patterns were most pronounced with less politically involved younger people (Media Monitor, 2000; Strope, 2000). Entertainment communication forms have therefore become an inordinately important channel through which politicians attempt to reach the most inaccessible members of the electorate.

Political professionals seem to acknowledge and account for the relevance of a new entertainment-oriented communication environment. Terry Edmonds, a speechwriter for Kerry, states that "it's almost become a staple in presidential politics that you make the rounds of late night comedy shows ... It's really an opportunity ... to humanize the candidate" (Zabarenko, 2004, para. 7). In an age of televised politics, a candidate's relational communication is theoretically an important scale on which voters weigh their voting preferences (Jamieson, 1988; Meyrowitz, 1992; Nimmo, 1974). Empirical evidence has confirmed this speculation (Pfau, 1990). As Davis and Owen (1998) claim, even highly educated voters "cite personal characteristics as reasons for voting for a particular candidate" (p. 71). In today's mass-mediated culture, sincerity has become an important test of reliability (Beninger, 1987; Jamieson & Waldman, 2003). Jamieson and Waldman (2003) report that Gore campaign workers faithfully read the monologues of each evening's entertainment talk shows. More specifically, these authors note that "late night caricatures typically reflect the criticisms being made elsewhere in the media" (p. 70). Moreover, the relationship is reciprocal. During the 2000 election season, late-night humor was rebroadcast by MSNBC as well as CBS and reprinted by the *New York Times* and the Associated Press. Cokie Roberts once warned that the late-night comics should be heeded, as "sometimes they have a lot more effect than any of us political analysts" (in Jamieson & Waldman, 2003, p. 70).

Anecdotal evidence demonstrating the impact of specific nontraditional communication forms is abundant. Davis and Owen (1998) report that conservative "talk radio hosts were credited with mobilizing young, male Republican voters, thus helping to secure GOP control of both Houses of Congress for the first time since 1954" (p. 4). Kurtz (1996) adds evidence to this claim by reporting that the 1994 exit polls showed that anywhere from 58 to 71 percent of talk radio listeners voted for Republican political candidates at all three levels of government. In 1992, Bill and Hillary Clinton famously diffused the impact of his alleged affair with Gennifer Flowers by subjecting themselves to a candid interview on the television newsmagazine *60 Minutes*. In 1989, conservative talk show hosts mobilized Americans to send scores upon scores of tea bags to congressional lawmakers in opposition to a pay raise (Barker, 2002). Even as early as the 1950s, Lyndon Johnson, then a Texas senator, prodded a radio talk show host to urge support for the B-52 bomber, the result of which was that Senate offices received more mail than they could reasonably process (Kurtz, 1996). After each of Franklin Roosevelt's *Fireside Chats*, his incoming mailbags grew, and people felt so close to Roosevelt that many of the letters requested personal advice (Davis, 1996). Kurtz (1996) argues that political talk shows (i.e., television and radio) "fertilize and spread the latest fodder down through the media food chain" (p. 14). Ultimately, the systematic literature concerning the influence of nontraditional media points toward a consistent and significant relationship between political talk radio, television talk, entertainment talk, and television newsmagazines.

Pfau and colleagues (2001) found that these four nontraditional communication forms exerted a significant impact on perceptions of the 2000 presidential contenders (Gore and Bush). In particular, they highlighted the role of entertainment talk. It was the first time a study found significant effects for this communication form on perceptions of presidential candidates. Pfau and colleagues (2002) note that "the reasons why television entertainment talk shows mainly worked to Gore's advantage are elusive" (p. 97). In this respect, Jamieson and Waldman (2003) provide some insight. Their content analysis of jokes directed at the 2000 presidential candidates by Letterman and Leno revealed that Bush was targeted 13 percent more often than Gore (62 vs. 49 percent). Finally, Baum (2003) reported that entertainment talk show viewing exerted influence on less politically involved viewers, particularly in terms of perceptions of candidate persona. His study of the 2000 presidential election revealed that "politically unengaged voters who watch entertainment-oriented TV talk shows are more likely to find the opposition party candidate likeable, as well as to cross party lines and vote for him" (p. 213). The results of these studies lend credence to the claim that late-night entertainment talk shows carry the potential to affect viewers' perceptions of political candidates. They exert influence when candidates appear as guests but also when hosts poke fun at candidates in their opening monologues.

Studies of other nontraditional forms also suggest influence. Pfau and Eveland (1996) found that television talk shows and television newsmagazines exerted significant impacts on perceptions of presidential candidates in the 1992 campaign. Like our present effort, they administered their survey in two phases. Effects on perceptions of the presidential candidates detected in early September persisted throughout the campaign and onto Election Day. In their study of talk radio's impact on political perceptions, Lee and Cappella (2001) found that "when an audience is exposed to an intense, one-sided message, their agreement with the positions advocated increases as exposure and reception increase" (p. 389). Using both quasi-experimental and purely experimental data, Barker (2002) supported the argument that Rush Limbaugh exercises influence through his ability and persistent willingness to employ what the author calls heurestethics, or, more specifically, "the strategic redefinition of an issue by manipulation of the salience (accessibility and importance) of consideration through frames and priming" (p. 389). With its emphases on convenience, entertainment, provocative content, and ideological orientation, talk radio is a paradigmatic illustration of the new, or nontraditional, media.

The empirical and anecdotal evidence allowed us to confidently predict that people's use of the following nontraditional communication forms during the 2004 presidential campaign would exert a significant impact on their perception of candidates: political talk radio, television talk shows, television newsmagazines, and television entertainment talk shows. However, the results failed to support this expectation, with the exception of one communication form: political talk radio.

Political talk radio listeners were more likely to support Bush both early in the campaign as well as later in the campaign. Their support manifested itself in terms of positive perception of Bush's overall character, a positive overall attitude toward Bush, and an intention to cast vote for Bush on Election Day. For Kerry, people's use of political talk radio was associated with unfavorable impressions of his character, negative attitude toward his political candidacy, and an expressed intention to vote against him on Election Day. This pattern of results for the Democrat was particularly pronounced at phase 1 of the survey's administration. However, by phase 2, political talk radio listeners' unfavorable impression of Kerry's character and their negative attitude toward his candidacy had dissipated, but their expressed intention to vote against him on Election Day remained. Within the context of political talk radio's traditionally conservative orientation as well as its demonstrated ability to mobilize its constituency, these results are comprehensible.

Since it matured in 1994, political talk radio has been a potent force for America's conservative movement. Davis and Owen (1998) report that "it is a well-established fact that the talk radio audience . . . is far more conservative than the general population" (pp. 184–185). The Annenberg Public Policy Center (2004a) found that the vast majority of listeners to the Rush Limbaugh radio program characterized themselves as dedicated Republicans. In addition, Hollander (1996) demonstrated that the talk radio audience "is not isolated but rather one open to political mobilization" (p. 110). In fact, this is the second study to demonstrate the potency of talk radio as a force for Republican presidential candidates (Pfau, 2002). On the basis of these and other findings, it is likely that talk radio will remain a relevant feature on the presidential communication landscape, but it may be imprudent to disregard the impact of the other three communication forms on the basis of this single study's results.

For the other nontraditional communication forms examined here, there was far less impact overall. While there was a weak association between watching television newsmagazines and an overall positive attitude toward Kerry, television talk and late-night entertainment talk failed to significantly influence viewers' perception of the political candidates at either phase of the survey's administration. Pfau, Cho, and Chong (2001) found that these forms exerted a statistically significant influence on voter perceptions in 2000, a pattern also revealed by Baum (2003), but just for entertainment television talk shows and limited to "politically unengaged voters." Television talk's impact was limited, but perhaps this isn't surprising given the timing of the surveys. Pfau and Eveland (1996) found that such programs exerted their influence early in the 1992 campaign. Recall that that campaign was marked by considerable fluidity, especially when one considers that Perot dropped out of the race and then rejoined it in the fall. Given that Bush and Kerry were well established as their parties' candidates by the spring of 2004, it is reasonable that the already limited impact of television talk shows may have been further undermined by the particular circumstances of this campaign season (see Becker & Kraus, 1978). The effects of late-night entertainment talk may have also been limited by these circumstances, but the lack of results here must not be considered too harshly until a content analysis can establish how late-night comics used humor to characterize the candidates. It is possible that a relative balance of jokes directed at Bush and Kerry may have resulted in their canceling each other's influence. Judgment here should be reserved until a content analysis of late-night comedy can properly assess the orientation of its humor in 2004.

Other Communication Venues

Nontraditional political communication forms are not monolithic. In fact, their most salient characteristic is their diversity. New communication forms employ a variety of media technologies, ideological orientations, and/or entertainment strategies. Particular media technologies implicated by the new political communication environment include film, DVDs, VCRs, the Web, traditional network television, and even radio broadcasts.

New communication forms also employ a variety of formats. Radio news includes everything from top-of-the-hour newsbreaks on commercial broadcast stations to all-news public radio stations, such as National Public Radio. Televised political drama includes formats such as *The West Wing*, a fictional look behind the scenes of a liberal presidential administration, and *K-Street*, a thinly fictionalized account of real-life political consultants Mary Madeline and James Carville's "staged" career as high-powered Washington lobbyists. The line between these political dramas and reality is thin. On *The West Wing*, the president copes with terrorism, and actual politicians frequently appear on *K-Street*. In particular, the political media establishment was shocked when presidential hopeful Howard Dean used "fictional" advice he received on an episode of *K-Street* against his opponents in an early debate with the other 2004 Democratic primary contenders. The political sketches of television comedic shows, such as *Saturday Night Live*, are regularly replayed on "serious" hard news programs, such as ABC's *This Week with George Stephanopoulos*. More recently, cinematic blockbusters have crossed the line from political commentary to political activism. Not only was Michael Moore's *Fahrenheit 9/11* a financial success, it was also the first of several documentaries that aimed to influence the 2004 presidential race. Although many of these films were not nationally released (e.g., *Control Room* and *Bush's Brain*), they became widely available in home formats, such as DVD or VHS. Other communication forms, such as printed materials, represent the coordinated efforts of political campaigns and political parties to target individual voters through direct mail, pamphlets, and yard signs.

Perhaps no new media form has received more attention than the Web. The Internet is a communication environment replete with both traditional and nontraditional political information. The Internet also offers the opportunity for interaction with other politically interested individuals. Very little is known about these "other" new communication media, either because they have been largely ignored by scholars, such as radio news (Chaffee, Zhao, & Leshner, 1994), or because they have only recently emerged as a source of political content, such as the Internet and movies. Anecdotal evidence suggests that they exerted notable influence during the 2004 presidential campaign. *Boston Globe* columnist Cathy Young went as far as to claim that "the election of 2004 . . . revealed that we live in a new media environment" (MIT Communications Forum, 2005, p. 1).

Movies, both in home-viewing formats (i.e., DVD or VHS) and on the big screen, emerged as a partisan-charged venue in 2004 with the airing of *Fahrenheit 9/11*, but it is unclear whether this form was able to extend its reach beyond partisan Democrats. In fact, this documentary seems unlikely to have had bipartisan appeal. The Annenberg Public Policy Center (2004b) reported that over 80 percent of *Fahrenheit 9/11* moviegoers identified themselves as liberals or Democrats. On the other hand, the universe of politically charged movies available in the 2004 campaign election season was not exhausted by Michael Moore's epic. Other partisan documentary-style films included *George W. Bush: Faith in the White House*, *Bush's Brain*, *The World according to Bush*, *Journeys with George*, *Stolen Honor: Wounds That Never Heal*, *Uncovered: The War in Iraq*, and *Celsius 41.11: The Temperature at Which the Brain Begins to Die*, to name only a few.

Although there may have been plenty of films available for Democrats and Republicans, the question remains as to whether political film produces a detectable influence on perceptions of candidates. Farhi (2004) reports that "scholars who study public opinion say . . . any message must be repeated and reinforced over and over, so any movie, book, or TV show, in isolation, is unlikely to have much effect" (para. 13). For example, public opinion polls taken before and after the antinuclear film *The Day After* did not register any significant change in attitudes toward nuclear weapons or disarmament. On the other hand, *The Day After*'s arguments were not nearly so direct or partisan as the previously mentioned films. Like many of the communication forms examined in this section, there is not enough consistent evidence on which to base a definitive prediction. Furthermore, movies have never been studied as a source of influence on people's perceptions of candidates during a political campaign.

The Internet, despite being the subject of extensive scholarly examination, also fails to offer a clear basis on which to predict its influence on perceptions of political candidates during an ongoing political campaign. Norris (2002b) points out that, since 1996, the Internet is one of only a few communication forms that are a growing source for political news. However, the Internet is more of a niche tool. In other words, it is not a communication venue likely to influence the political attitudes of the broader public. The Pew Center for the People and Press (2004b) found that 54 percent of Americans regularly go online to get political information (i.e., less than three days per week). The percentage of people who regularly get news online has increased to 29 percent from only 2 percent in 1996. Moreover, 71 percent of those who regularly access political information from the Web are also more likely to consume similar information from traditional news sources (e.g., televised news, newspapers, and newsmagazines). Of all those who get news online, 73 percent acquire that information while using the Web for other reasons; that is, they get the news incidentally.

Norris (2002a) argues that Internet use is a multidimensional phenomenon. Not everyone goes online for the same reasons. Because people use the Web for distinct purposes, their experiences with the medium are diverse. This is why Norris claims that the Internet is not a mass medium. Moreover, she observes that those who go online to access political information fall into two categories of users. The first is a general user who merely consumes political information. The second is a campaign activist who might seek information about a candidate's voting record, participate in online polls, send e-mail in support of or opposed to a candidate, download election information, provide information such as e-mail addresses, or even donate their offline time or money to a campaign. Using 1996 and 1998 Pew Research data, Norris (2002a) concluded that Internet political activism "involved no more than five percent of the total online community and therefore, an even smaller proportion of the larger population" (p. 68).

Kamarack (2002) argues that the Internet's impact on candidate perceptions is uncertain. She notes that as late as the "2000 election cycle the Internet was firmly entrenched in the routines of American political campaigns—although skepticism about its role remained" (p. 85). Even anecdotal evidence regarding the Internet's impact is nonexistent. "Web enthusiasts are still waiting for the Internet to 'make' a candidate in the same clear-cut, definitive way that television 'made' John Kennedy in 1960" (p. 100). Pfau and colleagues (2001) did not find any significant impact on the perception of voters who accessed political information online in 2000, but Kamarack (2002) argues that the Internet's impact is incremental. Therefore, researchers should closely monitor the Internet's influence as it continues to play a progressively more significant role in political campaigns.

For the remaining nontraditional communication forms addressed in this section, there is an appalling deficit of systematic scholarly inquiry. Patterson

(2002) argues that more and more Americans are turning to public radio news. He reports that, in the past decade, there has been a 300 percent increase in National Public Radio's audience, but, as noted by Chaffee and colleagues (1994), there is a paucity of systematic research with which to edify the impact of radio news. The same may be said for printed materials and, to a lesser degree, for televised drama and comedy. For these forms, one might explain their influence through the theoretical lens of cultivation theory. Its fundamental proposition is that "heavier viewers of television will be more likely to believe the real world is like the television world than will be lighter viewers" (Potter, 1993, p. 565). Given the thin separation between fictional television content and actual political events (e.g., Democratic primary debates) as well as politicians (e.g., Al Gore), one might expect enhanced cultivation effects for this genre; however, without a systematic content analysis of these programs, it is impossible to predict the direction or nature of their influence on perceptions of political candidates.

Given our lack of systematic or consistent knowledge regarding the influence of these communication forms, we simply ask if people's use of radio news, televised political drama, televised comedic shows, movies/DVDs/VCRs, the Web, or printed materials during presidential campaigns exerts an impact on their perceptions of candidates. Our results are very interesting.

Consumers of radio news demonstrated a relatively consistent preference for Kerry over Bush. At phase 1 of the survey's administration, radio news was weakly associated with an overall positive attitude toward Kerry. At phase 2, radio news listeners disapproved of Bush's character and expressed a negative overall attitude toward the incumbent president. This discontent with Bush was reflected in radio news listeners' expressed intention to vote for Kerry at phase 2. Pew Research (2004b) provides convergent evidence for the liberal orientation of radio news. Its biannual survey of media use found that "National Public Radio's audience has shown the most significant shift to the left. Today, three-in-ten regular NPR listeners describe themselves as liberal—up from 20% in 2002" (p. 15). Ultimately, these results may reflect the political climate of this particular election cycle. At phase 2, radio news listeners expressed discontent with Bush and an expressed intention to vote for Kerry, but the same radio listeners did not demonstrate significantly positive attitudes toward Kerry or evaluations of his character. In other words, liberals seemed willing to vote for anyone but Bush in 2004.

Politically oriented movies offered the most prominent pattern of influence on perceptions of political candidates. At phase 1, movies were associated with significantly negative evaluations of Bush's character and an expressed intention to vote against him on Election Day. At phase 2, the potency of anti-Bush sentiment among movie consumers remained strong. Intention to vote against Bush nearly doubled in strength, and the negative evaluations of his character intensified. Also at phase 2, political moviegoers developed a fundamentally unfavorable attitude toward Bush. Given the popularity of *Fahrenheit 9/11*—it dominated the box office for six days after its initial release and was the most financially successful documentary in the history of film (Farhi, 2004)—and its audience's liberal orientation (Annenberg Public Policy Center, 2004b), these results are hardly surprising. What is surprising is the apparent lack of impact for the several conservative films offered in 2004. Perhaps conservative films were "too little, too late." While *Fahrenheit 9/11* was nationally released in the early summer of 2004, movies such as *George W. Bush: Faith in the White House* and *Celsius 41.11: The Temperature at Which the Brain Begins to Die* received a limited distribution, were not released until late in the campaign, and were not available for home consumption until very late in the campaign season.

Surprisingly, printed materials exerted a significant influence on perceptions of Bush at phase 1. At that time, printed materials were associated with positive overall attitudes toward the incumbent president as well as favorable evaluations of his character. The boost that Bush received from printed materials may be related to the Republican National Committee's uniquely sophisticated overhaul of its direct-mail program. As reported by Edsall and Grimaldi (2004), Republican firms, such as TargetPoint Consultants and National Media Inc., used consumer-marketing data to identify "anger points" (e.g., late-term abortions, trial lawyer fees, estate taxes, and so on) among borderline voters. Republicans then used direct mail to target specific messages to specific constituencies. Matthew Dowd, a pollster for Bush, reported that this strategy helped the Republican National Committee quadruple the number of Republican voters who could be uniquely and profitably targeted by direct mail and other strategies.

The only other results detected by the survey occurred at phase 1. At that time, viewers of televised political drama expressed a negative overall attitude toward Bush. As Election Day approached, these evaluations dissipated. If the early influence of televised drama resulted from a cultivation-like effect, it seems possible that as these viewers' decisions become more urgent, they overcame their conditioning by centrally processing information about the presidential candidates. Shrum (2001) experimentally demonstrated that cultivation effects are obviated when subjects are induced to process systematically as opposed to heuristically. However, given our lack of theorizing relative to cultivation theory (e.g., a content analysis), one should cautiously employ this lens to interpret our results.

In the final analysis, our survey did not detect any significant influence on candidate perceptions originating from the Web or from televised comedy.

Despite claims by "cyber-optimists" (Norris, 2001, p. 232) that the Internet has revolutionized American politics, this is the second consecutive study that compared people's self-reports of communication use in presidential campaigns and found no impact for the Web (for a similar result, see Pfau et al., 2001). This finding supports Norris's (2000) position that the "proportion of Americans currently involved in any form of online election activity suggests the need for caution about the transformative capacity of the Web for democracy" (p. 82). The Internet simply lacks the wherewithal to "compete with television—the medium that goes out and 'pulls' often reluctant citizens into contact with candidates (Kamarack, 2002, p. 121). The Internet may be making a difference in the way campaigns raise contributions or mobilize volunteers, but so far there is no evidence that it is able to influence the broader public.

ROLE AND INFLUENCE OF POLITICAL CONVERSATIONS

People's political conversations are typically associated with a potential source of influence on their perceptions of candidates (Huckfeldt & Sprague, 1990). In fact, the amount of political talk during campaigns is considerable. Kingdon (in Chaffee, 1981, p. 192) reported that 20 to 40 percent of adults discuss political campaigns with others and that 20 percent of them are asked their advice about candidate choice. Greenberg (1975) calls people's conversations with others about public affairs content "crucial" in opinion formation, adding that attempts to persuade others occur in 47 percent of these interactions. This tendency is even more pronounced in political conversations. Patterson (1980) revealed that the proportion of people engaged in conversations about political content increases to nearly one-third in the final days of a presidential election campaign. Kendall and Yum (1991) found that, toward the end of a presidential campaign, 88 percent of adults take part in an average of seven political discussions per week.

The research regarding the influence of these exchanges on candidate perception is equivocal. Some studies reveal that political talk has a reinforcing effect. Their findings rely on the assumption that most prospective voters interact with people who are ideologically similar, such as family members and coworkers. In fact, the "homophily of primary groups" has been well documented by a number of empirical efforts (Beck, 1991; Chaffee, 1981; Huckfeldt & Sprague, 1987; Patterson, 1980; Yum & Kendall, 1995). On the other hand, Huckfeldt and Sprague (1990) contend that "many citizens . . . encounter other citizens with divergent viewpoints and perceptions" (p. 14). MacKeun (1990) insists that there are many interpersonal exchanges that result in "genuine debate and an exchange of ideas" (p. 60). Given the sheer volume of political talk, some influence on candidate perception was anticipated, and recent studies reveal such an impact (Harwood Group, 1993; National Election Studies, 2000; Patterson, 2002). Our position was that the empirical evidence warranted the expectation that people's conversations with others during presidential campaigns exert a significant influence on perceptions of candidates. Furthermore, we expect that the influence of political conversations will grow as presidential campaigns progress toward their conclusion on Election Day.

Our results offered partial support for the first component of our expectation. Those who engaged in political conversations at phase 1 of the study were significantly more likely to cast their votes for Kerry; alternatively, political conversations did not influence perceptions of Bush during the same time frame. Moreover, voting intentions was the only candidate perception ostensibly influenced by political conversations during either phase of the survey. The fact that conversation's influence was limited to voting intention may reveal a unique feature of political talk. In Pfau and Parrot's (1993) modified version of Colley's hierarchical model of purchase decision making, the choice stage is a synthetic moment when previous attitudes and perceptions dynamically interact with interpersonal communication (i.e., talk) in pursuit of an ultimate choice. Within this context, it makes sense that the salient perceptions of those engaging in political talk would relate to the decision-making component (i.e., voting intention) of their perception of candidates as opposed to the content of that decision-making process (i.e., overall candidate attitude or perceptions of candidate character).

We further expected that the impact of political talk would intensify as the election progressed. Once again, we received partial confirmation for this expectation. At phase 2 of the survey's administration, political conversations were significantly associated with intentions to vote for Bush. Reflecting this support for Bush was a weakly significant association between political talk and unwillingness to vote for Kerry. The statistical magnitude of results at phase 2, relative to voting intention and political conversation, was almost twice what it was at phase 1. We feel that these results confirm our expectation that the impact of political conversations intensifies as the election progresses toward its conclusion.

NOTES

1. *Macro Regression Results.* Hierarchical regression analyses were employed to assess all hypotheses and research questions about communication use and perceptions

of candidates. The full regression equations for the phase 1 surveys were significant for all dependent variables—for Bush: perceptions of character, $F(24, 380) = 11.82$, $p < .001$; overall attitude, $F(24, 380) = 13.97, p < .001$; and likelihood of voting for Bush, $F(24, 380) = 20.47, p < .001$; and for Kerry: perceptions of character, $F(24, 380) = 7.96, p < .001$; overall attitude, $F(24, 380) = 11.15, p < .001$; and likelihood of voting for Kerry, $F(24, 380) = 21.42, p < .001$.

The results of the second survey indicated that full regression equations were significant for all dependent variables—for Bush: perceptions of character, $F(24, 380) = 12.43, p < .001$; overall attitude, $F(24, 380) = 15.21, p < .001$; and likelihood of voting for Bush, $F(24, 380) = 19.73, p < .001$; and for Kerry: perceptions of character, $F(24, 380) = 10.19, p < .001$; overall attitude, $F(24, 380) = 10.83, p < .001$; and likelihood of voting for Kerry, $F(24, 380) = 21.84, p < .001$.

2. For phase 1, the combined sociodemographic variables accounted for 37 percent and communication use 5 percent of the variance in perceptions of Bush's character, 41 and 6 percent of variance in overall attitude toward Bush, and 52 and 4 percent of variance in likelihood of voting for Bush. Sociodemographic variables were responsible for 27 percent and communication use 8 percent of variance in perceptions of Kerry's character, 33 and 8 percent of variance in overall attitude toward Kerry, and 49 and 8 percent of variance in likelihood of voting for Kerry.

For phase 2, combined sociodemographic variables were responsible for 37 percent and communication use 7 percent of variance in perceptions of Bush's character, 41 and 8 percent of the variance in overall attitude toward Bush, and 49 and 7 percent of variance in likelihood of voting for Bush. Combined sociodemographic variables accounted for 30 percent and communication use 9 percent of variance in perceptions of Kerry's character, 33 and 8 percent of the variance in overall attitude toward Kerry, and 48 and 10 percent of variance in likelihood of voting for Kerry.

3. The Newspaper Association of America (2000) reports that only 50 percent of U.S. adults at least scan a newspaper on an average weekday but that the drop in newspaper readership will continue because readership is falling most precipitously among younger people (Hoenisch, 1991). Whereas more than half of Americans who are fifty years old and over read a newspaper each day, less than 20 percent of eighteen- to twenty-year-olds do so (Mindich, 2005). Network television news viewing is in an even faster free fall (Norris, 2000). The decline in the proportion of people who say they "regularly" watch network television news in recent years has been so dramatic that Norris (1999) called it a "hemorrhage of viewers" (p. 77). Viewership dropped 34 percent in the past decade alone (journalism.org, 2004). As with newspapers, the median age of users of network evening news has risen sharply during the past decade and now exceeds sixty (Mindich, 2005).

Table 4.1. Phase 1 Media Use and Perceptions of George Bush

	Bush Attitude	Voting for Bush	Bush Character
Control variables			
Gender (male)	.00	−.05	.00
Age	.01	−.01	.04
Education	−.10**	−.035	−.05
Income	.01	.015	.03
Party identification (Democrat)	−.32*	−.30*	−.27*
Party identification (Republican)	.41*	.44*	.33*
Political expertise	.03	.05	.00
R^2	.41*	.52*	.37*
Communication use			
Network television news	.05	.02	.12**
Local television news	.00	.00	−.05
Newspapers	−.05	−.06	−.05
Magazines	−.03	−.01	−.07
Political talk radio	.17*	.12**	.12**
Radio news	.00	.01	.025
Television talk	.01	−.01	.04
Television entertainment talk	.00	−.05	−.03
Television political drama	−.09**	−.02	−.06
Television comedic shows	−.04	−.055	−.01
Television newsmagazines	−.01	−.01	−.04
Movies/DVDs	−.06	−.09**	−.11**
Web	−.04	.01	−.04
Candidate debates	−.10**	−.09**	−.10**
Candidate ads	.05	.08+	.06
Conversations	−.02	.03	.00
Printed materials	.10**	−.02	.095**
Incremental R^2	.06*	.04*	.05*
Model $F(24, 380)$	13.97*	20.47*	11.82*

Note. Entries are standardized coefficients from ordinary-least-squares regression.
* Significant at $p < .01$.
** Significant at $p < .05$.
+ Significant at $p < .10$.

Table 4.2. Phase 1 Media Use and Perceptions of John Kerry

	Kerry Attitude	Voting for Kerry	Kerry Character
Control variables			
Gender (male)	.05	.03	.04
Age	−.06	−.015	.01
Education	.01	−.01	−.01
Income	−.035	.00	.02
Party identification (Democrat)	.27*	.39*	.25*
Party identification (Republican)	−.26*	−.32*	−.23*
Political expertise	−.09+	.01	−.10+
R^2	.33*	.49*	.27*
Communication use			
Network television news	−.03	−.04	−.02
Local television news	.01	.01	.03
Newspapers	.07	.04	.05
Magazines	.06	.06	.02
Political talk radio	−.13**	−.135*	−.17*
Radio news	−.09+	−.03	−.04
Television talk	.02	.04	.06
Television entertainment talk	.06	.065	.08
Television political drama	.02	.01	.03
Television comedic shows	−.01	.055	−.02
Television newsmagazines	.10+	.03	.045
Movies/DVDs	.12**	.11**	.07
Web	−.06	.02	−.06
Candidate debates	.17*	.13*	.145**
Candidate ads	−.07	−.07	−.045
Conversations	.01	.085**	.00
Printed materials	.01	−.03	−.01
Incremental R^2	.08*	.08*	.08*
Model $F(24, 380)$	11.15*	21.42*	7.96*

Note. Entries are standardized coefficients from ordinary-least-squares regression.
* Significant at $p < .01$.
** Significant at $p < .05$.
+ Significant at $p < .10$.

Table 4.3. Phase 2 Media Use and Perceptions of George Bush

	Bush Attitude	Voting for Bush	Bush Character
Control variables			
Gender (male)	.04	.02	.05
Age	.02	.01	.08+
Education	−.085**	−.08**	−.125*
Income	.07+	.02	.08+
Party identification (Democrat)	−.27*	−.29*	−.26*
Party identification (Republican)	.32*	.385*	.28*
Political expertise	.075+	.09**	.06
R^2	.41*	.49*	.37*
Communication use			
Network television news	.09+	.04	.01
Local television news	−.01	.05	.00
Newspapers	−.01	−.05	.01
Magazines	−.02	−.05	−.01
Political talk radio	.25*	.15*	.23*
Radio news	−.13*	−.06	−.14*
Television talk	−.04	.01	−.04
Television entertainment talk	.03	.00	.03
Television political drama	.05	−.04	.065
Television comedic shows	−.03	−.04	−.015
Television newsmagazines	−.06	−.04	−.09
Movies/DVDs	−.17+	−.14*	−.18*
Web	.03	.02	.01
Candidate debates	−.13**	−.14*	−.04
Candidate ads	.09+	.06	.10**
Conversations	.00	.09**	−.01
Printed materials	−.01	−.03	−.03
Incremental R^2	.08*	.07*	.07*
Model F(24, 380)	15.21*	19.73*	12.43*

Note. Entries are standardized coefficients from ordinary-least-squares regression.
* Significant at $p < .01$.
** Significant at $p < .05$.
+ Significant at $p < .10$.

Table 4.4. Phase 2 Media Use and Perceptions of John Kerry

	Kerry Attitude	Voting for Kerry	Kerry Character
Control variables			
Gender (male)	.05	−.01	.01
Age	.03	.02	.04
Education	.11**	.09**	.075+
Income	−.035	−.05	.01
Party identification (Democrat)	.21*	.37*	.18*
Party identification (Republican)	−.32*	−.28*	−.33*
Political expertise	−.06	−.035	−.06
R^2	.33*	.48*	.30*
Communication use			
Network television news	.04	−.02	−.02
Local television news	.07	.005	.05
Newspapers	.095+	.01	.11**
Magazines	.09+	.02	.07
Political talk radio	−.07	−.19*	−.06
Radio news	−.01	.10**	−.02
Television talk	−.01	−.02	−.06
Television entertainment talk	−.05	−.04	.01
Television political drama	.035	−.02	.04
Television comedic shows	.05	.05	.02
Television newsmagazines	.06	.06	.07
Movies/DVDs	.08	.22*	.12**
Web	.03	.01	−.03
Candidate debates	.09+	.17*	.11**
Candidate ads	−.06	−.08+	−.035
Conversations	−.05	−.06+	−.07
Printed materials	−.03	.04	−.01
Incremental R^2	.08*	.10*	.09*
Model $F(24, 380)$	10.83*	21.84*	10.19*

Note. Entries are standardized coefficients from ordinary-least-squares regression.
* Significant at $p < .01$.
** Significant at $p < .05$.
+ Significant at $p < .10$.

Chapter Five

The Media Landscape and Democratic Engagement

Democracy depends on the forms of communication by which we conduct politics.

—Journalism professor James W. Carey (1995, pp. 378–379)

Limitations in the communications environment are pinpointed as a primary reason why democratic practice falls short of normative expectations.

—Political scientist Michael Delli Carpini (2004, p. 395)

The elements of this research project that have been described in the previous chapters have addressed factors that impact communication use and the way in which communication forms, operating in a crowded multimedia environment, influence people's perceptions of presidential candidates. However, another issue, perhaps even more important to the modern media campaign environment, is the way in which various communication forms impact normative democratic outcomes. Normative outcomes concern core democratic values. In the context of this investigation about American presidential campaigns, normative questions address how campaigns *should* work. A normative investigation of presidential campaigns seeks to determine whether the outcomes produced by a campaign enhance the attitudes and values that benefit the electoral process and contribute to the health of our democratic system.

This investigation focuses on normative outcomes relevant to presidential campaigns, specifically the ways in which campaign communications affect people's attitude about the process used to elect candidates, contribute to political learning, and enhance the likelihood of participating in the political process. Ultimately, while the immediate impact of an American presidential election—and the campaign that leads up to the election—is to decide who will lead the nation for the next four years, the broader, long-term impact of a campaign is that it leaves an indelible imprint on the democratic process, and for this reason, campaign practices and communication "matter to the practice of democracy" (Geer & Lau, 1998, p. 1). Or, as Carey (1995) observes, "democracy depends on the forms of communication by which we conduct politics" (pp. 378–379). There are no more important effects of campaign communication.

This chapter embraces the insistence of McLeod, Kosicki, and McLeod (1994) that political communication research "cannot evade normative assumptions of how social institutions 'ought to' work" (p. 123). In the modern age, "the mass media are the public sphere" (Carpignano, Andersen, Aronowitz, & DiFazio, 1993, p. 93), but ultimately the media today comprise many diverse communication forms. The question this chapter seeks to answer is, Which communication forms promote and which communication forms degrade normative democratic outcomes? That is, to what degree do communication forms contribute to political learning, enhance positive attitudes about the electoral process, and increase the likelihood that people will participate in politics, including the likelihood of casting a ballot? Answers to these questions shed light on which communication forms contribute most to a healthy democratic system. This knowledge is important because, whether or not campaign communications are successful in influencing attitudes about candidates, if specific forms fail to enhance knowledge, interest, and political participation, then ultimately their use is detrimental to the health of the democracy.

We cannot take normative outcomes lightly, especially today. Political communication scholars point to dangerous levels of public cynicism about politicians and institutions and citizen disengagement in the American political process (e.g., Moy & Pfau, 2000; Nye, Zelikow, & King, 1997; Patterson, 2002; Putnam, 2000). The concern from a normative perspective is that current campaign communication practices may be exacerbating these problems and, hence, be detrimental to democracy. Blumler and Gurevitch (1995) maintain this is a problem. They argue that today's dominant political communication venues are more apt "to strain against, rather than with, the grain of citizenship" (p. 203). This is a serious claim that warrants attention. However, there is a paucity of empirical evidence about whether campaign communication, generally, is corrosive of democratic values and even fewer data about the impact of individual communication forms on normative outcomes. This investigation examined the influence of communication forms on normative democratic values during the 2004 presidential campaign.

THE IMPORTANCE OF NORMATIVE OUTCOMES

Democracy is a system of government in which a common societal will is developed through the participation of citizens (Schumpeter, 1947). Indeed, the opportunity for citizens to participate in decision-making processes is a fundamental criterion of a democracy (Dahl, 1998), and widespread participation of a society's citizens is a precondition for a healthy democracy. Specific citizen attitudes and behaviors lead to greater democratic support and participation, and, as such, these attitudes and behaviors—termed "outcomes" in this research—are of great interest to students of democracy. However, before such outcomes can be measured, it is first necessary to understand both the scope of such outcomes and their importance to democratic health.

Attitude about the Electoral Process

A general support of democratic principles constitutes Ichilov's (1990) narrowest construction of the citizen in a democracy. An individual who professes or maintains positive attitudes about democratic values is not antagonistic to the health of a democracy, but such an individual fails to provide the knowledge or action that a democracy requires to function effectively and is therefore not adding to the health of a democratic society. However, it seems commonsensical that support for democratic principles would precede both the seeking of political information in a democratic society and participation in the democratic decision-making process—both of which are activities that constitute a broader construction of democratic citizenship. So, if communication cultivates positive attitudes about the democratic process within an individual, such a function may, in fact, lay the groundwork for future, broader democratic interest and participation.

Thus, for our context of campaign communication, if use of a specific communication form results in more positive attitudes about the process of electing an American president, then it may motivate users to seek more information about an election or to participate in the process. In such a situation, the communication form is exerting a positive influence on normative democratic outcomes. Conversely, if use of a communication form results in negative attitudes about the American electoral process, then it may be responsible for users losing interest in politics and not participating in the process, a series of events that is, without question, unhealthy for a democracy. Positive attitudes about the democratic process are helpful in cultivating other normative outcomes that are critical to democratic well-being.

Political Knowledge

Simply put, political knowledge involves cognitions one attains through the process of learning about politics (Junn, 1991). Political knowledge is the raw material citizens use to make decisions in a democracy (Ichilov, 1990). Thus, citizens are expected to be knowledgeable about political issues (Berelson, Lazarsfeld, & McPhee, 1954). Political knowledge is essential if democratic government is to produce political decisions that benefit society. If effective decisions are to be made within a democracy, citizens must understand "what the issues are, what their history is, what the relevant facts are, what alternatives are proposed, what the party stands for, [and] what the likely consequences [of the policy] are" (Bereleson et al., 1954, p. 308). The lack of adequate levels of political knowledge by democratic citizens can result in poor choices both for the individual and for the broader society. As Moy and colleagues (Moy, Torres, Tanaka, & McCluskey, 2005) explain, "Political knowledge is a crucial element in the workings of a democracy. An informed electorate ideally allows its citizens not only to hold policy preferences that reflect their self-interests but also to protect these interests" (p. 63).

In addition, low levels of political knowledge constitute a barrier to voting in a democratic society. If an individual knows little about the candidates or the issues in an election, then there would be little use in taking the time to cast one's vote. Therefore, because political knowledge increases the likelihood that citizens will make political decisions that are beneficial to themselves and because political knowledge provides the cognitive abilities needed to participate in a democratic election, political knowledge is a normative democratic outcome. Since a more knowledgeable citizenry contributes to a healthy democracy, it is important to understand what communication forms impact political knowledge and how they do so because communication forms that enhance political learning also promote democracy.

Participation in the Electoral Process

Citizen participation in the governing process is central to a democratic society (Pateman, 1970), as an engaged citizenry is essential for a democracy to function properly (Fishkin, 1995; Putnam, 2000; Verba, Schlozman, & Brady, 1995). The broadest conception of a democratic citizen is an individual who is active in the political process (Ichilov, 1990). Democracy is a system of government through which a common will is expressed by citizens through the process of political participation (Schumpeter, 1947). Dahl (1971) writes that "a key characteristic of a democracy is the continuing responsiveness of the government to the preferences of its citizens" (p. 1). At the core of Schumpeter's (1947) "common will" and Dahl's (1971) "responsive democratic government" is decision making through the process of voting. By casting a vote, citizens in a democratic government decide public policy and select leaders. Therefore, the act of voting is the cornerstone of political participation.

However, political participation in a democracy includes other activities beyond the act of voting (Junn, 1991; Verba et al., 1995). Political participation also includes activities such as attending meetings, contributing time or money to political candidates, demonstrating for a political cause, and other related activities. Ultimately, an individual who participates politically may be someone who simply votes on Election Day, or it may be someone who always casts a vote and also spends several hours per week on political activities. What can be said for any of these forms of participation is that participating at any level begets future participation (Pateman, 1970). This is because when one participates politically, he or she acquires the knowledge and skills to participate more easily the next time. For example, voting once makes voting the next time easier as an individual is familiar with the polling location, the voting process, and how to understand a ballot. Likewise, someone who has volunteered for a campaign will likely find it easier to volunteer for another campaign in the future and will likely have a better understanding of what is involved in working for a campaign.

Ultimately, though, while political participation comprises numerous activities, the act of voting is a core component of democratic participation. The right to freely cast one's vote is the basis of a democratic government, and voting is often thought of as a fundamental obligation of citizens. Voting is important not just because it is the social mechanism by which decisions are made but also because the casting of a vote "is a civic act which displays commitment to the political institutions and processes of the country" (Petrocik & Shaw, 1991, p. 67). Voting also increases the likelihood that citizens accept the outcome of an election, as those who participate in an election—even though they may have voted for an alternative to that which was ultimately decided—have been allowed to voice their opinion through the vote and have taken advantage of such an opportunity. As such, citizens who vote have a stake in the electoral process and are more likely to accept an opinion to which they ultimately do not agree. Conversely, those who do not vote in an election are more apt to resist a decision they disagree with because, as a result of their nonparticipation, these individuals feel they have had no voice in that decision (Lipset, 1963).

Those who do not participate in an election also run the risk of not having their interests represented in the decision-making process. As the percentage of Americans who vote continues to decline, the citizens left voting are necessarily those individual's with higher levels of political involvement—those we call "political partisans." Patterson (2002) argues that when voter turnout declines, it is the "hard-core partisans (the 'wing-nuts')" who constitute a greater percentage of the electorate, the result of which is that moderate political candidates are defeated, and the government consists of more partisan officials who produce more "divided and rancorous" political institutions (p. 12). "Divided and rancorous" institutions, in turn, lead to reduced compromise and fewer policies that are beneficial to all members of society. Patterson (2002) argues that "as electorates shrink, they tend to calcify" (p. 12). Thus, those who do not vote in a democratic election ultimately harm the overall health of democracy because their absence results in partisan decisions that do not reflect the public will. Partisan-controlled institutions are often less responsive to the will or preferences of the people. If the will of the people is not actualized, then democratic institutions are weakened.

Ultimately, then, one can see why the normative outcomes of political knowledge and attitudes about the democratic process, as well as participation, are important to the overall health of a democracy. The question for media and political scholars is how the use of different communication forms impacts these values. Previous political communication has attempted to answer this question through a variety of approaches. The perspectives of these approaches and relevant findings are discussed in the following section.

THE SHORTCOMINGS OF PAST APPROACHES

The impact of campaign-related media consumption on normative democratic outcomes has been studied from a variety of perspectives. A general macroapproach treats the news media as monolithic institutions without regard for the individual communication forms that constitute their political content. Patterson's (1993, 2002) criticism of new journalism and Putnam's (1995, 2000) social erosion thesis are representative of the macrolevel approach. A general microapproach, on the other hand, narrows its focus to particular political communication forms or comparisons of communication forms, sometimes individually and sometimes in combinations of two or three at a time. To more fully understand the influence of campaign media use on normative political outcomes, we employ a simultaneous comparison of all the relevant political campaign communication forms relative to their association with political expertise, attitude about the political process, and political behavior. Previous approaches to the study of normative democratic outcomes and media use have cast their net either too widely or too narrowly.

Approaches

Macroapproaches to the influence of communication on normative political outcomes have produced a series of interesting studies and conclusions. Patterson (1993, 2002) argues that America's declining confidence in its public institutions is due, in part, to the media's negative coverage of politicians and political campaigns. He argues that there exists a fundamental disconnect between what information the public needs from news reporting and what journalists actually provide. The public needs political information packaged more in terms of a "governing schema" that defines "policy problems, leadership traits, policy debates, and the like as key dimensions of politics" (1993, p. 58). However, journalists are more interested in a "game schema," in which "candidates are strategic actors whose every move is significant" (p. 58). A game schema defines politicians as selfish opportunists who carry nothing for the public good. Patterson (1993) observed that the tone of campaign coverage had steadily worsened so that "in three of the last four [1980, 1984, 1988, and 1992] elections, bad news has outweighed good news" (p. 22). Patterson (2002) argues that the situation nine years later had not improved. In the 1990s, the advent of cable news divisions pulled the entire field of public affairs reporting toward a more entertainment-style focus of news coverage. A new form of "yellow journalism" was evidenced by a 9 percent increase in soft news coverage since 1980 with a corresponding 20 percent decline in public affairs coverage during the same period.

Unfortunately, the decline in journalistic optimism has real-world implications for America's faith in its political institutions and leaders. Patterson (2002) argues that the superficiality and negativity of political coverage are important reasons for the decline in American's confidence in its leaders. He documents his claim by showing a substantial correlation between negative news coverage and declining interest in political campaigns. Furthermore, Patterson documents this relationship for both primary and general election campaigns. Cappella and Jamieson (1997) provided convergent evidence for Patterson's (1993, 2002) arguments in their experimental investigation of the impact of negative news frames on normative political attitudes. Paralleling Patterson's (1993) "game" and "governing" schemas, Cappella and Jamieson (1997) tested the effects of a "strategic" and "public-issues" frames on their subject's levels of political alienation and indifference. They concluded that public cynicism is a mediated contagion.

Other scholars argue that the real culprit of declining confidence in America's public institutions is not journalists but the rise of television and television journalism. Putnam (2000) observes that civic engagement, the very bedrock of representative government, has sharply and steadily declined over the past thirty years. Putnam (1995) specifically indicts increasing television viewing as a primary determinant of the decline. He argues that television is "radically 'privatizing' or 'individualizing' our use of leisure time and thus disrupting many opportunities for social capital formation" (p. 74). Postman's (1985) indictment of television is more direct. He contends that it has cheapened political discourse by forcing politics to conform to a medium in which image is valued over substance. Perhaps the most incisive criticism of television relative to normative political outcomes was made by Robinson (1975, 1976), whose "video malaise" was based on the premise that the focus of network news on "conflict, its high credibility, its powerful audio-visual capabilities and its epidemicity, has caused the more vulnerable viewers first to doubt their own understanding of their political system . . . [and gives rise to] a new hostility toward politics and government" (1975, p. 99). With 1968 National Election Study data, Robinson (1975) revealed a powerful connection between reliance on television network news and three measures of nonnormative beliefs about American politics: that one cannot understand politics, that government leaders are crooked, and that elected officials lose touch with citizens after an election. Brehm and Rahn (1997) demonstrate that rising levels of television viewing correlate with falling levels of civic engagement as measured by several indices of social capital.

Microapproaches

Whereas macroapproaches employ broad strokes, examining media (especially television) in general terms, microapproaches are more complicated, nuanced, and equivocal. These efforts focus on individual communication forms, sometimes in isolation but sometimes in comparison to one or two other forms.

Bucy, D'Angelo, and Newhagen (1999) disputed Robinson's (1975, 1976) video-malaise position as well as Putnam's (1995, 2000) social erosion thesis by arguing that the electorate actively and critically consumes the "new media" as an actual form of indirect political activity. These authors define the new media as including "radio and television talk shows that incorporate responses to listener calls, faxes, e-mail messages, and online information services sponsored by major media organizations" (Bucy et al., 1999, p. 337). In a survey of Prince George, Maryland, residents, these authors found that most new media use significantly predicted voting behavior and political interest. These results strongly militate against the claim that television is "the agent of mass alienation that some critics would make it out to be" (p. 347). Similarly, Pan and Kosicki (1997) demonstrated that the interactive features of call-in radio and television programming transforms consumption of those communication forms into a manifest form of political participation. More specifically, they found that call-in audiences are more ideologically homogeneous, more likely to be concerned about national politics, more likely to contact public officials, and more likely to join or contribute money to a political cause.

In other cases, qualifications to the macroapproach's conclusions are more intricate. Wilkins (2000) argues that "blaming television for public disengagement from political life appears to be too simplistic" (p. 577). She finds that television news consumers are actually more likely to engage in political participation than those who do not watch the television news, but ultimately, she calls for more research. Norris (2002a), in a secondary analysis of National Election Survey data from the 2000 election season, found that those who consume a mix of television news and entertainment fare maintain relatively high levels of civic engagement defined as "knowledge, trust, efficacy, political discussion, and turn out" (p. 8). Only when respondents reported heavy consumption of entertainment television did she find higher levels of political disaffection, but she notes that "these findings were outweighed by the number of cases where exposure to campaign information from sources is positively related indicators of civic engagement" (p. 8). Even when studied alongside more traditional forms of campaign media consumption (e.g., newspaper use), the salutary associations with hard news television consumption persists. McLeod, Scheufele, and Moy (1999) found that, when seeking politically relevant information, citizens supplemented the television news with newspaper consumption and interpersonal political discussions. The authors concluded that each of these three communication forms uniquely enhanced the ability of respondents to execute their institutional duties.

Newspapers, both in isolation and compared to other communication forms, have also been evaluated for their impact on politically normative attitudes and behaviors. Eveland and Scheufele (2000) found that newspaper consumption enhances normative outcomes for more educated readers. They concluded that "newspapers seem to provide information that disproportionately benefits individuals who are already more likely to engage in participatory activities" (p. 231). McLeod and colleagues (1996) demonstrated that, in the 1992 election season, newspapers and television had the greatest beneficial impact on politically normative outcomes. The finding that newspaper readers are more politically active is hardly a novel or unexpected phenomenon.

Contrary to conventional wisdom, there is strong evidence that negative political advertising may not be as harmful to political attitudes and behaviors as once assumed, though the evidence is equivocal. On one side of the issue, Ansolabehere, Iyenger, Simon, and Valentino (1994) performed tightly controlled experiments to compare the effects of negative and positive political advertisements on their subjects' anticipated political behavior. They found that negative advertisements produce a 5 percent decrease in the willingness to cast a ballot. Kahn and Kennedy (1999) argue that the type of political advertisement is instrumental in determining its impact. When "constructive" negative commercials were compared to "destructive" commercials, they found that subjects exposed to constructive ads were significantly more likely to go to the polls than those in the other experimental group. Lau and Sigelman (2000) reviewed twenty-eight studies examining the impact of negative campaign ads on political mobilization. Sixteen studies showed no significant difference in the relative impact of positive and negative ads on political participation, nine studies demonstrated that exposure to negative ads actually increased voting behavior, and thirteen studies showed that negative campaign commercials demobilized their viewers. Interestingly, the majority of studies showed that negative advertising does not affect voter turnout or that, alternatively, it actually increases turnout. Finkel and Geer (1998) content analyzed campaign advertisements from 1960 through 1992. They found that there was no significant relationship between high levels of negative advertising and voting rates. In fact, they found that those who consumed more negative advertising were generally the most mobilized members of the electorate. Their findings even contradict Kahn and Kennedy's (1999) experimental evidence showing demobilization effects for independent voters. Finally, Goldstein and Freedman (2002) used network records of negative ad runs and National Election Survey data to locate and survey respondents who were most likely to have been exposed to televised negative commercials in the 2000 election season. They confirmed their hypothesis that negative attack ads "stimulate voters . . . , by raising interest, and by communicating the notion that something important is at stake in the outcome of an election" (p. 735). Ultimately, negative ads were significantly associated with greater levels of voter turnout regardless of "partisanship, information, or attention to the campaign" (p. 736).

If negative television advertising represents the dark side of campaign communication forms, candidate debates represent the light side. Researchers maintain a strong faith in debate viewing's potential to promote democratic values and participation. Patterson (2002) reports that viewing debates generates political interest; in fact, along with the Super Bowl and the Olympics, they are among the most-watched televised events. Pfau (2002) notes: "political communication scholars operate from the premise that debates matter—that they make a difference: in people's knowledge and perceptions and, therefore, in campaign outcomes; and by strengthening the democratic process itself" (p. 251). Hart (2000) documents that debates produce less bombast and assertion, resulting in "an almost philosophical, or idealistic, discourse" that contains "space for examining basic premises" (pp. 118, 121). His data suggest that presidential debates are superior to other venues, that they are comparatively "sober," "focused," and "plainspoken," "with . . . potential to create genuine dialogue" (p. 126).

Unfortunately, hard evidence on debate viewing and normative outcomes is sparse and generally inconclusive. Spiker and McKinney (1999) experimentally associated debate viewing with heightened levels of political malaise; however, they argue that cynicism does not automatically depress political activity and that, in some cases, it might enhance it. Ultimately, political malaise was most pronounced for subjects given an opportunity to discuss the debates with other subjects in a focus group–like setting. Weaver, Drew, and Wu (1998) investigated candidate debate watching but failed to find any significant relationships with their outcome variables. Hellweg, Pfau, and Brydon (1992) report that campaign context impacts the potential for all debate effects, including normative outcomes. Their argument agrees with Becker and Kraus's (1978) classic observation that the impact of campaign communication is relative to a variety of factors: when "one of the candidate's is not well-known, many voters are undecided, the contest appears to be a close one, and party allegiances are weak" (p. 267).

The effects of political talk radio on normative political outcomes are much more surprising and much less ambiguous. Moy and Pfau (2000) found that talk radio exposure was associated with political cynicism, but other research shows that this cynicism is more likely to mobilize than to depress political activity. Bucy et al. (1999) documented that talk radio listeners are more likely to vote. Hofstetter and colleagues (1994) found that "frequent listeners to political talk radio are more interested in politics, pay more attention to politics in mass media, vote more, and participate more than others in a variety of political activities" (p. 477). Owen (1996) employed a nationwide survey and discovered that citizens use political talk radio to "become more personally engaged with political problems, and this, in turn can inspire participation" (p. 145). On the other hand, researchers need to be aware of the potential for the hostile tone of political talk radio to depress normative outcomes. Mutz (2004) used experimental data to show the potential for uncivil political discourse, within the context of a *Hardball*-like television program, to instill negative attitudes toward implicated government institutions.

Impossible to ignore in any discussion of political media is the Internet. Many have hailed the Internet's arrival as a revolution in normative political activity, but in fact the empirical data have yet to confirm their hopes. Norris (1999) contends that "the proportion of Americans currently involved in any form of online election activity suggests the need for caution about the transformative capacity of the Web for democracy, at least in the short term" (p.

82). She further suggests that the Internet is a venue for activists and "may never be a mass medium in terms of a shared political experience" (p. 75). Davis and Owen (1998) failed to find any significant relationship between Internet use and political interest. On the other hand, Johnson and Kaye (1998) documented an opposite finding. Ultimately, it seems that, at least in the short term, the Internet is likely to exacerbate the knowledge gap in political knowledge and attitudes. Davis (1999) concludes that "rather than acting as a revolutionary tool rearranging power and instigating direct democracy, the Internet is destined to become dominated by the same actors in American politics who currently utilize other mediums" (p. 5).

The best that scholars of political communication can do is to continue monitoring the impact of the Internet as well as the impact of the other communication forms discussed in this book. Because both the technique and the content of politically relevant communication forms are in a constant state of flux, it has become ever more necessary to develop sensitive instruments capable of tracking the relationship between media use and normative political outcomes as well as other outcome variables. We believe that our multiple approach offers the best mechanism for acting on this prescription.

A Third Approach

This investigation examines the relative impact of seventeen communication forms on normative political outcomes. It uses a statistical technique that allows simultaneous assessment of the unique impact of specific communication forms while controlling for the impact of all other forms. This approach combines the breadth of the macroapproach with the sensitivity to subtle nuances characterized by the microapproach.

This study assumes that "we should look at what all the media have to say," systematically examining "the totality of political information that is made available" to the electorate (Page, 1996, p. 1). Delli Carpini (2004) eloquently conveyed the need for this approach:

> Politically relevant information can take many forms . . . , emanate from many sources (from face-to-face exchanges to newspapers to television to the Internet), and have many different impacts . . . beginning with the questions, "What information matters?" and "Where do people get this information?" and letting the answers to these questions determine the particular media and genres we study, would, I believe, produce a more nuanced, integrated, and ultimately accurate picture of how media affects democratic engagement. (p. 423)

In this spirit, we next assess the influence of seventeen communication forms on normative political outcomes.

We know of only one other effort that has employed this approach to examine normative political outcomes. Pfau, Cho, and Chong (2001), in a survey of Dane County, Wisconsin, during the 2000 presidential election, found that newspapers, televised presidential debates, and political conversations were positively associated with most normative outcomes (e.g., political interest, positive attitudes about the process, and democratic participation). The study also found that television network news and radio news were associated with at least one positive normative political outcome. On the other hand, newsmagazines, print materials, campaign ads, political talk radio, television newsmagazines, television talk shows, and the Internet were not associated with any normative political outcomes.

INFLUENCE OF COMMUNICATION FORMS ON NORMATIVE OUTCOMES

The specific methods employed in this investigation are spelled out in detail in the appendix. However, it is worth reviewing the specific normative democratic outcomes assessed in this study: political expertise, attitude toward the democratic process, and likelihood of participating in the democratic process.

The political expertise of individuals was measured as a respondent's awareness of, interest in, and knowledge of the presidential campaign. Attitude toward the democratic process was a measure of how positively or negatively a respondent viewed the electoral process by which an American president is selected. Finally, likelihood of participating in the democratic process assessed how likely an individual was to perform each of the following tasks: seek out information about a presidential candidate and/or his positions, contribute time or money to a presidential political campaign, and go to the polls and vote. The study assessed the influence of relevant sociodemographic variables and the seventeen communication forms on each normative outcome.[1] What follows are the results of this research, with each phase of the campaign examined in turn.

The Mid- and Late-September Phase of the Campaign

Sociodemographic Variables

During the first phase of this research project,[2] several sociodemographic variables were related to normative democratic outcomes (see table 5.1). The gender of respondents impacted their level of political expertise, with males exhibiting higher levels of political expertise during this phase of the campaign. Respondents' age was related to level of political expertise, with older respondents demonstrating more knowledge about politics. Interestingly, the age of respondents was negatively related to participation in the political process, although this relationship was weak. Older respondents were less likely to participate: to vote, seek information, or volunteer time or money to a candidate.

Respondents' level of education impacted all three normative democratic outcomes, positively impacting two of the variables—political expertise and participation in the electoral process—and negatively influencing attitude about the process. More educated respondents knew more about the campaign and were more likely to vote, volunteer, or seek information about the candidates. However, more educated citizens possessed more negative attitudes about the electoral process.

Respondents' party identification impacted all the normative democratic measures, although some of the relationships were weak. Specifically, Republican identification positively impacted political expertise, attitude toward democratic process, and participation, although the latter two relationships were weak. Democratic identifiers exhibited greater political expertise and were more likely to participate in the process, though again these relationships were weak. However, Democratic identifiers reported a more negative attitude about the democratic process, perhaps because the Democratic ticket was trailing in most polls in September, when the phase 1 survey was conducted.

Finally, respondents' level of political expertise was positively related to the two other normative outcomes measured in this research—attitude about the democratic process and likelihood of participating. This finding suggests that the more an individual knows about and is interested in a presidential campaign, the more positive he or she perceives the process of electing a president and the more likely he or she is to vote, seek out political information, and contribute to a campaign. In this case, then, improving one normative outcome—that of political expertise—seems to positively impact the other normative outcomes of interest in this project.

Communication Use

During the mid- and late-September phase of the 2004 presidential election, political conversations with others impacted all the normative democratic outcomes investigated as part of this project[3] (see table 5.1). The relationship between conversations and the normative outcomes were all positive. Talking to other people about the political campaign was related with higher levels of political expertise, a greater likelihood of participating in the democratic process, and more positive attitude about the process, although this last relationship was weak. Ultimately, for all three of the normative outcomes, political conversations had the most robust, positive effects during phase 1 of the study. In addition to conversations, people's anticipation of the upcoming presidential debates was related with greater political expertise and a greater likelihood of participating in the democratic process. Therefore, anticipation of debates also exhibited a pattern of leading to positive democratic outcomes.

Additional communication forms impacted one of three normative outcomes examined during phase 1. Use of local television news, political talk radio, and television talk shows was related to higher levels of political expertise. On the other hand, use of television comedic shows led to lower levels of political expertise. The use of movies/DVDs was related to more positive thoughts about the democratic process, while use of newspapers had the opposite effect, leading to more negative thoughts about the democratic process. Beyond these specific impacts, no other communication forms impacted normative democratic outcomes at phase 1.

Late-October/Early-November Phase of the Campaign

Sociodemographic Variables

Compared to phase 1, late-October/early-November results revealed less influence of sociodemographic variables on normative political outcomes (see table 5.2). Republican identification and respondent political expertise were associated with more positive attitudes about the electoral process. This means that Republicans and those who assess themselves as being very interested in and knowledgeable about politics manifested more positive attitudes about the electoral system. No other sociodemographic variables were related to political expertise.

A number of sociodemographic variables impacted political participation. Gender was positively related to participation, with men significantly more likely to participate in the political process. Age was negatively associated with participation. Older people were less likely to participate. Greater education was positively related to participation. More educated respondents were more likely to participate. Finally, Democratic identifiers and individuals reporting higher levels of political expertise were more likely to participate in the political process.

Communication Use

The phase 2 survey[4] found that, overall, a number of specific communication forms affected normative political outcomes most positively (see table 5.2).

These results contradict the macroviews that generally associate media campaign coverage with overall reductions in normative political outcomes (Cappella & Jamieson, 1997; Patterson, 1993, 2002).

In terms of the influence of particular communication forms, the pattern of results revealed that use of movies/DVDs was associated with negative attitudes about the political process and that use of television comedic programming was associated with less political participation, whereas television entertainment talk use was associated with positive attitudes about the democratic process. We believe that the results for movies and television comedy make a statement about those who rely more on entertainment as a source of political information. We suspect that reliance on diversionary sources of political information is indicative of preexisting nonnormative political attitudes and behaviors. Heavier users are citizens who are already on the electoral fringe. The positive impact of television entertainment talk shows is probably due to the unique nature of those programs. The National Annenberg Election Survey (2004) revealed that viewers of late-night entertainment talk shows (*The Tonight Show* and *Late Night with David Letterman*) and late-night comedy shows (*The Daily Show with Jon Stewart*) were more likely than nonviewers to know information about the candidates and their positions on issues.

In accordance with previous research that indicates a strong relationship between political talk radio and normative outcomes, our survey documented strong normative outcomes for political talk radio on two of our three measures (attitudes about process and participation). These results contradict Owen's (1996) assertion that political talk radio was unique to the 1990s and that its influence would soon fade. Our results indicate that political talk radio remains a vital force in American presidential politics. Viewing presidential debates was also related to the two normative outcomes assessed in this research. Debate viewing was associated with increased levels of political expertise and greater participation in the electoral process.

During phase 2, political conversations were associated with political interest as well as with political participation. Given Eveland's (2004) finding that political conversations are associated with in-depth cognitive processing and given that such processing is effortful, it makes sense that more interest would be a prerequisite for political talk. In addition, it makes sense that people who talk about politics would be more likely to participate in democratic processes. In fact, social capital theorists define interpersonal contact and trust as a form of civic engagement (Brehm & Rahn, 1997). In addition, Wilkins (2000) has found that civic engagement is predictive of democratic participation.

The only normative outcome associated with network television news was a positive relationship with political knowledge. This finding is consistent with Robinson's (1975, 1976) video-malaise argument. He argues that television network news enhances political interest while at the same time instilling a sense of impotence and despair. Caught in a web of malaise, network news viewers may find themselves caged on the sidelines of American politics. Our results would lend support for that conclusion.

Use of newspapers was found to be positively related to likelihood of participation but not related to the two other normative outcomes assessed in this project. This result is consistent with the changing nature of the communication landscape. In light of these findings, it may be time to readjust prior assumptions. As Pan and Kosicki (1997) observe, political communication scholars should expect that the electorate may be finding new and more interactive means of engaging political information (e.g., call-in talk shows). Under such a rubric of change, it makes sense that cold, cognitive-oriented newsprint would be among the first casualties.

For the remaining communication forms, only one exhibited any impact on the normative democratic outcomes. Radio news was positively associated with political interest but negatively related to attitudes about the democratic process. Patterson's (2002) finding that dissatisfied hard news consumers have flocked to radio news is a plausible explanation for why radio news users may be dissatisfied with the process. Their dissatisfaction could stem from what they perceive as the superficial campaign coverage by the mainstream media. Patterson (2002) further reports that since 1990, radio news listenership has increased by as much 300 percent. Radio news listeners are both dissatisfied and politically interested. This profile conforms perfectly to our findings.

The remaining communication forms exerted no impact on normative outcomes. This includes newsmagazines, print materials, local television news, campaign ads, television newsmagazines, television talk shows, and the Internet.

CONCLUSION

The results of this investigation indicate that communication use exerts more influence on normative democratic outcomes as Election Day approaches. The impact of communication use was greater in late October and early November, particularly on the indices of attitude toward the democratic process and likelihood of participating in the electoral process (9 vs. 5 percent on the former and 14 vs. 8 percent on the latter).

Overall, the pattern of results indicates that many traditional communication forms—and some of the "new" or alternative forms—exerted a positive influence on normative outcomes.

The most significant influence was found for political conversations. Political talk—that is, people talking to friends, family, or coworkers about politics or the presidential election—led to higher levels of political expertise and a greater likelihood of participating in the election for both phases of this research. These results support previous findings (Chaffee, 1986; Fishkin, 1995; Pfau et al., 2001; Scheufele, 2002) that support the utility of political talk in enhancing normative outcomes. As Moy, Torres, et al. (2005) observe, "Discussion of political issues is critical to key processes of well-functioning democratic systems" (p. 115).

Ultimately, political conversations are likely microinstances of public deliberation. If a democracy is built on the principle of citizen participation in political decision making, then discussion about politics among friends and family serves as an appropriation of this function in contemporary American society. With political conversations, the discussion is not taking place in the town hall format envisioned by the Founding Fathers, but if personal political conversations are actually derivative of a basic democratic principle, then it is not surprising that conversations would facilitate values such as the acquisition of political knowledge and greater participation. Further, the process of talking with others about politics—a cognitive process—should contribute to political knowledge. Through communicating about politics with friends or family, one discovers new political facts.

In addition to political conversations, greater use of political talk radio was found to be associated with multiple normative outcomes across both phases of this study. This finding is in line with previous research that found a positive relationship between using talk radio and normative democratic outcomes (Bennett, 1998; Bucy et al., 1999; Hofstetter et al., 1994; Moy et al., 2005; Owen, 1996; Pan & Kosicki, 1997). Political talk radio positively impacted each of the three normative outcomes investigated here at some point during either of the two phases of this research. The finding that political talk radio increases political expertise, leads to a more positive attitude about the electoral process, and increases the likelihood of participating in an election is interesting since talk radio appeals primarily to Republicans (Hollander, 1996; Kurtz, 1996; Lee & Cappella, 2001). Political talk radio functions as both a political educator and a motivator for conservatives in America. Our results find no comparable communication form that provides such a robust, positive impact on normative outcomes for Democratic identifiers.

The use of presidential debates was also found to positively impact multiple normative outcomes. In both phases of this study, the use of presidential debates was found to lead to greater political expertise and enhanced likelihood of participating in the democratic process. Again, this finding supports previous research that has produced similar results (Hart, 2000; Patterson,

2002; Pfau, 2002; The Racine Group, 2002). American presidential debates continue to function as a media event, gathering large television audiences and generating large-scale discussion across many diverse communication forms (Patterson, 2002). The attention generated by presidential debates, along with the continued talk about debates on other media forms, means that presidential debates continue to echo through the media landscape long after the event has occurred.

Beyond these examples of broad communication form impact, other traditional forms exerted a more limited influence on normative outcomes. In September, local television news and, during late October, network television news were positively related to political expertise. Also during October, use of newspapers was positively associated with likelihood of participating in the democratic process. Among traditional communication forms, only the use of radio news was negatively linked to normative outcomes, and only on one of the normative outcomes: in late October, it was negatively associated with attitude toward the democratic process. Therefore, overall, this pattern of results suggests that most traditional communication forms promote normative democratic outcomes, thus confirming the previous findings of other political communication researchers (Bucy et al., 1999; McLeod et al., 1996; Moy, Torres, et al., 2005; Norris, 2002a; Pfau et al., 2001).

In contrast to the findings for traditional communication forms, more entertainment-oriented communication forms exerted mixed influence on the normative outcomes examined in this project. Most corrosive to normative outcomes was people's use of television comedic programs. During September, this usage was negatively associated with political expertise, and in late October it was negatively related to the likelihood of participating in the democratic process.

However, the influence of television entertainment talk shows such as *Late Night with David Letterman* and *The Tonight Show with Jay Leno* was associated with a greater likelihood of participating in the democratic process. In addition, use of television entertainment talk shows was positively associated with political expertise during phase 1 and positively associated with the individual's attitude about the democratic process at phase 2. The finding that entertainment talk show use is positively linked to normative outcomes supports similar findings by the Annenberg Public Policy Center (2004d) and a recent study by Moy, Xenos, and Hess (2005).

Finally, the influence of movies/DVDs was mixed. People's use of movies/DVDs was positively associated with attitude toward the democratic process earlier in the campaign but was negatively related to attitude toward the process late in the campaign. Perhaps the themes of Michael Moore's film *Fahrenheit 9/11*—that the 2000 presidential election was a fraud and that the

George W. Bush administration functions with a modus operandi of distortion, lies, and deceit—eventually sank in with the audience that was receptive to the film, so that as the campaign progressed, the film's enthusiasts turned from a hopeful view of the election to a pessimistic outlook as to whether the 2004 presidential election would produce political change.

Other communication forms besides the ones discussed to this point exerted no influence on normative democratic outcomes. People's use of newsmagazines, television talk shows, prime-time television political drama, television newsmagazines, the Internet, televised candidate advertising, and printed materials affected no normative outcomes. The finding that the Internet exerted no impact on normative outcomes contradicts some research that the use of the Internet promotes political interest (Johnson & Kaye, 1998), but the results are consistent with most previous studies examining Internet use and political interest and/or participation in the democratic process (e.g., Davis, 1999; Davis & Owen, 1998; Norris, 2001; Pfau et al., 2001).

Despite the uproar over whether political attack ads stimulate, suppress, or have no effect on voter turnout in an election, this is the second consecutive investigation that examined people's use of political advertising in tandem with other relevant communication forms that reported no effects on normative democratic outcomes (Pfau et al., 2001). It should be noted, however, that all research that asks respondents to self-report their exposure and attention paid to political advertisements probably underreports the amount of people's political ad use. This is because people are particularly hesitant to acknowledge the use of political ads, as they claim to dislike political advertising more than other political communication forms.

Ultimately, this research finds that many communication forms exert a positive impact, many communication forms exert no impact, and a few communication forms exert a negative impact on the normative democratic outcomes. So what do these findings mean for the study of normative democratic theory? There has been a concerted effort to determine the cause of what is seen as a continuing decline in the level of participation in both American elections and civic or political organizations (Patterson, 2002; Putnam, 2000). As mentioned previously, such a decline in participation is potentially very hazardous for the continued health of a democratic society. However, the claim that the modern media environment is partially to blame for such a decline in political participation (Patterson, 2002) is not supported by the data analyzed here, as, overall, many communication forms were positively related to normative democratic outcomes, while only a few forms exhibited a negative relationship with these outcomes.

Political communication researchers need to collect data in future campaigns to see how the relationships between communications use and democratic values evolve. It is imperative that we ascertain not only how all communication forms are impacting normative democratic outcomes in the present but also how such influence is changing. Ultimately, there may be no more important question political communication scholars can pose than, What is the impact of campaign communication on normative democratic outcomes? For, as Delli Carpini (2004) has argued, "limitations in the communications environment are pinpointed as a primary reason why democratic practice falls short of normative expectations" (p. 395).

NOTES

1. Hierarchical regression analyses were employed to assess the relative influence of communication forms on normative outcomes. The variables were entered causally: sociodemographic variables in block 1 and communication forms in block 2. This method permitted a judgment of the influence of each block of variables on normative outcomes and ensured a net judgment of communication effects, assessed after controlling for other influence.

2. The results of the first survey revealed that the full regression equations were significant for all dependent variables: political expertise, $F(23, 381) = 13.19$, $p < .001$; attitude toward the process used to elect a president, $F(24, 380) = 2.87, p < .001$; and likelihood of participating in the political process, $F(24, 380) = 13.69, p < .001$.

3. Overall variances accounted for by combined communication forms on normative indicators were modest: 24 percent for political expertise and, with expertise incorporated into analyses as a control variable, 5 percent on attitude toward process and 8 percent on the likelihood of participating.

4. The results of the second survey indicated that full regression equations were significant for all three dependent variables: political expertise, $F(23, 378) = 8.33, p < .001$; attitude toward the process used to elect a president, $F(24, 377) = 4.54, p .001$; and likelihood of participating in the political process, $F(24, 377) = 13.97, p < .001$. Overall variances accounted for in late October were greater than those reported during the September phase of the study: 29 percent for political expertise and, with expertise incorporated into analyses as a control variable, 9 percent on attitude toward process and 12 percent on the likelihood of participating

Table 5.1. Mid- and Late-September Media Use and Attitudes about the Democratic Process

	Attitude about Process	Political Expertise	Participation
Control variables			
Gender (male)	.08	−.11*	.015
Age	.03	.19*	−.08+
Education	−.11+	.17*	.09**
Income	−.10+	.045	.07
Party identification (Democrat)	−.12**	.10**	.08+
Party identification (Republican)	.11+	.17*	.09+
Political expertise	.15**	—	.42*
R^2	.105*	.21*	.38*
Communication use			
Network television news	−.095	.04	.01
Local television news	.10	.11**	−.02
Newspapers	−.11**	−.025	.00
Magazines	.00	.02	.01
Political talk radio	.01	.11**	−.03
Radio news	.04	−.06	.08
Television talk	−.02	.11**	−.06
Television entertainment talk	−.02	.07	−.01
Television political drama	−.08	−.05	−.06
Television comedic shows	−.05	−.16*	−.03
Television newsmagazines	.01	.04	−.06
Movies/DVDs	.13**	.03	.00
Web	−.01	.01	.06
Candidate debates	.07	.24*	.14*
Candidate ads	−.045	−.08	−.03
Conversations	.09+	.24*	.19*
Printed materials	.09+	.05	−.09+
Incremental R^2	.05	.24*	.08*
Model $F(24, 380)$	2.87*	13.19*	13.69*

Note. Entries are standardized coefficients from ordinary-least-squares regression.
* Significant at $p < .01$.
** Significant at $p < .05$.
+ Significant at $p < .10$.

Table 5.2. Mid- and Late-September Media Use and Attitudes about the Democratic Process

	Attitude about Process	Political Expertise	Participation
Control variables			
Gender (male)	.08+	−.08+	.10**
Age	−.03	.10+	−.11**
Education	−.09+	.08+	.10**
Income	.00	.04	.045
Party identification (Democrat)	.015	.04	.13*
Party identification (Republican)	.20*	.08	.03
Political expertise	.20*	—	.33*
R^2	.14*	.05*	.33*
Communication use			
Network television news	.09	.14**	.02
Local television news	.09	−.10+	−.05
Newspapers	.02	.05	.10**
Magazines	−.03	.055	−.01
Political talk radio	.13**	.03	.15*
Radio news	−.12**	.15*	.04
Television talk	−.04	.01	.04
Television entertainment talk	.15**	.02	.05
Television political drama	.07	.05	−.01
Television comedic shows	−.04	−.09	−.16*
Television newsmagazines	−.08	−.025	−.06
Movies/DVDs	−.17*	.05	.06
Web	−.01	.00	.07
Candidate debates	−.08	.32*	.11**
Candidate ads	.07	.05	−.04
Conversations	.08	.115**	.24*
Printed materials	.04	−.05	.04
Incremental R^2	.09*	.29*	.14*
Model $F(24, 380)$	4.54*	8.33*	13.97*

Note. Entries are standardized coefficients from ordinary-least-squares regression.
* Significant at $p < .01$.
** Significant at $p < .05$.
+ Significant at $p < .10$.

Appendix: Design of the Studies

> We do not doubt the power and the promise of the survey method. . . . Always, the challenge is to allow ourselves to learn more. . . . In a positive as well as negative sense, there are many unanswered questions about both questions and answers.
>
> —Howard Schuman, University of Michigan, and Stanley Presser, University of Maryland (1996, p. 316)

Questions about the influence of communication media in political campaigns are difficult and, in many respects, still unresolved (McGuire, 1986; Zaller, 1992). However, in the twenty-first century, the task of addressing such questions has grown even more intricate because of "the decline of certain media that have defined the context of communication and democracy since the end of World War II and perhaps longer" (Carey, 1995, p. 379) and the emergence of a variety of new communication forms. Indeed, we are living in an era of expanding communication options and the growing fragmentation of what once was a broad, general mass media audience into a myriad of smaller, niche audiences (Chaffee & Metzger, 2001).

But it isn't just the sheer number of communication forms that poses problems for assessing the influence of communication in political campaigns. It is also the interwoven nature of the communication environment (Owen, 1991; Pfau, Cho, & Chong, 2001). More and more, prospective voters rely on multiple communication forms, some of which intend to provide information about candidates and campaigns but others that seek to offer pure entertainment. Moreover, effects of communication are commingled. What candidates might say in one forum finds its way into other communication venues. For example, a candidate's statement in televised debates is covered in news, is dissected on talk radio and television, finds its way into ads, and is parodied in late-night comedic shows. The same utterance may influence some people who viewed the televised debate, affect others who experienced it for the first time in news or on talk radio or television, and impact others who encountered it in ads or on late-night comedy.

This is an era of diverse communication forms, and people's perceptions about candidates are, in part, the product of their communication use patterns, consisting of a unique blending of traditional and alternative communication forms. This development makes the task of ascertaining the influence of particular communication forms all the more difficult. West (2000) refers to the contemporary political communication environment as "fragmented," explaining that such an environment results in "massive measurement and conceptual problems . . . in disentangling the impact of various sources of information" (p. 155).

The once-common microapproach of examining the influence of communication forms individually, in isolation, is no longer appropriate. In today's interwoven campaign communication environment, campaign communication that is initiated in one forum spreads quickly into other forums, some of them traditional campaign communication venues such as newspapers or network television news, but some best characterized as alternative communication forms, such as late-night entertainment talk shows or comedic programming (Pfau et al., 2001), what Davis and Owen (1998) call "new media." However, political communication scholars have largely ignored the influence of these alternative communication venues in election campaigns (Baum, 2003), or, when they have studied the influence of new communication forms, they have examined them in isolation from the broader contemporary communication matrix.

What is needed is a macrocomprehensive approach, examining the simultaneous influence of all relevant communication forms: assessing the impact of each form in turn while controlling the influence of all other forms. This approach is required because, as Holbert (2004) maintains, "no one type of media content functions in a vacuum relative to other media" (p. 645). Hence, this investigation employs a macroapproach. It presumes that "we should look at what all the media have to say," systematically examining "the totality of political information that is made available" to citizens (Page, 1996, p. 7). This comprehensive media approach is appropriate because "politically relevant information can take many forms . . . , emanate from many sources (from face-to-face exchanges to newspapers to television to the Internet), and have many different impacts" (Delli Carpini, 2004, p. 423). Thus, Delli Carpini (2004) recommends that political communication scholars should attempt to determine where people acquire all politically relevant information in order to provide a more accurate and complete sense of the role and influence of the media in political campaigns.

The study assessed the relative impact of seventeen communication forms on people's perceptions of presidential candidates and democratic process during two periods of the 2004 presidential campaign: the first in September (from September 9, following the Republican National Convention, through the afternoon of September 30, on the eve of the first presidential debate) and the second during the last two weeks of the general election campaign (from October 18 through November 1).

SURVEY METHOD

Two national telephone surveys were conducted by the University of Oklahoma Public Opinion Learning Laboratory. The first survey consisted of 467 partially completed interviews (406 fully completed interviews), and the second survey consisted of 458 partially completed interviews (402 fully completed interviews). All respondents were prospective voters who resided in the forty-eight contiguous states. The national sample was obtained from Survey Sampling Inc. and was screened of nonresidential numbers. One adult from each eligible household was chosen as respondent. The survey instrument was pilot-tested before actual fieldwork. The two surveys featured the same measures, which are described in detail in the "Variables and Instruments" section.

The surveys achieved satisfactory response rates and operated within acceptable margins of error, as described in table A.1. Response rate is important since it ensures that completed interviews reflect the sample from which they are drawn and, therefore, the population to which researchers want to generalize findings. Survey margin of error is important because it addresses how accurate findings are. For example, using the 95 percent confidence interval employed in this investigation, the margins of error of less than ±5 percent in both surveys means that there is a 95 percent chance that the true population values lie within plus or minus 5 percent of the results obtained from the sample. Together, the response rate and margin of error speak to the stability of survey findings. Satisfactory response rates and relatively low margins of error increase the likelihood that replications involving other samples drawn from the same population would yield similar results.

As indicated previously, response rates for each of the two surveys conducted for this investigation were satisfactory, a relative judgment in the sense that response rates of all surveys have been declining for more than a decade. Surveys with acceptable response rates produce findings that are more likely to generalize to the population of potential voters. Another way to ensure generalizability is to check the sample statistics against population parameters to make sure that samples reasonably reflect the populations from which they were drawn. This minimizes concerns over external validity because, when samples reasonably reflect the population from which they are drawn, generalizability is usually ensured even if the overall response rate is less than optimal (Merkle, 1996).

Table A.2 compares sample statistics and population parameters on a number of sociodemographic factors. The samples reasonably reflected the population benchmark on most items. However, compared to the population, both of the surveys were somewhat skewed toward females and greater education levels. More troubling is the fact that both of the surveys featured more Republicans and fewer Independents than the population benchmark. However, this is less alarming than appears at first glance. The surveys asked respondents, "Generally speaking, do you consider yourself a Democrat, Republican, or Independent, or do you have no affiliation?" It asked not what their registration was but what they considered themselves to be. Since the 2004 presidential campaign featured an incumbent Republican who led in most polls conducted during both survey periods, the question may have elicited respondents' preferences in the 2004 election more than their actual party registration. Both surveys closely mirrored the population in terms of age and household income.

In sum, response rate was satisfactory, but there were some discrepancies between the sample statistics and population parameters. Nonetheless, concerns over generalizability of the study's findings are less than for other purely descriptive surveys. The focus of this investigation was not simply to describe people's perceptions about either the presidential candidates or the democratic process, as is true of most polls that are conducted during a presidential campaign. If it were, the question of whether those interviewed reflected the sample and whether the sample mirrored the population would be paramount. Instead, this investigation was about linkages between people's media use and their perceptions of candidates and the democratic process. In this context, the obtained response rate, which is typical of response rates of most contemporary surveys, and the modest discrepancies between the sample statistics and the population parameters are much less of a concern.

VARIABLES AND INSTRUMENTS

The surveys gathered relevant sociodemographic data, probed communication use patterns during the 2004 presidential election campaign, and assessed people's perceptions of candidates' character, their overall attitudes about the candidates, their likelihood of voting for the candidates, and the affective and cognitive basis of these perceptions. In addition, surveys evaluated respondents' attitudes toward the process by which we elect a president and the likelihood of participating in that process.

All instruments employed in this study are proven measures with impressive track records. All of the multiple-item measures featured in the study were assessed for internal consistency using Cronbach's (1951) coefficient alpha. The specific measures are described next.

Sociodemographics

Respondents' sociodemographic characteristics, including sex, age, education, household income, and political party affiliation, served as control variables in all analyses. Respondents' political expertise served as a control variable in analyses addressing the influence of communication use on perceptions of candidates, but it functioned both as a control and a dependent variable in analyses about the impact of communication use on the democratic process.

Respondents' sex was determined without specifically asking and was operationalized as male or female. Age was assessed by asking respondents to indicate their age on their last birthday as less than thirty, thirty to forty-four, forty-five to fifty-nine, or sixty or more years. Education was operationalized as some high school, high school degree, some post–high school education, college or professional school degree, or a master's or advanced professional degree. Household income was operationalized as less than $15,000, between $15,000 and $29,999, between $30,000 and $44,999, between $45,000 and $59,999, between $60,000 and $74,999, and more than $75,000. Respondent political party affiliation was gauged as Democrat, Republican, Independent, or no affiliation. Prior to data analyses, researchers computed dummy variables for Democratic and Republican affiliation from the party identification variables.

Political expertise captures people's knowledge and interest in political objects (Fiske, Lau, & Smith, 1990). Political expertise was operationalized as respondents' awareness of, interest in, and knowledge of the presidential campaign. It was assessed using three seven-interval, bipolar scales employed in past research by Fiske and colleagues (1990), Price and Zaller (1993), and Moy and Pfau (2000).

For initial correlation analysis, respondents' communication use during the two phases of the campaign was examined in relation to their party identification, strength of party identification, and political interest. Operationalization of communication use is described here. Political party identification was described previously. Strength of party identification was assessed for those people who identified with one of the two political parties using a single seven-interval scale that ranged from weak affiliation to strong affiliation. Political interest was measured with a single seven-interval scale drawn from the political expertise measure, as described previously. The scale ranged from very low to very high.

Measures of Communication Use

Communication use was the primary variable of interest in this study. It served as the independent variable in all regression analyses. The study featured multiple communication sources, reflecting the "transformational" nature of contemporary use patterns (Chesebro & Bertelsen, 1996, p. 134). Scholars justify this more comprehensive approach to media use. For example, Moy and Pfau (2000, p. 65) argue that "today's media environment embodies a complex mosaic of communication sources." Holbert (2004, p. 645) advises that "no one type of media content functions in a vacuum relative to other media." The implication of this position is that researchers should examine the entire array of communication forms in tandem, which enables a parsing of the influence of any one form while simultaneously controlling for the influence of all other forms.

This study operationalized communication use as exposure to a particular communication form and the attention paid to the communication form as a source of information about presidential candidates or the presidential campaign. Respondents' exposure to and attention paid to communication forms were each assessed with seven-interval Likert-type scales based on measures used previously by Chaffee and Schleuder (1986) and McLeod and McDonald (1985). The exposure scale ranged from "rarely use" to "frequently use," whereas the attention scale ranged from "little attention" to "close attention." The exposure item was asked about all communication forms before moving on to the attention item. The first time a communication form was mentioned, examples were offered to ensure clarity (e.g., national network television news programs such as ABC or CNN or television entertainment talk shows such as Leno or Letterman). The examples were selected on the basis of their relative popularity within that genre at the time of the study.

The combined approach using exposure plus attention, especially with studies that seek to compare different media, is highly recommended and has become the norm, although exposure-alone measures were once common. Chaffee and Schleuder (1986) explain the need for the combined measures: "If . . . one anticipates making comparisons between media, . . . then media attention measures are essential." They add that the addition attention measures "reduce the spurious influence of third variables on tests of cognitive effects" (p. 103).

The communication forms included in the investigation and any exemplars featured in the survey instrument were newspapers, newsmagazines (e.g., *Time*), national network television news (e.g., ABC or CNN), local television news, political talk radio (e.g., Rush Limbaugh), radio news programs, television talk shows (e.g., *Larry King Live* or *Hardball*), television entertainment talk shows (e.g., Leno or Letterman), prime-time television political drama (e.g., *The West Wing*), television comedic shows (e.g., *Saturday Night Live*), television newsmagazines (e.g., *60 Minutes* or *20/20*), movies or DVDs (e.g., *Fahrenheit 9/11*), the Web, televised candidate debates, televised candidate advertising, conversations with others, and printed materials (e.g., direct mail or flyers). The reliability ratings of communication use measures are depicted in table A.3.

Measures of Affect and Cognition

Measures of affect and cognition were the first in a series of three groups of dependent variables in this investigation. We were interested in determining whether communication forms varied in eliciting more feelings or thoughts about candidates. Reliability ratings of all dependent variables are shown in table A.4.

Affect involves people's emotional responses. Political communication scholars have only recently begun to empirically assess emotional response. This study focused on two affect dimensions: feelings of contentment about a candidate, which is positive, and feelings of anger, which is negative. The study utilized scales developed by Dillard and colleagues (Dillard, Plotnick, Godbold, Freimuth, & Edgar, 1996; Smith & Dillard, 1997). The interval scales of 0 to 6 measured the extent to which the candidate conveyed contentment (mellow, tranquil, peaceful, and contented) and anger (annoyed, irritated, aggravated, and angry).

Thinking about candidates involves people's cognitive responses. Five seven-interval Likert-type scales were used to assess cognitive responses to candidates. The items were adapted from true/false belief items employed in recent National Election Studies (2000). The respondents were asked the extent to which they perceived the following items to be false or true (the response options ranged from extremely false to extremely true): compared to John Kerry, George W. Bush is the most qualified to be president; George W. Bush really cares about people like me; George W. Bush, generally, holds the right position on domestic issues; George W. Bush, generally, holds the right position on foreign policy issues; and George W. Bush has what it takes to be an effective leader. The same items were repeated later in the survey, but for John Kerry. The items were summed to provide an overall measure of cognitive responses to Bush and to Kerry.

Measures of Perceptions of Candidates

The next series of dependent variables addressed people's perceptions of the 2004 presidential candidates. Three measures were designed to measure overall perceptions of the candidates during the two periods. Respondents' overall attitude toward candidates was assessed using six seven-interval bipolar adjective pairs developed by Burgoon, Cohen, Miller, and Montgomery (1978). This attitude measure has attained excellent reliabilities in past political communication research (e.g., Pfau et al., 1999; Pfau et al., 2001). The adjective-opposite pairs included foolish/wise, unfavorable/favorable, wrong/right, unacceptable/acceptable, bad/good, and negative/positive.

People's perceptions of the character of the candidates were assessed using three seven-interval adjective-opposite scales that were developed in factor analytic research by McCroskey and colleagues (see McCroskey, 1966; McCroskey & Jenson, 1975). The character measure has been used extensively in past research (Rubin, Palmgreen, & Sypher, 1997), including studies of public perceptions of political candidates (e.g., Pfau, Diedrich, Larson, & Van Winkle, 1993; Pfau et al., 1997). The specific items used to assess people's perceptions of the character of candidates were dishonest/honest, unsympathetic/sympathetic, and unselfish/selfish.

Finally, a single item was used to measure people's voting disposition. Respondents were asked, using a scale from 0 to 100, where 0 indicates "no chance" and 100 indicates "near-certain likelihood," "How likely are you to vote for George W. Bush for president?" The item was repeated later in the survey for John Kerry.

Measures of Perceptions of Democratic Process

The final series of dependent variables addressed normative outcomes, which concern core democratic values. The normative phase of the study featured three dependent variables (political expertise served as a dependent variable for one analysis and as a control variable in two analyses; it was described previously). Attitude toward the process by which a president is elected was assessed using six seven-interval bipolar adjective pairs developed by Burgoon and colleagues (1978). The adjective opposite pairs included foolish/wise, bad/good, unacceptable/acceptable, negative/positive, wrong/right, and unfavorable/favorable.

Four behavioral disposition items were employed to assess the likelihood of participating in the political process. Respondents were asked, on a scale from 0 to 100, where 0 indicates "no chance" and 100 indicates "near-certain probability," what is the likelihood that they would "actively seek information about the presidential candidates and/or their positions," "engage in conversations with other people about the presidential candidates and/or their positions," "contribute either time or money to a presidential political campaign," and "go to the polls and vote on November 2." The participation items subsequently were summed.

DATA ANALYSIS PROCEDURES

This investigation focused on people's communication use and its relationship to partisanship, perceptions of candidates, and normative outcomes. Different analytic tools were employed, depending on the questions raised. Simple Pearson r correlations were computed to examine associations involving people's communication use and their political party identification, strength of identification, and political interest.

Hierarchical regression analyses were employed to assess the relative impact of people's use of communication forms on their perceptions of the 2004 presidential candidates and the relative influence of communication forms on normative outcomes. The variables were entered causally: relevant sociodemographic variables were entered in block 1, and communication forms were entered in block 2. This method permitted a judgment of the influence of each block of variables on perceptions of candidates or on normative outcomes and ensured a net judgment of communication effects, assessed after controlling for other influences.

Multicollinearity is a concern intrinsic to all studies using regression analyses to simultaneously assess the impact of multiple communication sources. Multicollinearity refers to the interrelationships of what are assumed to be independent variables (in this case, the seventeen communication forms). However, this did not prove to be a serious problem in this study. Intercorrelations of communication form were modest, most not exceeding .30 and none exceeding .50, with the exceptions of network and local television news at phase 1 (.55) and phase 2 (.60) and local television news and television newsmagazines during phase 1 (.51). However, these associations did not reveal symptoms that are normally associated with multicollinearity. The issue of multicollinearity in regression is not just whether variables are related but also whether levels of intercorrelation are sufficiently severe as to undermine the integrity of the results. Asher (1983, p. 52) explains that "there is no automatic level at which collinearity becomes a problem," and other experts maintain that collinearity does not pose a serious problem until correlations reach levels of .70 and beyond (see Asher, 1984).

A final caveat concerns causation. Correlational and regression analyses are able to determine with precision the relationships involving communication forms and various dependent variables, but, by themselves, these tools cannot prove that communication use is the antecedent or causal variable. For example, the data may reveal that people's use of political talk radio is associated with more favorable perceptions of George W. Bush. What can we infer about causality? People's political talk radio use may enhance their perceptions of President Bush, or people with positive perceptions of President Bush may be increasingly drawn to political talk radio. In all likelihood, both are true. Delli Carpini (2004) advises that the relationship between media use and political effects is "bidirectional" (p. 418). This book has attempted to marry logic and data. Each chapter made the logical case for the influence of specific communication forms on dependent variables, documenting claims with past research, and then data were provided that may or may not support our claims. Ultimately, we ask reader to judge the strength of the claims we have advanced the basis of the combination of our logic and our data.

Table A.1. Fieldwork of Public Opinion Surveys

Date of Fieldwork	N	Response Rate	Margin of Error
September 9–30, 2004	406	33.9%*	±4.86%
October 18–November 1, 2004	402	39.8%	±4.89%

Note. The response rate is defined as the number of completed interviews divided by the sum of the number of completed interviews, number of refusals, and number of eligible household nonresponses. It was computed using the American Association of Public Opinion Research Standard Definitions. The margin of error was computed at a 95 percent confidence interval. A 95 percent confidence interval means that, if a survey was conducted 100 times with 100 different random samples, the results obtained would fall within the limits of error at least 95 times.

* Response rate in survey 1 was affected by two hurricanes that hit the state of Florida during the calling period. Calls to Florida represented 6 percent of numbers dialed, but residents of Florida were twice as difficult to locate compared to residents of other states.

Table A.2. Characteristics of Survey Samples versus U.S. Adult Population Benchmark

	Survey Samples		
Category	Survey 1	Survey 2	Population
Sex			
Female	63.5%	60.9%	55.1%
Male	36.4%	39.1%	44.8%
Age			
18–44 years	38.9%	38.3%	38.9%
45–59 years	30.8%	36.1%	24.8%
60 or over	29.3%	24.4%	22.2%
Refused	1.0%	1.2%	
Education			
Some high school	4.4%	4.0%	9.0%
High school degree	23.2%	22.9%	32.1%
Some college	26.4%	27.1%	25.3%
College degree	29.1%	28.1%	17.7%
Advanced degree	16.5%	16.7%	9.0%
Refused	0.5%	1.2%	
Household income			
Less than $15,000	6.4%	4.0%	15.8%
$15,000–$44,999	29.1%	31.1%	37.3%
$45,000–$74,999	23.4%	24.4%	24.4%
Over $75,000	30.3%	28.4%	22.5%
Refused/don't know	10.8%	12.2%	
Party identification			
Democrat	27.3%	29.6%	34.6%
Republican	37.7%	35.8%	31.8%
Independent	16.0%	15.2%	25.2%
No affiliation	17.7%	18.2%	8.4%
Refused	1.2%	1.2%	

Note. National population data (restricted to people eighteen years of age and older) are based on 2003 U.S. Census Bureau statistics (U.S. Census Bureau, 2005). Party identification data are based on the results of the 2004 National Annenberg Election Survey (Annenberg Public Policy Center, 2004d).

Table A.3. Communication Use Measures and Alpha Reliability Ratings

Measure	Reliability Ratings Survey 1	Reliability Ratings Survey 2
Communication form	N = 467	N = 458
Newspapers	.82	.83
Newsmagazines	.77	.79
Network television news	.73	.78
Local television news	.81	.81
Political talk radio	.77	.83
Radio news	.75	.79
Television talk shows	.78	.77
Television entertainment talk shows	.76	.79
Prime-time television political drama	.76	.70
Television comedy	.68	.77
Television newsmagazines	.77	.84
Movies/DVDs	.79	.77
Web	.85	.85
Televised candidate debates	.85	.90
Televised candidate ads	.69	.73
Conversations with others	.79	.86
Direct mail/flyers	.71	.73

Note. Reliability ratings were computed on the summed exposure and attention measures. Because all the communication use measures consisted of only two items, alpha reliability ratings were lower than those of other measures employed in this investigation.

Table A.4. Dependent Variables: Measures and Alpha Reliability Ratings

	Reliability Ratings	
Measure	Survey 1	Survey 2
Affective responses		
Bush	N = 431	N = 423
Contentment	.96	.98
Anger	.98	.97
Kerry	N = 408	N = 408
Contentment	.98	.97
Anger	.98	.98
Cognitive responses		
Bush	N = 443	N = 431
Thinking	.96	.97
Kerry	N = 409	N = 411
Thinking	.96	.97
Perceptions of candidates		
Bush	N = 457	N = 449
Attitude	.97	.98
Character	.95	.95
Kerry	N = 419	N = 417
Attitude	.98	.98
Character	.94	.95
Perceptions of the democratic process	N = 407	N = 405
Political expertise	.87	.87
Attitude	.92	.96
Participation	.63	.65

References

Abramson, P. R. (1983). *Political attitudes in America*. San Francisco: W. H. Freeman.

Allen, M., & D'Alissio, D. (2000). Media bias in presidential elections: A meta-analysis. *Journal of Communication, 50*, 133–156.

Alter, J. (2005, June 13). If Watergate happened now. *Newsweek*, p. 33.

Annenberg Public Policy Center. (2004a, August 20). *Cable and talk radio boost public awareness of swift boat ad: National Annenberg Election Survey shows*. Retrieved September 23, 2004, from http://www.naes04.org

Annenberg Public Policy Center. (2004b, August 3). *Fahrenheit 9/11 viewers and Limbaugh listeners about equal in size even though they perceive two different nations, Annenberg data show*. Retrieved September 10, 2004, from http://www.naes04.org

Annenberg Public Policy Center. (2004c, September 15). *Issue advertising in the 1999–2000 election cycle*. Retrieved September 15, 2001, from http://www.annenbergpublicpolicycenter.org

Annenberg Public Policy Center. (2004d, November 19). *NAES04 National Annenberg Election Survey Annenberg Public Policy Center, University of Pennsylvania*. Retrieved June 1, 2005, from http://www.naes04.org

Ansolabehere, S., & Iyengar, S. (1995). *Going negative. How political advertisements shrink and polarize the electorate*. New York: Free Press.

Ansolabehere, S., Iyengar, S., Simon, A., & Valentino, N. (1994). Does attack advertising demobilize the electorate? *American Political Science Review, 88*, 829–838.

Arendt, H. (1961). *Between past and future: Eight essays in political thought*. New York: Viking Press.

Aristotle. (1991). *The Nicomachean ethics* (D. Ross, Trans.). New York: Oxford University Press.

Armstrong, R. (1988). *The next hurrah: The communications revolution in American politics*. New York: Beech Tree Books.

Asher, H. B. (1983). *Causal modeling* (2nd ed.). Beverly Hills, CA: Sage.
Asher, H. B. (1984). Regression analysis. In H. B. Asher, H. F. Weisberg, J. H. Kessel, & W. P. Shively (Eds.), *Theory-building and data analysis in the social sciences* (pp. 237–261). Knoxville: University of Tennessee Press.
Atkin, C., & Heald, G. (1976). Effects of political advertising. *Public Opinion Quarterly, 40,* 216–228.
Atkin, C. K. (1980). Political campaigns: Mass communication and persuasion. In M. E. Roloff & G. R. Miller (Eds.), *Persuasion: New directions in theory and research* (pp. 280–308). Beverly Hills, CA: Sage.
Atkinson, M. (1984). *Our masters' voices: The language and body of politics.* London: Metheun.
Axelrod, R. (1986). Presidential election conditions in 1984. *American Political Science Review, 80,* 281–285.
Barber, B. R. (2003). *Strong democracy: Participatory politics for a new age (twentieth-anniversary edition).* Berkeley: University of California Press.
Barker, D. C. (2002). *Rushed to judgment: Talk radio, persuasion, and American political behavior.* New York: Columbia University Press.
Baum, M. A. (2003). *Soft news goes to war: Public opinion and American foreign policy in the new media age.* Princeton, NJ: Princeton University Press.
Beck, P. A. (1991). Voters' intermediation environments in the 1988 presidential contest. *Public Opinion Quarterly, 55,* 371–394.
Beck, P. A. (2002). Encouraging political defection: The role of personal discussion network in partisan desertions to the opposition party and Perot voters in 1992. *Political Behavior, 24,* 309–337.
Becker, L. B., & Dunwoody, S. (1982). Media use, public affairs knowledge and voting in a local election. *Journalism Quarterly, 59,* 212–218.
Becker, S. L., & Kraus, S. (1978). The study of campaign '76: An overview. *Communication Monographs, 45,* 265–267.
Beninger, J. R. (1987). Personalization of mass media and the growth of pseudo-community. *Communication Research, 14,* 352–371.
Bennett, S. E. (1986). *Apathy in America 1960–1984: Causes and consequences of citizen political indifference.* Dobbs Ferry, NY: Transnational Publishers.
Bennett, S. E. (1998). Political talk radio shows' impact on democratic citizenship. In T. J. Johnson, C. E. Hays, & S. P. Hays (Eds.), *Engaging the public: How government and media can reinvigorate American democracy* (pp. 111–122). New York: Rowman & Littlefield.
Bennett, S. E., Flickinger, R. S., & Rhine, S. L. (2000). Political talk over here, over there, over time. *British Journal of Political Science, 30,* 99–119.
Benoit, W. L., & Hansen, G. J. (2004). The changing media environment of presidential campaigns. *Communication Research Reports, 21,* 164–173.
Benoit, W. L., Hansen, G. J., & Holbert, R. L. (2004). Presidential campaigns and democracy. *Mass Communication and Society, 7,* 177–190.
Benoit, W. L., Hansen, G. J., & Verser, R. M. (2003). A meta-analysis of the effects of viewing U.S. presidential debates. *Communication Monographs, 70,* 335–350.

Benoit, W. L., Pier, P. M., Brazeal, L. M., McHale, J. P., Klyukovski, A., & Airne, D. (2002). *The primary decision: A functional analysis of debates in presidential primaries.* Westport, CT: Praeger.

Berelson, B. R., Lazarsfeld, P. F., & McPhee, W. N. (1954). *Voting: A study of opinion formation in a presidential campaign.* Chicago: University of Chicago Press.

Berkowitz, D., & Pritchard, D. (1989). Political knowledge and communication resources. *Journalism Quarterly, 66,* 697–701.

Berry, J. P., Jr. (1987). *John F. Kennedy and media: The first television president.* Lanham, MD: University Press of America.

Bimber, B., & Davis, R. (2003). *Campaigning online: The Internet in U.S. elections.* New York: Oxford University Press.

Blair, J. A. (1996). The possibility and actuality of visual arguments. *Argumentation and Advocacy, 33,* 23–39.

Blum, J. M., Catton, B., Morgan, E. S., Schlesinger, A. M., Jr., Stampp, K. M., & Van Woodward, C. (1968). The national experience: A history of the United States. *European Journal of Communication, 14,* 241–250.

Blumler, J. G. (1999). Political communication systems all change: A response to Kees Brants. *European Journal of Communication, 14,* 241–250.

Blumler, J. G., & Gurevitch, M. (1995). *The crisis of public communication.* New York: Routledge.

Boyer, P. S., Clark, C. E., Kett, J. E., Salisbury, N., Sitkoff, H., & Woloch, N. (1993). *The enduring vision: A history of the American people* (2nd ed.). Lexington, MA: D. C. Heath.

Brehm, J., & Rahn, W. (1997). Individual-level evidence for the causes and consequences of social capital. *American Journal of Political Science, 41,* 999–1023.

Brians, C. L., & Wattenberg, M. P. (1996). Campaign issue knowledge and salience: Comparing reception from TV commercials, TV news, and newspapers. *American Journal of Political Science, 40,* 172–193.

Bucy, E. P., D'Angelo, P., & Newhagen, J. E. (1999). The engaged electorate: New media use as political participation. In L. L. Kaid & D. G. Bystrom (Eds.), *The electronic election: Perspectives on the 1996 campaign communication* (pp. 335–347). Mahwah, NJ: Lawrence Erlbaum Associates.

Burgoon, M., Cohen, M., Miller, M. D., & Montgomery, C. L. (1978). An empirical test of resistance to persuasion. *Human Communication Research, 5,* 27–39.

Butler, L. D., Koopman, C., & Zimbardo, P. G. (1995). The psychological impact of viewing the film *JFK*: Emotions, beliefs, and political behavior intentions. *Political Psychology, 16,* 237–257.

Cacioppo, J. T., Petty, R. E., & Green, T. R. (1989). Attitude structure and function: From the tripartite to the homeostasis model of attitudes. In A. Pratkanis, S. Breckler, & A. Greenwald (Eds.), *Attitude structure and function* (pp. 39–69). Hillsdale, NJ: Lawrence Erlbaum Associates.

Calhoun, C. (1988). Populist politics, communication media, and large-scale societal integration. *Sociological Theory, 6,* 219–241.

Campbell, A., Converse, P. E., Miller, W. E., & Stokes, D. E. (1960). *The American voter.* New York: John Wiley & Sons.

Campbell, A., Gurin, G., & Miller, W. E. (1954). *The voter decides*. Evanston, IL: Row, Peterson and Co.

Campbell, J. E., Munro, M., Alford, J. R., & Campbell, B. A. (1986). Partisanship and voting. *Research in Micropolitics, 1*, 99–126.

Cappella, J. N., & Jamieson, K. H. (1997). *Spiral of cynicism: The press and the public good*. New York: Oxford University Press.

Carey, J. W. (1995). The press, public opinion, and public discourse. In T. L. Glasser & C. T. Salmon (Eds.), *Public opinion and the communication of consent* (pp. 373–402). New York: Guilford Press.

Carpenter, E. (1986). The new languages. In G. Gumpert & R. Cathcart (Eds.), *Inter/Media: Interpersonal communication in a media world* (3rd ed., pp. 353–367). New York: Oxford University Press.

Carpignano, P., Andersen, R., Aronowitz, S., & DiFazio, W. (1993). Chatter in the age of electronic reproduction: Talk television and the "public mind." In B. Robbins (Ed.), *The phantom public sphere* (pp. 93–120). Minneapolis: University of Minnesota Press.

Carter, S. L. (1998). *Civility: Manners, morals, and the etiquette of democracy*. New York: Basic Books.

Chaffee, S. H. (1981). Mass media in political campaigns: An expanding role. In R. E. Rice & W. J. Paisley (Eds.), *Public communication campaigns* (pp. 181–198). Beverly Hills, CA: Sage.

Chaffee, S. H. (1986). Mass media and interpersonal channels: Competitive, convergent, or complementary? In G. Gumpert & R. Cathcart (Eds.), *Inter/media: Interpersonal communication in a media world* (3rd ed., pp. 62–80). New York: Oxford University Press.

Chaffee, S. H. (2001). Studying the new communication of politics. *Political Communication, 18*, 237–244.

Chaffee, S. H., & Hockheimer, J. L. (1985). The beginnings of political communication research in the United States: Origins of the "limited effects" model. In E. M. Rogers & F. Balle (Eds.), *The media revolution in America and in Western Europe* (pp. 267–296). Norwood, NJ: Ablex.

Chaffee, S. H., & Metzger, M. (2001). The end of mass communication? *Mass Communication and Society, 4*, 365–379.

Chaffee, S. H., & Schleuder, J. (1986). Measurement and effects of attention to media news. *Human Communication Research, 13*, 76–107.

Chaffee, S. H., & Tims, A. R. (1982). News media use in adolescence: Implications for political cognitions. In M. Burgoon (Ed.), *Communication yearbook* (Vol. 6, pp. 736–758). Beverly Hills, CA: Sage.

Chaffee, S. H., Zhao, X., & Leshner, G. (1994). Political knowledge and the campaign media of 1992. *Communication Research, 21*, 305–324.

Chaiken, S. (1980). Heuristic versus systematic information process and the use of source verses message cues in persuasion. *Journal of Personality and Social Psychology, 39*, 752–766.

Chaiken, S., & Eagly, A. H. (1976). Communication modality as a determinant of message persuasiveness and message comprehensibility. *Journal of Personality and Social Psychology, 34*, 605–614.

Chaiken, S., & Eagly, A. H. (1983). Communication modality as a determinant of persuasion: The role of communicator salience. *Journal of Personality and Social Psychology, 45*, 241–256.

Chesebro, J. W. (1984). The media reality: Epistemological functions of media in cultural systems. *Critical Studies in Mass Communication, 1*, 111–130.

Chesebro, J. W., & Bertelsen, D. A. (1996). *Analyzing media: Communication technologies as symbolic and cognitive systems.* New York: Guilford Press.

Christ, W. B., Thorson, E., & Caywood, C. (1994). Do attitudes toward political advertising affect information processing of televised political commercials? *Journal of Broadcasting and Electronic Media, 38*, 251–270.

Comstock, G., & Scharrer, E. (2005). *The psychology of media and politics.* Burlington, MA: Elsevier Academic Press.

Conlin, J. R. (1990). *The American past: Part two: A survey of American history since 1865* (3rd ed.). Orlando, FL: Harcourt Brace Jovanovich.

Crites, S. L., Farbrigar, L. R., & Petty, R. E. (1994). Measuring the affective and cognitive properties of attitudes: Conceptual and methodological issues. *Personality and Social Psychology Bulletin, 20*, 619–634.

Cronbach, L. J. (1951). Coefficient alpha and the internal structure of tests. *Psychometrika, 16*, 297–334.

Crossen, C. (1994). *Tainted truth: The manipulation of fact in America.* New York: Simon & Schuster.

Dahl, R. A. (1971). *Polyarchy: Participation and opposition.* New Haven, CT: Yale University Press.

Dahl, R. A. (1998). *On democracy.* New Haven, CT: Yale University Press.

Damasio, A. (2003). *Looking for Spinoza: Joy, sorrow, and the feeling brain.* New York: Harvest.

Davis, R. (1996). *The press and American politics: The new mediator* (2nd ed.). Upper Saddle River, NJ: Prentice Hall.

Davis, R. (1999). *The web of politics: The Internet's impact on the American political system.* New York: Oxford University Press.

Davis, R., & Owen, D. (1998). *New media and American politics.* New York: Oxford University Press.

Dayman, D., & Katz, E. (1992). *Media events: The live broadcasting of history.* Cambridge, MA: Harvard University Press.

Delli Carpini, M. X. (2004). Mediating democratic engagement. The impact of communications on citizens' involvement in political and civic life. In L. L. Kaid (Ed.), *Handbook of political communication research* (pp. 395–434). Mahwah, NJ: Lawrence Erlbaum Associates.

Delli Carpini, M. X., & Williams, B. A. (1998). Constructing public opinion: The uses of fictional and nonfictional television in conversations about the environment. In A. N. Crigler (Ed.), *The psychology of political communication* (pp. 149–175). Ann Arbor: University of Michigan Press.

Dillard, J. P., Plotnick, C. A., Godbold, L. C., Freimuth, V. S., & Edgar, T. (1996). The multiple affective outcome of AIDS PSAs: Fear appeal do more than scare people. *Communication Research, 23*, 44–72.

Dimberg, U., Thunberg, M., & Elmehed, K. (2000). Unconscious facial reactions to emotional facial expressions. *Psychological Science*, *11*, 86–89.

Drew, D., & Weaver, D. (1990). Media attention, media exposure, and media effects. *Journalism Quarterly*, *67*, 740–748.

Eagly, A. H., & Chaiken, S. (1993). *The psychology of attitudes*. Fort Worth, TX: Harcourt Brace.

Edsall, T. B., & Grimaldi, J. V. (2004, December 30). On Nov. 2, GOP got more bang for its billion, analysis shows. *The Washington Post*, p. A01.

Eliosoph, N. (1998). *Avoiding politics: How Americans produce apathy in everyday life*. New York: Cambridge University Press.

Eveland, W. P., Jr. (2004). The effect of political discussion in producing informed citizens: The roles of information, motivation, and elaboration. *Political Communication*, *21*, 177–193.

Eveland, W. P., Jr., & Dunwoody, S. (2002). An investigation of elaboration and selective scanning as mediators of learning from the Web versus print. *Journal of Broadcasting and Electronic Media*, *46*, 34–53.

Eveland, W. P., Jr., Marton, K., & Seo, M. (2004). Moving beyond "just the facts." *Communication Research*, *31*, 82–108.

Eveland, W. P., Jr., & Scheufele, D. A. (2000). Connecting news media use with gaps in knowledge and participation. *Political Communication*, *17*, 215–237.

Eveland, W. P., Jr., Seo, M., & Marton, K. (2002). Learning from the news in campaign 2000: An experimental comparison on TV news, newspapers, and on-line news. *Media Psychology*, *4*, 353–378.

Faber, R. J., Tims, A. R., & Schmitt, K. G. (1993). Negative political advertising and voting intent: The role of involvement and alternative information sources. *Journal of Advertising*, *22*, 67–76.

Fan, D. P., & Tims, A. R. (1989). The impact of the news media on public opinion: American presidential election 1987–1988. *International Journal of Public Opinion Research*, *1*, 151–163.

Farhi, P. (2004, July 2). Pop culture and the 2004 election: Movies and books could help choose a president. *The Washington Post*, p. A01.

Finkel, S. E., & Geer, J. G. (1998). A spot check: Casting doubt on the demobilizing effect of attack advertising. *American Journal of Political Science*, *42*, 573–595.

Fiorina, M. P., Abrams, S. J., & Pope, J. C. (2005). *Culture war? The myth of a polarized America*. New York: Pearson.

Fishkin, J. S. (1995). *The voice of the people: Public opinion and democracy*. New Haven, CT: Yale University Press.

Fiske, S. T., Lau, R. R., & Smith, R. A. (1990). On the varieties and utilities of political expertise. *Social Cognition*, *8*, 31–48.

Forgas, J. P., & Moylan, S. (1987). After the movies: Transient mood and social judgment. *Personality and Social Psychology Bulletin*, *13*, 467–477.

Freedman, J. L., & Sears, D. O. (1965). Selective exposure. In L. Berkowitz (Ed.), *Advances in experimental social psychology* (Vol. 2, pp. 57–95). New York: Academic Press.

Freedman, P., Frantz, M., & Goldstein, K. (2004). Campaign advertising and democratic citizenship. *American Journal of Political Science*, *48*, 723–741.
Garry, P. (2003–2004). The roots of political incivility. *American Experiment Quarterly*, pp. 35–37.
Geer, J., & Lau, R. R. (1998, August). *A new way to model campaign effects*. Paper presented at the annual meeting of the Political Science Association, Boston, MA.
Global Language Monitor. (2004). *Myth of 24-hour news cycle directly impacts (and undermines) the 2004 presidential campaign: October surprise short-lived compared to August surprise according to exclusive analysis by GLM*. Retrieved June 11, 2005, from http://www.languagemonitor.com/wst_page12.html
Goldstein, K., & Freedman, P. (2002). Campaign advertising and voter turnout: New evidence for a stimulation effect. *Journal of Politics*, *64*, 721–740.
Graber, D. (1976). Press and TV as opinion resources in presidential campaigns. *Public Opinion Quarterly*, *40*, 285–303.
Graber, D. (2001). *Processing politics: Learning from television in the Internet age*. Chicago: University of Chicago Press.
Graber, D. (2004). Mediated politics and citizenship in the twenty-first century. *Annual Review of Psychology*, *55*, 545–571.
Green, D. P., & Shapiro, I. (1994). *Pathologies of rational choice theory: A critique of applications in political science*. New Haven, CT: Yale University Press.
Greenberg, S. R. (1975). Conversations as units of analysis in the study of personal influence. *Journalism Quarterly*, *52*, 128–131.
Gross, J. J., & Levenson, R. W. (1995). Emotion elicitation using films. *Cognition and Emotion*, *9*, 87–108.
Gunther, A. C., Christen, C. T., Liebhart, J. L., & Chia, S. C.-Y. (2001). Congenial public, contrary press and biased estimates of the climate of opinion. *Public Opinion Quarterly*, *65*, 295–320.
Habermas, J. (1989). *The structural transformation of the public sphere*. Cambridge, MA: MIT Press.
Hajela, D. (2004, October 2). Brokaw, Jennings show support for Rather. *The Miami Herald*, p. D1.
Hallin, D. C. (1992). Sound bite news: Television coverage of elections, 1968–1988. *Journal of Communication*, *42*, 5–24.
Hansen, G. J. (2004). *The informational function of communication sources in presidential campaigns: Effects on issue knowledge and character evaluation*. Unpublished doctoral dissertation, University of Missouri, Columbia.
Harrison, A. A. I. E. (1977). Mere exposure. In L. Berkowitz (Ed.), *Advances in experimental social psychology* (Vol. 10, pp. 39–83). New York: Academic Press.
Hart, R. A. (2000). *Campaign talk: Why elections are good for us*. Princeton, NJ: Princeton University Press.
Harwood Group. (1993). *Meaningful chaos: How people form relationships with public concerns*. Bethesda, MD: Kettering Foundation.
Hearold, S. (1986). A synthesis of 1043 effects of television on social behavior. In G. Comstock (Ed.), *Public communication and behavior* (Vol. 1, pp. 65–144). Orlando, FL: Academic Press.

Hellweg, S. A., Pfau, M., & Brydon, S. R. (1992). *Televised presidential debates: Advocacy in contemporary America*. New York: Praeger.

Herbst, S. (1995). On electronic public space: Talk shows in theoretical perspective. *Political Communication, 12*, 263–274.

Hetherington, M. J. (2001). Resurgent mass partisanship: The role of elite polarization. *American Political Science Review, 95*, 619–631.

Hill, K. A., & Hughes, J. E. (1998). *Cyberpolitics: Citizen activism in the age of the Internet*. Lanham, MD: Rowman & Littlefield.

Hitchon, J. C., & Chang, C. (1995). Effects of gender schematic processing on the reception of political commercials for men and women candidates. *Communication Research, 22*, 430–458.

Hoenisch, S. (1991). *The future of American newspapers*. Retrieved September 21, 2004, from http://www.criticism.com/md/future.html

Hofstetter, C. R., Donovan, M. C., Klauber, M. R., Cole, A., Huie, C. J., & Yuasa, T. (1994). Political talk radio: A stereotype reconsidered. *Political Research Quarterly, 47*, 467–479.

Holbert, R. L. (2004). Soft news goes to war: Public opinion and American foreign policy in the new media age/war and the media: Reporting conflict 24/7. *Public Opinion Quarterly, 68*, 644–648.

Holbert, R. L. (2005). Intramedia mediation: The cumulative and complementary effects of news media use. *Political Communication, 22*, 430–458.

Holbrook, T. M. (1996). *Do campaigns matter?* Thousand Oaks, CA: Sage.

Holbrook, T. M. (2002). Presidential campaigns and the knowledge gap. *Political Communication, 19*, 437–454.

Hollander, B. (1995). The new news and the 1992 presidential campaign: Perceived vs. actual political knowledge. *Journalism and Mass Communication Quarterly, 72*, 786–798.

Hollander, B. A. (1994). Patterns in the exposure and influence of the old news and the new news. *Mass Communication Review, 21*, 144–155.

Hollander, B. A. (1996). Talk radio: Predictors of use and effects on attitudes about government. *Journalism and Mass Communication Quarterly, 72*, 102–113.

Holmes, O. W. (2001). Letter to Harold J. Laskey. In L. Menand (Ed.), *The metaphysical club: A story of ideas in America* (p. 62). New York: Farrar, Straus and Giroux.

Howard, P., & Rainie, L. (2000, May). Insights: The revolution that hasn't begun yet. Information IMPACTS magazine. Retrieved January 9, 2003, from http://www.cisp.org/imp/may_2000/05_00rainie-insight.htm

Huckfeldt, R., & Sprague, J. (1987). Networks in context: The social flow of political information. *American Political Science Review, 81*, 1197–1216.

Huckfeldt, R., & Sprague, J. (1990). Social order and political chaos: The structural setting of political information. In J. A. Ferejohn & J. H. Kuklinski (Eds.), *Information and democratic processes* (pp. 23–58). Urbana: University of Illinois Press.

Hunt, A. R. (2002, October 31). Election 2002: Greed over duty. *The Wall Street Journal*, p. A19.

Hunter, J. D. (1991). *Culture wars: The struggle to define America.* New York: Basic Books.
Huston, A. C., Donnerstein, E., Fairchild, H., Feshbach, N. D., Katz, P. A., Rubenstein, E. A., et al. (1992). *Big world, small screen.* Lincoln: University of Nebraska Press.
Ichilov, O. (1990). Dimensions and role patterns of citizenship in democracy. In O. Ichilov (Ed.), *Political socialization, citizenship education, and democracy* (pp. 11–24). New York: Teachers College Press.
Iyengar, S., & Kinder, D. R. (1987). *News that matters: Television and American opinion.* Chicago: University of Chicago Press.
Iyengar, S., & Valentino, N. A. (2000). Who says what? Source credibility as a mediator of campaign advertising. In A. Lupia, M. D. McCubbins, & S. L. Popkin (Eds.), *Elements of reason: Cognition, choice and the bounds of rationality* (pp. 108–129). New York: Cambridge University Press.
Jamieson, K. H. (1984). *Packaging the presidency: A history and criticism of presidential campaign advertising.* New York: Oxford University Press.
Jamieson, K. H. (1988). *Eloquence in the electronic age: The transformation of political speechmaking.* New York: Oxford University Press.
Jamieson, K. H. (1992). *Dirty politics: Deception, distraction, and democracy.* New York: Oxford University Press.
Jamieson, K. H. (1996). *Packaging the presidency: A history and criticism of presidential campaign advertising* (3rd ed.). New York: Oxford University Press.
Jamieson, K. H., & Waldman, P. (2003). *The press effect: Politicians, journalists, and the stories that shape the political world.* New York: Oxford University Press.
Jefferson, T. (1807). Letter to John Norvell. In E. Dumbauld (Ed.), *The political writings of Thomas Jefferson: Representative selections* (pp. 94–95). New York: The Liberal Arts Press.
Jeffres, L. W. (1986). *Mass media processes and effects.* Prospect Heights, IL: Waveland Press.
Johnson, T. J., & Kaye, B. K. (1998). A vehicle for engagement or a haven for the disaffected? Internet use, political alienation and voter participation. In T. J. Johnson, C. F. Hays, & S. P. Hays (Eds.), *Engaging the public: How government and media can reinvigorate American democracy* (pp. 123–135). New York: Rowman & Littlefield.
Jordan, D. L. (1983). Newspaper effects on policy preferences. *Public Opinion Quarterly, 57,* 191–204.
Joslyn, R. A. (1990). Election campaigns as occasions for civic education. In D. L. Swanson & D. Nimmo (Eds.), *New directions in political communication: A resource book* (pp. 86–119). Newbury Park, CA: Sage.
journalism.org. (2004). *The state of the news media 2004: An annual report on American journalism.* Retrieved June 22, 2005, from http://stateofthenewsmedia.org/narrative_networktv_audience.asp?cat=3&media=4
Junn, J. (1991). Participation and political knowledge. In W. Crotty (Ed.), *Political participation and American democracy* (pp. 192–212). New York: Greenwood Press.

Just, M. R., Crigler, A. N., Alger, D. E., Cook, T. E., Kern, M., & West, D. M. (1996). *Crosstalk: Citizens, candidates, and the media in a presidential campaign.* Chicago: University of Chicago Press.

Kahn, K. F., & Kenney, P. J. (1999). Do negative campaigns mobilize or suppress turnout? Clarifying the relationship between negativity and participation. *American Political Science Review, 93,* 877–889.

Kahn, K. F., & Kenney, P. J. (2000). How negative campaigning enhances knowledge of Senate elections. In C. J. N. J. A. Thurber & D. A. Dulio (Eds.), *Crowded airwaves: Campaign advertising in elections* (pp. 65–95). Washington, DC: Brookings Institution Press.

Kaid, L. L. (1982). Paid television advertising and candidate name information. *Campaigns and Elections, 3,* 34–36.

Kaid, L. L. (1997). Effects of the television spots on images of Dole and Clinton. *American Behavioral Scientist, 40,* 1085–1094.

Kaid, L. L., Chanslor, M., & Hovind, M. (1992). The influence of program and commercial type on political advertising effectiveness. *Journal of Broadcasting and Electronic Media, 36,* 303–320.

Kaid, L. L., & Johnston, A. (2001). *Videostyle in presidential campaigns.* Westport, CT: Praeger.

Kaid, L. L., & Sanders, K. (1978). Political television commercials: An experimental study of type and length. *Communication Research, 5,* 57–70.

Kamarack, E. C. (1999). Campaigning on the Internet in the elections of 1998. In E. C. Kamarack & J. S. Nye, Jr. (Eds.), *Democracy.com? Governance in a networked world* (pp. 99–123). Hollis, NH: Hollis Publishing.

Kamarack, E. C. (2002). Political campaigning on the Internet: Business as usual? In E. C. Kamarack & J. S. Nye, Jr. (Eds.), *Governance.com: Democracy in the information age* (pp. 81–103). Washington, DC: Brookings Institution Press.

Kellner, D. (2005). The media and election 2004. *Critical Studies in Media Communication, 22,* 178–186.

Kendall, K. E., & Yum, J. O. (1991, March). *Interpersonal communication in a presidential campaign: A profile.* Paper presented at the annual meeting of the Southwestern Political Science Association, San Antonio, TX.

Kennamer, J. D. (1990). Political discussion and cognition: A 1998 look. *Journalism and Mass Communication Quarterly, 67,* 348–352.

Kern, M., Just, M., & Crigler, A. (1997, November). *Citizen use of World Wide Web sites in the 1996 presidential election.* Paper presented at the annual meeting of the National Communication Association, Chicago.

Kernell, S. (1997). *Going public: New strategies of presidential leadership* (3rd ed.). Washington, DC: Congressional Quarterly.

Kim, J., Wyatt, R. O., & Katz, E. (1999). News, talk, opinion, participation: The part played by conversation in deliberative democracy. *Political Communication, 16,* 361–385.

Kinder, D. R. (1983). Diversity and complexity in American public opinion. In A. Finifter (Ed.), *Political Science: The state of the discipline* (pp. 389–425). Washington, DC: American Political Science Association.

Klapper, J. T. (1960). *The effects of mass communication*. New York: Free Press.
Krugman, H. E. (1971). Brain wave measures of media involvement. *Journal of Advertising Research, 11*, 3–9.
Krugman, H. E. (1977). Memory without recall, exposure without reception. *Journal of Advertising Research, 12*, 7–12.
Kuklinski, J. H., & Quirk, P. J. (2000). Reconsidering the rational public: Cognition, heuristics, and mass opinion. In A. Lupia, M. D. McCubbins, & S. L. Popkin (Eds.), *Elements of reason: Cognition, choice and the bounds of rationality* (pp. 153–182). New York: Cambridge University Press.
Kurtz, H. (1996). *Hot air: All talk, all the time*. New York: Times Books.
Lau, R. R., & Sigelman, L. (2000). Effectiveness of negative political advertising. In J. A. Thurber, C. J. Nelson, & D. A. Dulio (Eds.), *Crowded airwaves: Campaign advertising in elections* (pp. 10–43). Washington, DC: Brookings Institution Press.
Lazarsfeld, P., Berelson, B., & Gaudet, H. (1948). *The people's choice: How the voter makes up his mind in a presidential campaign*. New York: Columbia University Press.
Lazarus, R. S. (1982). Thought on the relations between emotion and cognition. *American Psychologist, 37*, 1019–1024.
Lazarus, R. S. (1984). On the primacy of cognition. *American Psychologist, 39*, 124–129.
Lazarus, R. S., & Lazarus, B. N. (1994). *Passion and reason: Making sense of our emotions*. New York: Oxford University Press.
Lee, G., & Cappella, J. N. (2001). The effects of political talk radio on political attitude formation: Exposure versus knowledge. *Political Communication, 18*, 369–394.
Lenart, S. (1994). *Shaping political attitudes*. Thousand Oaks, CA: Sage.
Levy, S. (2005, May 30). Television reloaded. *Newsweek*, pp. 49–55.
Lichter, S. R., & Noyes, R. E. (1995). *Good intentions make bad news: Why Americans hate campaign journalism*. Lanham, MD: Rowman & Littlefield.
Liebes, T. (2001). Look me straight in the eye: The political discourse of authenticity, spontaneity, and sincerity. *The Communication Review, 4*, 499 510.
Lippman, W. (1922). *Public opinion*. New York: Harcourt Brace Jovanovich.
Lipset, S. M. (1963). *Political man: The social bases of politics*. Baltimore: The Johns Hopkins University Press.
Lodge, M., & Taber, C. (2000). Three steps toward a theory of motivated political reasoning. In A. Lupia, M. D. McCubbins, & S. L. Popkin (Eds.), *Elements of reason: Cognition, choice and the bounds of rationality* (pp. 183–213). New York: Cambridge University Press.
Lohmann, S. (1995). The poverty of Green and Shapiro. *Critical Review, 9*, 127–154.
Lowi, T. (1985). *The personal president: Power invested promise unfulfilled*. Ithaca, NY: Cornell University Press.
Lupia, A., McCubbins, M. D., & Popkin, S. L. (2000). Beyond rationality: Reason and the study of politics. In A. Lupia, M. D. McCubbins, & S. L. Popkin (Eds.), *Elements of reason: Cognition, choice and the bounds of rationality* (pp. 1–20). New York: Cambridge University Press.

MacKeun, M. (1990). Speaking of politics: Individual conversational choice, public opinion, and the prospects for deliberative democracy. In J. A. F. J. H. Kuklinski (Ed.), *Information and democratic processes* (pp. 59–99). Urbana: University of Illinois Press.

Marcus, G. E., Neuman, W. R., & MacKuen, M. (2000). *Affective intelligence and political judgment*. Chicago: University of Chicago Press.

Martinelli, K. A., & Chaffee, S. H. (1995). Measuring new-voter learning via three channels of political information. *Journalism and Mass Communication Quarterly, 72*, 18–32.

Mauldin, J. (2004). Don't confuse me with the facts: The emotional contrarian. Frontline thoughts. Retrieved January 22, 2005, from http://www.assetbase.co.za/press/mauldin/frontline6.htm

Mayer, J. P. (Ed.). (1969). *Alexis de Tocqueville: Democracy in America*. Garden City, NJ: Anchor Books.

McCroskey, J. C. (1966). Scales for the measurement of ethos. *Speech Monographs, 33*, 65–72.

McCroskey, J. C., & Jenson, T. A. (1975). Image of mass media news sources. *Journal of Broadcasting and Electronic Media, 19*, 169–180.

McGinniss, J. (1969). *The selling of the president, 1968*. New York: Trident Press.

McGuire, W. J. (1986). The myth of massive media impact: Savagings and salvagings. In G. Comstock (Ed.), *Public communication and behavior* (Vol. 1, pp. 173–257). Orlando, FL: Academic Press.

McLeod, J. M., Guo, Z., Daily, K., Steele, C. A., Huang, H., Howowitz, E., et al. (1996). The impact of traditional and nontraditional media forms in the 1992 presidential election. *Journalism and Mass Communication Quarterly, 73*, 401–416.

McLeod, J. M., Kosicki, G. M., & McLeod, D. M. (1994). The expanding boundaries of political communication effects. In J. Bryant & D. Zillmann (Eds.), *Media effects: Advances in theory and research* (pp. 123–162). Hillsdale, NJ: Lawrence Erlbaum Associates.

McLeod, J. M., & McDonald, D. G. (1985). Beyond simple exposure: Media orientations and their impact on political processes. *Communication Research, 12*, 3–33.

McLeod, J. M., Scheufele, D. A., & Moy, P. (1999). Community, communication, and participation: The role of mass media and interpersonal discussion in local political participation. *Political Communication, 16*, 315–336.

McLuhan, M. (1964). *Understanding media: Extensions of man*. New York: McGraw-Hill.

McLuhan, M. (1967). *The medium is the massage: An inventory of effects*. New York: Bantam Books.

McLuhan, M. (1995). Playboy interview. In E. McLuhan & F. Zingrone (Eds.), *Essential McLuhan* (pp. 233–269). New York: Basic Books.

Media Monitor. (2000, November/December). Campaign 2000 final: How TV news covered the general election campaign. Retrieved September 13, 2004, from http://www.cmpa.com/Mediamon/mm111200

Merkle, D. M. (1996). The polls—Review: The National Issues Convention deliberative poll. *Public Opinion Quarterly, 60*, 588–619.

Meyrowitz, J. (1985). *No sense of place: The impact of electronic media on social behavior*. New York: Oxford University Press.

Meyrowitz, J. (1992). The life and death of media friends: New genres of intimacy and mourning. In S. J. Drucker & R. S. Cathcart (Eds.), *American heroes in a media age* (pp. 62–81). Cresskill, NJ: Hampton Press.

Mill, J. S. (1859). *On liberty* (C. V. Shields, Ed.). Indianapolis: Bobbs-Merrill.

Mindich, D. T. Z. (2005). *Tuned out: Why Americans under 40 don't follow the news*. New York: Oxford University Press.

MIT Communications Forum. (2005). Election 2004 and beyond: Did the media fail? Retrieved June 5, 2005, from http://web.mit.edu/comm-forums/elections_did_media_fail.html

Morgan, E. S. (1992). *The birth of the republic: 1763–1789* (3rd ed.). Chicago: University of Chicago Press.

Morris, D. (1999). *Vote.com*. Los Angeles: Renaissance.

Morris, J. S., Ohman, A., & Dolan, R. J. (1998). Conscious and unconscious emotional learning in the human amygdala. *Nature*, *393*, 467–470.

Moy, P., & Pfau, M. W. (2000). *With malice toward all? The media and public confidence in democratic institutions*. New York: Praeger.

Moy, P., Torres, M., Tanaka, K., & McCluskey, M. R. (2005). Knowledge or trust? Investigating linkages between media reliance and participation. *Communication Research*, *32*, 59–86.

Moy, P., Xenos, M. A., & Hess, V. K. (2005). Communication and citizenship: Mapping the political effects of infotainment. *Mass Communication and Society*, *8*, 111–131.

Moyers, B. (1984). *The thirty-second president* [Video]. New York: PBS.

Mutz, D. (2004). Hostile political TV leads to negative attitudes about politics. Retrieved October 23, 2004, from http://researchnews.osu.edu/archive/uncivil.htm

Mutz, D. C. (2002). Cross-cutting social networks: Testing democratic theory in practice. *American Political Science Review*, *96*, 111–126.

Mutz, D. C., & Martin, P. S. (2001). Facilitating communication across lines of political difference: The role of the mass media. *American Political Science Review*, *95*, 97–114.

National Annenberg Election Survey. (2004). Daily Show *viewers knowledgeable about the campaign, National Annenberg election survey shows*. Retrieved October 23, 2004, from http://www.annenbergpublicpolicycenter.org/naes/2004_03_late-night-knowledge-2_9-21_pr.pdf

National Election Studies. (2000). *Electronic resources from the NES World Wide Web site*. Retrieved January 23, 2005, from http://www.umich.edu/nes

Neuman, W. R. (1986). *The paradox of mass politics: Knowledge and opinion in the American electorate*. Cambridge, MA: Harvard University Press.

Neuman, W. R., Just, M. R., & Crigler, A. N. (1992). *Common knowledge*. Chicago: University of Chicago Press.

Newhagen, J. E., & Reeves, B. (1991). Emotion and memory responses for negative political advertising: A study of television commercials used in the 1988 presidential election. In F. Biocca (Ed.), *Television and political advertising* (pp. 197–220). Hillsdale, NJ: Lawrence Erlbaum Associates.

Newspaper Association of America. (2000). Facts about newspapers. Retreived October 23, 2004, from http://www.naa.org/info/facts00/02.html

Nimmo, D. D. (1974). *Popular images of politics: A taxonomy*. Englewood Cliff, NJ: Prentice Hall.

Norris, P. (1999). Who surfs? New technology, old voters and virtual democracy. In E. C. Kamarck & J. S. Nye, Jr. (Eds.), *Democracy.com? Governance in a networked world* (pp. 71–94). Hollis, NH: Hollis Publishing.

Norris, P. (2000). *A virtuous circle: Political communication in postindustrial societies*. Cambridge, England: Cambridge University Press.

Norris, P. (2001). *Digital divide: Civic engagement, information poverty, and the Internet worldwide*. Cambridge, England: Cambridge University Press.

Norris, P. (2002a). Revolution, what revolution? The Internet in U.S. elections, 1992–2000. In E. C. Kamarck & J. S. Nye, Jr. (Eds.), *Governance.com: Democracy in the information age* (pp. 71–94). Washington, DC: Brookings Institution Press.

Norris, P. (2002b, May 3). *Tuned out voters? Media impact on campaign learning*. Paper presented at the Politeia Conference, Brussels, Belgium.

Norris, P., & Sanders, D. (2003). Message or medium? Campaign learning during the 2001 British general election. *Political Communication, 20,* 233–262.

Nye, J. S., Jr., Zelikow, P. D., & King, D. C. (Eds.). (1997). *Why people don't trust government*. Cambridge, MA: Harvard University Press.

O'Brien, G. (2004, August 12). Is it all just a dream? *New York Review of Books,* p. 51.

Ottati, V. C., & Wyer, R. S., Jr. (1993). Affect and political judgment. In S. Iyenger & M. J. McGuire (Eds.), *Explorations in political psychology* (pp. 296–315). Durham, NC: Duke University Press.

Overholser, G., & Jamieson, K. H. (2005). Afterword. In G. Overholster & K. H. Jamieson (Eds.), *The press* (pp. 433–442). New York: Oxford University Press.

Owen, D. (1991). *Media messages in American presidential elections*. New York: Greenwood Press.

Owen, D. (1995). Who's talking? Who's listening? The new politics of radio and television talk shows. In S. C. Craig (Ed.), *Breaking contract: Changing relationships between citizens and their government in the United States* (pp. 127–146). Boulder, CO: Westview Press.

Owen, D. (1996). Who's talking? Who's listening? The new politics of radio talk shows. In S. C. Craig (Ed.), *Broken contract: Changing relationships between Americans and their government* (pp. 127–146). Boulder, CO: Westview Press.

Owen, D. (1997). The press' performance. In L. J. Sabato (Ed.), *Toward the millennium: The elections of 1996* (pp. 205–223). Boston: Allyn & Bacon.

Page, B. I. (1996). *Who deliberates? Mass media in modern democracy*. Chicago: University of Chicago Press.

Pan, Z., & Kosicki, G. M. (1997). Talk show exposure as an opinion activity. *Political Communication, 14,* 371–388.

Park, R. E. (1975). The natural history of the newspaper. In W. B. Schramm (Ed.), *Mass communications* (2nd ed., pp. 8–23). Urbana: University of Illinois Press.

Pateman, C. (1970). *Participation and democratic theory.* New York: Cambridge University Press.
Patterson, T., & Sieb, P. (2005). Informing the public. In G. Overholster & K. H. Jamieson (Eds.), *The press* (pp. 189–202). New York: Oxford University Press.
Patterson, T. E. (1980). *The mass media election: How Americans choose their president.* New York: Praeger.
Patterson, T. E. (1993). *Out of order.* New York: Alfred A. Knopf.
Patterson, T. E. (2002). *The vanishing voter: Public involvement in an age of uncertainty.* New York: Alfred A. Knopf.
Patterson, T. E., & McClure, D. (1974). *Political advertising: Voter reaction to televised political commercials.* Princeton, NJ: Citizens Research Foundation.
Patterson, T. E., & McClure, R. D. (1976). *The unseeing eye: The myth of television power in national politics.* New York: Putnam.
Pennington, G. (2002, September 30). *Network news: Incredible shrinking audience share.* The Augusta Chronicle. Retrieved March 15, 2004, from http://augustachronicle.com/stories/020402/fea
Perloff, R. M. (1989). Ego-involvement and the third-person effect of televised news coverage. *Communication Research, 16,* 236–262.
Petrocik, J. R., & Shaw, D. (1991). Nonvoting in America: Attitudes in context. In W. Crotty (Ed.), *Political participation and American democracy* (pp. 67–88). New York: Greenwood Press.
Petty, R., & Cacioppo, J. (1979). Issue-involvement can increase or decrease persuasion by enhancing message-relevant cognitive responses. *Journal of Personality and Social Psychology, 37,* 1915–1926.
Petty, R. E., & Cacioppo, J. T. (1986). *Communication and persuasion: Central and peripheral routes to attitude change.* New York: Springer-Verlag.
Pew Research Center for the People and the Press. (2004a, May 2). *News audiences increasingly politicized: Online news audiences larger, more diverse.* Retrieved May 2, 2005, from http://people-press.org/reports/display.php3?PageID-833
Pew Research Center for the People and the Press. (2004b, June 8). *Online news audience larger, more diverse: News audiences increasingly politicized. Pew research center biennial consumption survey.* Retrieved June 16, 2004, from http://www.people-press.org
Pfau, M. (1990). A channel approach to television influence. *Journal of Broadcasting and Electronic Media, 34,* 195–214.
Pfau, M. (2002). The subtle nature of presidential debate influence. *Argumentation and Advocacy, 38,* 251–261.
Pfau, M. (2003), *The changing nature of presidential debate influence in the new age of mass media communication.* Paper presented at the 9th Annual Conference on Presidential Rhetoric, Texas A&M University, College Station, TX.
Pfau, M., Diedrich, T., Larson, K. M., & Van Winkle, K. M. (1993). Relational and competence perceptions of presidential candidates during primary election campaigns. *Journal of Broadcasting and Electronic Media, 37,* 275–292.
Pfau, M., & Eveland, W. P. (1996). Influence of traditional and non-traditional news media in the 1992 election campaign. *Western Journal of Communication, 60,* 214–232.

Pfau, M., & Kang, J. G. (1991). The impact of relational messages on candidate influence in televised political debates. *Communication Studies*, *42*, 114–128.

Pfau, M., Kendall, K. E., Reichert, T., Hellweg, S. A., Lee, W., Tusing, K. J., et al. (1997). Influence of communication during the distant phase of the 1996 presidential primary campaign. *Journal of Communication*, *47*, 6–26.

Pfau, M., Moy, P., Holbert, R. L., Szabo, E. A., Lin, W., & Zhang, W. (1999). The influence of political talk radio on confidence in democratic institutions. *Journalism and Mass Communication Quarterly*, *75*, 730–745.

Pfau, M. W., Cho, J., & Chong, K. (2001). Impact of communication forms in presidential campaigns: Influences on candidate perceptions and democratic process. *Harvard International Journal of Press/Politics*, *6*, 88–105.

Pfau, M. W., & Parrot, R. (1993). *Persuasive communication campaigns.* Needham Heights, MA: Allyn & Bacon.

Popkin, S. L. (1991). *The reasoning voter: Communication and persuasion in presidential campaigns.* Chicago: University of Chicago Press.

Popkin, S. L. (1994). *The reasoning voter: Communication and persuasion in presidential campaigns* (2nd ed.). Chicago: University of Chicago Press.

Postman, N. (1985). *Amusing ourselves to death: Public discourse in the age of show business.* New York: Penguin Books.

Postman, N. (1993). *Technopoly: The surrender of culture to technology.* New York: Vintage.

Postman, N. (2001). *Building a bridge to the eighteenth century: How the past can improve our future.* New York: Alfred A. Knopf.

Potter, J. W. (1993). Cultivation theory and research: A conceptual critique. *Human Communication Research*, *19*, 564–601.

Powers, W. (2005, January/February). The massless media. *Atlantic Monthly*, pp. 122–126.

Price, V., & Zaller, J. (1993). Who got the news? Alternative measures of news reception and their implications for research. *Public Opinion Quarterly*, *57*, 133–164.

Putnam, R. D. (1995). Bowling alone: America's declining social capital. *Journal of Democracy*, *6*, 65–78.

Putnam, R. D. (2000). *Bowling alone: The collapse and revival of American community.* New York: Simon & Schuster.

Rahn, W. M. (2000). Affect as information: The role of public mood in political reasoning. In M. D. M. A. Lupia & S. L. Popkin (Eds.), *Elements of reason: Cognition, choice and the bounds of rationality* (pp. 130–150). New York: Cambridge University Press.

Rahn, W. M., & Hirshorn, R. M. (1999). Political advertising and public mood: A study of children's political orientations. *Political Communication*, *16*, 387–407.

Ranney, A. (1983). *Channels of power: The impact of television on American politics.* New York: Basic Books.

Rauch, J. (2005, January/February). Bipolar disorder. *Atlantic Monthly*, pp. 102–110.

Reinsch, J. L. (1998). *Getting elected: From radio and Roosevelt to television and Reagan.* New York: Hippocrene Books.

Richards, B. (2004). The emotional deficit in political communication. *Political Communication*, *21*, 339–352.

Roberts, C. L. (1979). Media use and difficulty of decision in the 1976 presidential campaign. *Journalism Quarterly*, *56*, 794–802.

Roberts, M., & McCombs, M. (1994). Agenda setting and political advertising: Origins of the news agenda. *Political Communication*, *11*, 249–262.

Robertson, L. (2000). Talk-show campaigning: Late night with Al and Dubya. *American Journalism Review*, *22*, 10–11.

Robins, R. S., & Post, J. M. (1997, September). *Paranoia in a political context*. Paper presented at the annual meeting of the American Political Science Association, Washington, DC.

Robinson, J. P., & Levy, M. R. (1986). Comprehension of a week's news. In J. P. Robinson & M. R. Levy (Eds.), *The main source: Learning from television news* (pp. 87–105). Beverly Hills, CA: Sage.

Robinson, M. (1975). American political legitimacy in an era of electronic journalism. In D. Cater & R. Adler (Eds.), *Television as a social force: New approaches to TV criticism* (pp. 97–141). New York: Praeger.

Robinson, M. (1976). Public affairs television and the growth of political malaise: The case of "The selling of the Pentagon." *American Political Science Review*, *70*, 409–432.

Roper Organization. (1981). *Evolving public attitudes towards television and other mass media 1959–1980*. New York: Television Information Office.

Rosenburg, M. J., & Hovland, C. I. (1960). Cognitive, affective, and behavioral components of attitude. In M. Rosenburg, C. Hovland, W. McGuire, R. Abelson, & J. Brehm (Eds.), *Attitude organization and change* (pp. 39–69). New Haven, CT: Yale University Press.

Rosenstiel, T. (1993). *Strange bedfellows: How television and the presidential candidates changed American politics in 1992*. New York: Hyperion.

Rossiter, C. L. (1961). *The Federalist Papers*. New York: New American Library.

Rottenberg, J., Ray, R. R., & Gross, J. J. (in press). Emotion elicitation using films. In J. A. Coan & J. J. B. Allen (Eds.), *The handbook of emotion elicitation and assessment*. New York: Oxford University Press.

Rubin, R. B., Palmgreen, P., & Sypher, H. E. (1997). *Communication research measures: A sourcebook*. New York: Guilford.

Ryfe, D. M. (2003). The principles of public discourse: What is good public discourse? In J. Rodin & S. P. Steinberg (Eds.), *Public discourse in America: Conversation and community in the twenty-first century* (pp. 163–177). Philadelphia: University of Pennsylvania Press.

Salomon, G. (1987). *Interactions of media, cognition, and learning: An exploration of how symbolic forms cultivate mental skills and affect knowledge acquisition*. San Francisco: Jossey-Bass.

Samuelson, R. J. (2004, June 28). Picking sides for the news. *Newsweek*, p. 37.

Scheufele, D. A. (2000). Talk or conversation? Dimensions of interpersonal discussion and their implications for participatory democracy. *Journalism and Mass Communication Quarterly*, *77*, 727–743.

Scheufele, D. A. (2002). Examining differential gains from mass media and their implications for participatory behavior. *Communication Research, 29*, 46–65.

Scheufele, D. A., & Nisbet, M. C. (2002). Being a citizen online: New opportunities and dead ends. *Harvard International Journal of Press/Politics, 7*, 55–75.

Schroeder, A. (2000). *Presidential debates: Forty years of high-risk TV.* New York: Columbia University Press.

Schuman, H., & Presser, S. (1996). *Questions and answers in attitude surveys: Experiments on question form, wording, and context.* Thousand Oaks, CA: Sage.

Schumpeter, J. A. (1947). *Capitalism, socialism and democracy* (2nd ed.). New York: Harper and Brothers.

Schwartz, B. (2004). *The paradox of choice: Why more is less.* New York: HarperCollins.

Schwartz, T. (1973). *The responsive chord.* Garden City, NJ: Doubleday.

Sears, D. O., & Chaffee, S. H. (1979). Uses and effects of the 1976 debates: An overview of empirical studies. In S. Kraus (Ed.), *The great debates: Carter vs. Ford, 1976* (pp. 223–261). Bloomington: Indiana University Press.

Sears, D. O., & Freedman, J. L. (1967). Selective exposure to information: A critical review. *Public Opinion Quarterly, 31*, 194–213.

Shaw, D. R. (1999). A study of presidential campaign event effects from 1952 to 1992. *Journal of Politics, 61*, 387–422.

Shively, W. P. (1980). The nature of party identification: A review of recent developments. In J. C. Pearce & J. L. Sullivan (Eds.), *The electorate reconsidered* (pp. 219–236). Beverly Hills, CA: Sage.

Shrum, L. J. (2001). Processing strategy moderates the cultivation effect. *Human Communication Research, 27*, 94–120.

Simon, H. A. (1995). Rationality in political behavior. *Political Psychology, 16*, 45–63.

Smith, B. A., & Dillard, J. P. (1997, November). *Affect and persuasion: Evidence for cognitive coloration of message processing.* Paper presented at the annual meeting of the National Communication Association, Chicago.

Smith, T. J., Lichter, S. R., & Harris, L. (1997). *What people want from the press.* Washington, DC: Center for Media and Public Affairs.

Sniderman, P. M. (1983). The new look in public opinion research. In A. Finifter (Ed.), *Political science: The state of the discipline* (pp. 218–223). Washington, DC: American Political Science Association.

Sniderman, P. M., Brody, R. A., & Tetlock, P. E. (1991). *Reasoning and choice: Explorations in political psychology.* New York: Cambridge University Press.

Spiker, J. A., & McKinney, M. S. (1999). Measuring political malaise in the 1996 presidential election. In L. L. Kaid & D. G. Bystrom (Eds.), *The electronic election: Perspectives on the 1996 campaign communication* (pp. 319–334). Mahwah, NJ: Lawrence Erlbaum Associates.

Stauffer, J., Frost, R., & Rybolt, W. (1981). Recall and learning from broadcast news: Is print better? *Journal of Broadcasting and Electronic Media, 25*, 253–262.

Strope, L. (2000, October 22). Pols' images are live from New York. *Wisconsin State Journal*, p. A-4.

Stuckey, M. E. (1991). *The president as interpreter-in-chief*. Chatham, NJ: Chatman House.
Sunstein, C. R. (2001). *Republic.com*. Princeton, NJ: Princeton University Press.
Surlin, S. H. (1978). "Roots" research: A summary of findings. *Journal of Broadcasting and Electronic Media*, 22, 309–320.
The Racine Group. (2002). White paper on televised political campaign debates. *Argumentation and Advocacy*, 38, 199–218.
The small screen continued to expand its empire in 2003. (2003, December 23). *St. Louis Post-Dispatch*, p. C8.
Trent, J. S., & Friedenberg, R. V. (2000). *Political campaign communication: Principles and practices* (4th ed.). Westport, CT: Praeger.
Tulis, J. K. (1987). *The rhetorical presidency*. Princeton, NJ: Princeton University Press.
Turrow, J. (1997). *Breaking up America: Advertisers and the new media world*. Chicago: University of Chicago Press.
U.S. Census Bureau. (2005). *USA statistics in brief—Population by sex, age, and region*. Retrieved June 1, 2005, from http://www.census.gov/statab/www/pop.html
Vallone, R. P., Ross, L., & Lepper, M. R. (1985). The hostile media phenomenon: Bias perception and perceptions of media bias in coverage of the Beirut massacre. *Journal of Personality and Social Psychology*, 49, 577–585.
Verba, S., Schlozman, K. L., & Brady, H. E. (1995). *Voice and equality: Civic voluntarism in American politics*. Cambridge, MA: Harvard University Press.
Wattenberg, M. P. (1986). *The decline of American political parties, 1952–1984*. Cambridge, MA: Harvard University Press.
Wayne, S. J. (2001). *The road to the White House 2000: The politics of presidential elections, post-election edition*. Boston: Bedford/St. Martin's.
Weaver, D., & Drew, D. (1995). Voter learning in the 1992 presidential election: Did the "nontraditional" media and debates matter? *Journalism and Mass Communication Quarterly*, 72, 7–17.
Weaver, D., Drew, D., & Wu, W. (1998). Voter interest and participation in the 1996 presidential election: Did the debates matter? In T. J. Johnson, C. E. Haysm & S. P. Hays (Eds.), *Engaging the public: How government and the media can reinvigorate American democracy* (pp. 87–95). Lanham, MD: Rowman & Littlefield.
Webster, J. G. (2005). Beneath the veneer of fragmentation: Television audience polarization in a multichannel world. *Journal of Communication*, 55, 366–382.
West, D. (1994). Political advertising and news coverage in the 1992 California U.S. Senate campaigns. *Journal of Politics*, 56, 1056–1075.
West, D. M. (2000). How issue ads have reshaped American politics. In J. A. Thurber, C. J. Nelson, & D. A. Dulio (Eds.), *Crowded airwaves: Campaign advertising in elections* (pp. 149–170). Washington, DC: Brookings Institution Press.
Wilkins, K. G. (2000). The role of media in public disengagement from public life. *Journal of Broadcasting and Electronic Media*, 44, 569–580.
Wilkinson, E. J. (2002, June 6). *Confronting the newspaper youth readership puzzle*. Paper presented at the Newspaper Association of America Newspapers in Education Conference, Hershey, PA.

Will, G. F. (2005, May 23). The oddness of everything. *Newsweek*, p. 84.

Williamson, J. (1978). *Decoding advertisements: Ideology and meaning in advertising*. New York: Marion Boyars.

Worchel, S., Andreoli, V., & Eason, J. (1975). Is the medium the message? A study of the effects of media, communication, and message characteristics on attitude change. *Journal of Applied Psychology, 5*, 157–172.

Wright, P. L. (1974). Analyzing media effects on advertising responses. *Public Opinion Quarterly, 38*, 192–205.

Yum, J. O., & Kendall, K. E. (1995). Sex differences in political communication during presidential campaigns. *Communication Quarterly, 43*, 131–141.

Zabarenko, D. (2004, September 22). American campaign comedy: Being funny is optional. *Reuters*. Retrieved September 25, 2004, from http://today.reuters.com

Zajonc, R. B. (1980). Feeling and thinking: Preferences need no inferences. *American Psychologist, 35*, 151–175.

Zajonc, R. B. (1984). On the primacy of affect. *American Psychologist, 39*, 117–123.

Zaller, J. R. (1992). *The nature and origins of mass opinion*. New York: Cambridge University Press.

Zhao, X., & Bleske, G. L. (1995). Measurement effects in comparing voter learning from television news and campaign advertisements. *Journalism and Mass Communication Quarterly, 72*, 72–83.

Zhao, X., & Chaffee, S. H. (1995). Campaign advertisements versus television news as sources of political issue information. *Public Opinion Quarterly, 59*, 41–65.

Index

20/20, 34, 137
48 Hours, 73
527 advertising. *See* Advertising
60 Minutes, 23, 34, 73, 92, 137
abolitionists, 12
Abrams, S. J., 42
Adams, John Quincy, 10–11
Adams, Samuel, 8
advertising, 13, 17–18, 36–37, 57–59, 115–16, 132, 137; 527 advertising, 36, 39; affect and (*see* affect); attack advertising, 39, 115–16; cognition and (*see* cognition); democratic outcomes and (*see* democratic outcomes); television (*see* television); marginally attentive and (*see* marginally attentive); partisanship and (*see* partisanship); perception of political candidate and (*see* perception of political candidate); political party identification and (*see* political party identification); printed materials, 95, 98
affect, 50–79, 135, 137
—advertising and, 57–58, 69–71
—attitude formation and, 49–50, 53–54, 63, 68, 73–74
—debate and, 63–65
—education and, 55–57
—impact on candidate evaluation (*see* perception of political candidate)
—internet use and, 59
—as elicited by media forms, 49–50
—movie use and, 67–69, 74
—new media use and, 72
—newsmagazine use and, 59
—newspaper use and, 59
—political talk radio use and, 66–67
—radio use and, 70–71
—partisanship and, 51
—perception of George W. Bush and, 55–59, 62, 65–66, 69, 71, 73–74
—perception of John F. Kerry and, 55–60, 62, 65–66, 69, 71, 73–74
—political decision making and, 50–54
—political expertise and, 55–57
—political party identification and, 55–57
—sociodemographics and, 55–57
—statistical analysis of, 76*n*1–2
—television: comedy use and, 73; network news use and, 57; prime-time political drama use and, 73; talk show use and, 73
—*See also* Rational Choice Theory
age. *See* sociodemographics
aggravated. *See* affect

Allen, M., 33
Alter, Jonathan, 40
American Broadcasting System (ABC), 33, 136–37
American National Election Studies (ANES), 88, 91, 114–16, 137
Amerika, 67
ANES. *See* American National Election Studies
anger. *See* affect
Annenberg Public Policy Center, 68, 72, 90–91, 94, 96 122, 125
annoyed. *See* affect
Ansolabehere, S., 115
AP. *See* Associated Press
Arendt, Hannah, 39
Aristotle, 53
Armstrong, Richard, 16
Articles of Confederation, 9
Associated Press (AP), 92
association, 11
Atlantic, The, 90
attention, 136
attitude, 4–5, 49–50, 53–54, 63, 68, 73–74, 81–83, 138; affect and (*see* affect); cognition and (*see* cognition); about democratic process (*see* democratic outcomes); about political candidate (*see* perception of political candidate)

Barber, B. R., 83
Barker, D. C., 93
Baum, M. A., 93–94
Becker, L. B., 117
Beltway Boys, The, 34
Bennett, S. E., 30, 60, 62
Benoit, W. L., 91
bias. *See* media bias
Birth of a Nation, The, 67
Blair, J. A., 68–69
Blumler, J. G., 43, 108
books, 31
Boston Globe, 96
Brehm, J., 114

Brokaw, Tom, 34
Brydon, S. R., 63, 117
Bucy, E. P., 114, 117
Burgoon, M., 138
Bush, George H. W., 22
Bush, George W., 24, 28, 33–34, 36, 39, 63, 67, 137–38, 140; affect and (*see* Affect); cognition and (*see* Cognition); perception of (*see* perception of political candidate)
Bush's Brain, 67, 95–96

Cable News Network (CNN), 26, 37, 39, 136–37
cable television. *See* television
Cacioppo, J., 61
campaign, 10–11, 15, 19, 21–31, 35–42, 67, 71–72, 82, 86, 90–98, 107–8, 132; cognition and (*see* cognition); media use and, 2, 3, 23, 35–39; television and (*see* television)
Campbell, A., 84
candidate, 23, 25, 30–31, 51–52, 90, 113, 132; media use and, 2–3. *See also* perception of political candidate
Cappella, J. N., 93, 113
Captain Planet, 72
Carey, James W., 1, 107–8
Carter, Jimmy, 20–22, 63
Carter, Stephen, 34–35, 40–41
Carville, James, 95
causation, 140
CBS. *See* Columbia Broadcasting System
Celsius 41.11: The Temperature at Which the Brain Begins to Die, 96, 99
Chaiken, S., 73
Chaffee, S. H., 63–64, 98, 136
Chang, C., 57
Chanslor, M., 17
character. *See* perception of political candidate
Cho, J., 94, 119
Chong, K., 94, 119

citizens. *See* Democracy
civic engagement, 113–15, 122. *See also* democratic outcomes
Civil War, 40
Clay, Henry, 10
Clinton, Bill, 22–25, 71–72, 90, 92
Clinton, Hillary, 92
Clansmen, The, 67
CNN. *See* Cable News Network
coefficient alpha, 135
cognition, 50–75, 135, 137
—advertising and, 57–58, 70–71, 74
—attitude formation and, 49–50, 53–54, 63, 68, 73–74
—campaigns and, 23
—conversation and, 60–61, 72, 124
—debate and, 63–65
—education and, 55–67
—impact on candidate evaluation (*see* perception of political candidate)
—internet use and, 59
—as elicited by media forms, 49–50
—movie use and, 69
—new media use and, 72
—newsmagazine use and, 59
—newspaper use and, 59
—political talk radio use and, 65–67
—radio use and, 70–71
—television: comedy use and, 73; network news use and, 57; newsmagazine use and, 74; prime-time political drama use and, 73; talk show use and, 73
—perception of George W. Bush and, 55–59, 62, 65–66, 69, 73–74
—perception of John F. Kerry and, 55–60, 62, 65–66, 69, 73–74
—political decision making and, 50–54
—political expertise and, 55–57
—political party identification and, 55–57
—sociodemographics and, 55–57
—statistical analysis of, 76*n*1–2
—*See also* rational choice theory
Cohen, M., 138

Columbia Broadcasting System (CBS), 33, 37, 92; *CBS Nightly News,* 90
commercials. *See* advertising
Common Sense, 9
communication: definition, 7
communication effects, 127*n*1
communication form, 1, 82, 132, 136, 139
Comstock, G., 31
Conservative. *See* Republican Party
Constitution of the United States of America, 9, 14; First Amendment, 9
contented. *See* affect
contentment. *See* affect
Continental Congress, 9
Control Room, 67, 95
conversation, 30–31, 34, 38–43, 60–62, 72, 100–1, 115, 124, 137; affect and (*see* affect); cognition and (*see* cognition); democratic outcomes and (*see* democratic outcomes); political information and (*see* political information); political knowledge and (*see* political knowledge); political party identification and (*see* political party identification); perception of political candidate and (*see* perception of political candidate). *See also* public sphere
Cook Political Report, 2
correlation, 139–40
Crigler, A., 28, 88
Cronbach, L. J., 135
Crossen, Cynthia, 40
Crossfire, 39, 43
cultivation theory, 98–99
cynicism, 108, 113, 117

D'Alissio, D., 33
D'Angelo, P., 114
Dahl, R. A., 110–11
Daily Show with Jon Stewart, The. *See* Stewart, Jon
"Daisy Girl" commercial, 17
Damasio, Antonio, 52, 75

Davis, R., 25, 72, 89–92, 94, 118, 132
Day After, The, 67, 72, 96
Dane County, Wisconsin, 119
Dean, Howard, 24, 95
Debs, Eugene, 14
debate, 20, 25, 36, 63–65, 87, 116–17, 124–25, 131, 137; affect and (*see* affect); cognition and (*see* cognition); democratic outcomes and (*see* democratic outcomes); marginally attentive and (*see* marginally attentive); partisanship and (*see* partisanship); perception of political candidate and (*see* perception of political candidate); political party identification and (*see* Political party identification); voter learning and (*see* learning, voter)
Deep Throat, 40
Delli Carpini, Michael, 7, 71–73, 107, 118, 127, 132, 140
democracy, 31, 34, 41–43, 107–12, 126–27, 131; attitude about (*see* democratic outcomes); citizens, 109–10, 124, 132; decision-making process, 109; perceptions of media and, 33; print media, and (*see* print media); values, 3, 108, 138. *See also* affect; cognition; participation; political knowledge; voting
democratic dialogue. *See* conversation
democratic outcomes, 30, 107–27, 135, 138
— conversation and, 115, 120, 122, 124
— education and, 120–21
— in statistical analysis, 127n1–4
— media: advertising and, 115–16, 123, 126; debate and, 116–17, 120, 122, 124; internet use and, 117–19, 123, 126; movie use and, 121–22, 125–26; newspaper use and, 115, 119, 123; political talk radio use and, 117, 121, 124; radio use and, 119, 123, 125; television use and, 115, 119–23, 125–26

— partisanship and (*see* partisanship)
— political expertise and (*see* political expertise)
— political party identification and, 121
— sociodemographics and, 119–20
Democratic Party, 11, 15, 31, 35–38, 42, 56, 67–68, 96, 124, 134–35; affect and (*see* affect); media use and, 34–37. *See also* political party identification
democratic process, perception of. *See* democratic outcomes
democratic values. *See* democracy
de Tocqueville, Alexis, 11
dialogue. *See* conversation
digital video disc (DVD). *See* movie
Dillard, J. P., 137
direct mail. *See* advertising
discourse. *See* conversation
Dole, Bob, 90
Donahue, 73
Douglas, Stephen, 63
Dowd, Matthew, 99
Drew, D., 117
Dukakis, Michael, 22, 63, 90
DVD. *See* movie

Eagly, A. H., 73
Edsall, T. B., 99
education, 55, 134–35; affect and (*see* affect); candidate evaluation and (*see* perception of political candidate); cognition and (*see* cognition); democratic outcomes and (*see* democratic outcomes); perception of political candidate and (*see* perception of political candidate); public education, 12
Eisenhower, Dwight, 16–18
Elaboration Likelihood Model (ELM), 53, 61
election, 12, 24; attitude about (*see* democratic outcomes); election day, 2, 7, 60, 65, 83, 91, 93–94, 98–99, 101, 111, 123; "horse race," 30, 64

election day. *See* election
electoral process. *See* election
electronic town meeting, 89
Eliosoph, N., 62
ELM. *See* Elaboration Likelihood Model
emotion. *See* affect
entertainment television. *See* television
Eveland, W. P., 60–62, 64, 93–94, 115, 122
exposure, 136
external validity. *See* validity

Fahrenheit 911, 34, 36, 67–69, 95–96, 99, 125, 137
Faith of George W. Bush, The, 67
FCC. *See* Federal Communications Commission
Fear and the Selling of American Empire, 67
Federal Communications Commission (FCC), 15
Federal Radio Commission, 15
Federalist Papers, 9–10
Federalists, 9–10
feelings. *See* affect
film. *See* movie
Finkel, S. E., 116
Fiorina, M. P., 42
fireside chats. *See* Roosevelt, Franklin D.
First Amendment. *See* Constitution of the United States of America
Fiske, S. T., 135
Flicklenger, R. S., 60
Flowers, Gennifer, 92
flyers. *See* advertising
Ford, Gerald, 20–22, 63
Founding Fathers, the, 9, 42, 124
Fox New Channel (FOX), 26, 34, 37, 39–40
fragmentation. *See* mass media
Freedman, P., 116

game schema, 113
Geer, J. G., 116

gender. *See* Sociodemographics
generalizability, 134
George W. Bush: Faith in the White House, 96, 99
Global Language Monitor, 36
Goldstein, K., 116
Goldwater, Barry, 17
Gore, Al, 24, 90
Graber, D., 75
Great Depression, the, 16
Greenberg, S. R., 100
Griffith, W. D., 67
Grimaldi, J. V., 99
Gross, J. J., 69
Grunwald, Mandy, 23
Gurevitch, M. 108

Hall, Arsenio, 23
Hallin, Daniel, 30
Hamilton, Alexander, 9
Hannity and Colmes, 34
Hansen, G. J., 91
Hardball, 39, 43, 117, 137
Harrison, A. A., 70
Hart, R. A., 116
Hearst, William Randolph, 13
Hellweg, S. A., 63–64, 117
Hess, V. K., 29, 125
Hetherington, M. J., 32
Heuristics, 52. *See also* Rational Choice Theory
Heuristic-Systematic Model (HSM), 53. *See also* Elaborated Likelihood Model
hierarchical regression. *See* regression
Hirshorn, R. M., 57
Hitchon, J. C., 57
Hofstetter, C. R., 117
Holbert, R. L., 132, 136
Hollander, B., 88, 94
Holocaust, 67
horse race. *See* election
hostile media effect. *See* media bias
hostile media perception. *See* media bias
Hovind, M., 17

HSM. *See* Heuristic-Systematic Model
Huckfeldt, R., 100
Humphrey, Hubert, 19–20
Hunter, J. D., 42–43
Huston, A. C., 69

Ichilov, O., 109
illiteracy, 13
income. *See* sociodemographics
Independent, 22, 32, 85, 116, 134–35. *See also* Political party identification; Ross Perot
Independent voters. *See* Independent
information. *See* political information
information processing, 61
Internet, 2, 22, 24–28, 34–35, 37, 40, 95–97, 100, 117, 137; affect and (*see* affect); cognition and (*see* cognition); democratic outcomes and (*see* democratic outcomes); perception of political candidate and (*see* perception of political candidates); political knowledge and (*see* political knowledge); political party identification and (*see* political party identification)
interview, 133
irritated. *See* affect
Iyengar, S., 115

Jackson, Andrew, 11
Jamieson, Kathleen Hall, 11, 32, 63, 67, 89–92, 113
Jay, John, 9
Jefferson, Thomas, 9–10, 18, 29, 42
JFK, 67
Johnson, Lyndon, 17, 92
Johnson, T. J., 118
Joslyn, R. A., 64
journalism, 89–90; journalists, 12, 30, 113; muckraking, 13; press, the, 14; yellow journalism, 13, 113
journalists. *See* journalism
Journeys with George, 96
Just, M., 28, 88

Kahn, K. F., 116
Kaid, L. L., 17
Kamarack, E. C., 97
Kang, J. G., 63, 73
Kaye, B. K., 118
Kellner, D., 43
Kendall, K. E., 100
Kennamer, J. D., 61
Kennedy, John F., 19, 25
Kennedy, P. J., 116
Kern, M., 28, 88
Kernell, Samuel, 15
Kerry, John F., 28, 33–34, 36, 39, 137–38; affect and (*see* affect); cognition and (*see* cognition); perception of (*see* perception of political candidate)
Kosicki, G.M., 108, 114, 123
Kraus, S., 117
Krugman, H. E., 72
K-Street, 73–74, 95
Kurtz, H., 89, 92

Ladies Home Journal, 13
Larry King Live, 22, 71, 73, 90, 137
late-night entertainment talk show. *See* Letterman, David; Leno, Jay; Stewart, Jon; television
Late Show with David Letterman. *See* Letterman, David
Lau, R. R., 116
Laugh In, 21
Lauper, Cyndi, 72
Lazarsfeld, P., 29
Lazarus, B. N., 75
Lazarus, R. S., 53, 69, 75
League of Nations, 15
learning, voter: debate and, 64–65
Lee, G., 93
Lenart, S., 60–61
Leno, Jay, 2, 27, 31, 72–73, 90, 92, 122, 125, 136–37
Letterman, David, 27–28, 72, 90, 92, 122, 125, 136–37
Levenson, R. W., 69

Levy, M. R., 60
Liberal. *See* Democratic party
Liddy, G. Gordon, 34
Liebes, T., 19
likelihood of participating. *See* democratic outcomes
likelihood of voting. *See* democratic outcomes
likelihood of voting for a candidate. *See* perceptions of political candidate
Limbaugh, Rush, 34, 37, 137
Lincoln, Abraham, 12, 63
Live with Regis and Kathy Lee, 90
Locke, John, 8
Lodge, M., 52
low-information rationality. *See* Rational Choice Theory

MacKeun, M., 51, 100
Mad TV, 73
Madeline, Mary, 95
Madison, James, 10–18
magazine. *See* newsmagazine
Marcus, G. E., 51
margin of error, 133
marginally attentive, 27–28, 31, 43–44; advertising and, 43; debate and, 43; political information and (*see* political information); television comedic programs and, 44; television entertainment programs and, 43–44. *See also* political interest; political involvement
Martin, P. S., 41
mass media, 7–45, 131; fragmentation of, 28, 31, 43, 83, 131; political party identification and (*see* political party identification); specialized, 5; technology and, 8, 10, 13; McCain, John, 24
McCombs, M., 18
McCroskey, J. C., 138
McDonald, D. G., 136
McGovern, George, 20
McKinley, William, 13–14

McKinney, M. S., 117
McLaughlin Group, The, 43
McLeod, D. M., 108
McLeod, J. M., 108, 115, 136
McLuhan, Marshall, 9
media. *See* journalism; mass media
media bias, 33, 89; hostile media perception, 33
media effects, 81–82, 86
medium theory, 9
mellow. *See* affect
mere exposure, 69–70
meta-analysis, 33
Meyrowitz, J., 71
Microsoft/National Broadcasting System (MSNBC), 39, 92
middle way. *See* presidential leadership, American
Miller, M. D., 138
Montgomery, C. L., 138
Moore, Michael, 34, 67, 95–96, 125
Morris, Dick, 24
MoveOn.org, 36
movie, 34–38, 67, 95–96; affect and (*see* affect); cognition and (*see* cognition); democratic outcomes and (*see* democratic outcomes); partisanship and (*see* partisanship); perception of political candidate and (*see* perception of political candidate); political party identification and (*see* political party identification)
Moy, P., 27, 29, 72, 89, 110, 115, 117, 124, 125, 135–36
MSNBC. *See* Microsoft/National Broadcasting System
MTV. *See* Music Television
muckraking. *See* journalism
multicollinearity, 139
Music Television (MTV), 23, 72, 89–90
Mutz, D. C., 41, 117–18

NAES. *See* Annenberg Public Policy Center

National Annenberg Election Survey (NAES). *See* Annenberg Public Policy Center
National Broadcasting System (NBC), 33
National Election Study. *See* American National Election Studies
National Media Inc., 99
National Public Radio (NPR), 33, 37, 70, 95, 98
NBC. *See* National Broadcasting System
NES. *See* American National Election Studies
network television news. *See* television
Neuman, Russell, 2, 4, 27, 51
new way. *See* presidential leadership, American
new media, 20–26, 37, 72, 81–83, 88–93, 96, 114, 132; affect and (*see* affect); cognition and (*see* cognition); perception of political candidate and (*see* political candidate perception); political knowledge and (*see* political knowledge). *See also* Internet; political talk radio; television
New York Times, The, 92
New Yorker, The, 90
Newhagen, J. E., 114
news media. *See* journalism
News Hour, The, 37, 91
newsmagazine, 2, 12–13, 25, 29, 31, 40, 59–60, 137; affect and (*see* affect); cognition and (*see* cognition); perception of political candidate and (*see* perception of political candidate); political party identification and (*see* political party identification)
newspaper, 2, 10–11, 13, 18, 20, 25, 28–29, 31, 36–37, 40, 59–60, 87, 115, 132, 137; affect and (*see* affect); cognition and (*see* cognition); decline of, 25; democratic outcomes and (*see* democratic outcomes);

Newspaper Association of America, 102*n*3; partisan use of, 11–13; political knowledge and (*see* political knowledge); political party identification and (*see* political party identification)
Newsweek, 33
Nixon, Richard, 19–23, 25, 40
normative democratic outcomes. *See* democratic outcomes
Norris, P., 2, 26, 91, 96–97, 100, 117
North, Oliver, 34
Norvell, John, 29
NPR. *See* National Public Radio

O'Brien, G., 68
old way. *See* presidential leadership, American
Olympics, the, 64, 116
opinion leaders, 29, 61
O'Reilly, Bill, 34, 37, 91
O'Reilly Factor. See O'Reilly, Bill
Ottati, Victor C., 49–50
Outfoxed, 67
Overholser, G., 32
Owen, D., 72, 89–92, 94, 117–18, 122, 132

Paine, Thomas, 9
Pan, Z., 114, 123
Parrot, R., 101
participation in Democratic process. *See* democratic outcomes
participation in Election. *See* democratic outcomes
partisan press. *See* partisanship
partisanship, 31–33, 35, 37–38, 40, 42–43, 112
—affect and (*see* affect)
—media use and, 2, 10, 13, 27. 33–35, 37–38; advertising and, 38; debate and, 38; movie use and, 67–68; political talk radio use and, 37, 66; radio use and, 38; television talk show use and, 37

—partisan press, 13
—perceptions of media and, 33
—political information and (*see*
  political information)
—*See also* political party identification
party. *See* political party
party identification. *See* political party
  identification
Patterson, T. E., 18, 64, 70, 89, 97–98,
  100, 112–13, 123
peaceful. *See* affect
Pearson *r*. *See* correlation
Penny press, the, 12–13
perception of political candidate,
  82–101, 135, 138; advertising use
  and, 86–87, 98–99; conversation and,
  100–101; debate use and, 86–87;
  education and, 85; internet use and,
  96–100; late-night entertainment talk
  show use and, 93–94; movie use and,
  96, 98–99; new media use and,
  88–95; newsmagazine use and,
  86–88, 93–94; newspaper use and,
  86–88; political party identification
  and, 84–85; political talk radio use
  and, 65, 93–94; radio use and, 98;
  sociodemographics and, 84;
  statistical analysis of, 76n1–2,
  101n1, 102n2; television program
  use and, 86–88, 93–94, 98–99
perception of democratic process. *See*
  democratic process
Perot, Ross, 22, 90, 94
Petty, R., 61
Pew Research Center for the People and
  the Press, 2, 24, 26, 33, 37, 88,
  90–91, 97–98
Pfau, M., 27, 63, 72–73, 89, 92–94, 97,
  101, 116–17, 119, 135–36
political conversation. *See* conversation
political decision making. *See*
  democracy
political discourse. *See* conversation
political expertise, 55, 135; affect and
  (*see* affect); cognition and (*see*

  cognition); democratic outcomes
  and, 119–20. *See also* political
  knowledge
political information, 5, 26, 28, 61–62,
  132; conversations and, 61–62;
  marginally attentive and, 43; network
  television news and, 26; partisanship
  and, 26. *See also* democratic
  outcomes; political knowledge
political interest, 32, 135; media use
  and, 43–45. *See also* marginally
  attentive; partisanship; political
  involvement
political involvement, 26. *See also*
  democratic outcomes; marginally
  attentive; partisanship; political
  interest
political knowledge, 61–62, 110, 135;
  conversations and, 61–62; internet
  use and, 59; new media use and, 72;
  newspaper use and, 59. *See also*
  democratic outcomes; political
  information
political learning. *See* democratic
  outcomes
political party, 10, 15, 33, 52; decline
  of, 18–19. *See also* Democratic
  Party; Independent; marginally
  attentive; partisanship; political party
  identification; Republican Party
political party identification, 18, 31–33,
  36, 55, 84, 135–36; affect and (*see*
  affect); cognition and (*see*
  cognition); decline of, 32;
  democratic outcomes and (*see*
  democratic outcomes); impact on
  candidate evaluation (*see* perception
  of political candidate); rise of, 32;
  media use and, 34–38; advertising
  and, 36; local television news use
  and, 35; internet use and, 35; movie
  use and, 35–36; newsmagazine use
  and, 37; newspaper use and, 37;
  perception of political candidate and
  (*see* perception of political

candidate); political talk radio use and, 36–37; prime-time political drama use and, 37; radio use and, 35; television comedy use and, 36–37; television entertainment talk show use and, 35–36; television network news use and, 37; television newsmagazine use and, 35–36. *See also* Democratic Party; Independent; marginally attentive; partisanship; political party; Republican Party
political speeches. *See* speeches
political talk. *See* conversation
political talk radio, 23, 26–27, 34, 36–38, 40, 65, 89, 91–92, 94, 117, 124, 132, 137; affect and (*see* affect); cognition and (*see* cognition); democratic outcomes and (*see* democratic outcomes); partisanship and (*see* partisanship); perception of political candidate and (*see* perception of political candidate); political party identification and (*see* political party identification); Republican use of, 92, 94, 124; Political Sensitivity Quotient (PQ), 36
politics, 5
Pope, J. C., 42
Popkin, S. L., 27, 52
population, 134
Post, J. M., 67
Postman, N., 9–10, 17, 63, 114
PQ. *See* Political Sensitivity Quotient
presidential campaign. *See* campaign
presidential candidate. *See* candidate
presidential debate. *See* debate
presidential election. *See* election
presidential leadership, American, 14–15
presidential speeches. *See* speeches
press, the. *See* journalism
Presser, Stanley, 131
Price, V., 135
prime-time television political drama. *See* Television

Prince George, Maryland, 114
print media, 8, 9–10, 12, 29, 59–61; democracy and, 8–10; democratic outcomes and (*see* democratic outcomes)
printed materials. *See* advertising
psychological theory of voting. *See* voting
Public Broadcasting System (PBS), 33, 91
public education. *See* education
Public Opinion Learning Laboratory (POLL), 133
public sphere, 41, 108 *See also* conversation
Pure Food and Drug Act, 14
Putnam, R. D., 112–14

Racine Group, the, 65
radio, 15–16, 20, 22, 24, 35, 37, 61, 70: affect and (*see* affect); cognition and (*see* cognition); democratic outcomes and (*see* democratic outcomes); partisanship and (*see* partisanship); perception of political candidate and (*see* perception of political candidate); political party identification and (*see* political party identification); political talk radio (*see* political talk radio); radio news, 2, 37, 70, 95–96, 98, 137
radio news programs. *See* radio
Rahn, W., 57, 75, 114
Rational Choice Theory (RCT), 51–52, 64; low-information rationality, 27
rationality. *See* Rational Choice Theory
Ray, R. R., 69
RCT. *See* Rational choice theory
Reagan, Ronald, 16, 21–22
Reeves, Rosser, 17
regression, 75n1, 101–2n1, 127n1–4, 139–40
Republican National Committee. *See* Republican Party
Republican Party, 12–13, 15, 18, 22–23, 26, 31, 34–38, 42, 56, 67, 96,

134–35; affect and (*see* affect); media use and, 34–37; perceptions of media and, 33; political talk radio use and (*see* political talk radio); Republican National Committee, 99. *See also* political party identification
respondents, 133
response rate, 133
Rhine, S. L., 60
Richards, B., 54, 75, 89
Roberts, Cokie, 92
Roberts, M., 18
Robins, R. S., 67
Robinson, J. P., 60
Robinson, M., 114, 123
Roosevelt, Franklin D., 14–16, 92; Fireside chats, 16, 92
Roosevelt, Theodore, 13–14
Roots, 67
Rottenberg, J., 69
Rough Riders, 13
Ryfe, D. M., 74–75

sample statistics, 134
Saturday Evening Post, 13
Saturday Night Live, 2, 21, 31, 73, 90, 95, 137
Scharrer, E., 31
Scheufele, D. A., 61–62, 115
Schleuder, J., 136
Schuman, Howard, 131
Schumpeter, J. A., 111
Schwartz, Barry, 27, 68
Schwartz, Tony, 17, 70
Sears, D. O., 63–64
selective avoidance. *See* selective exposure
selective exposure, 32–33, 40
Sherman Anti-Trust Act, 14
Shrum, L. J., 65, 99
Sigelman, L., 116
Simon, A., 115
Simon, H. A., 51
Simpsons, The, 72
social capital, 114, 122

sociodemographics, 55–57, 84, 134–35, 139; affect and (*see* affect); cognition and (*see* cognition); democratic outcomes and (*see* democratic outcomes); perception of political candidate and (*see* perception of political candidate); variables in statistical analysis, 76n2, 102n2, 127n1. *See also* education
sound bite, 30
speeches, 13
Spiker, J. A., 117
Sprague, J., 100
Stamp Act of 1765, 8
State of the Union Address, 14–15
Stewart, Jon, 72–73, 91, 122
Stolen Honor: Wounds That Never Heal, 96
Stowe, Harriet Beecher, 12
Stuckey, M. E., 16, 20–21, 23
Sunstein, C. R., 24
Super Bowl, the, 64, 116
survey, 133–39
Survey Sampling Inc., 133
Swift Boat Veterans for Truth, 36

Taber, C., 52
talk radio. *See* political talk radio
TargetPoint Consultants, 99
telegraph, 11
televised debate. *See* debate
televised candidate advertising. *See* advertising
television, 15 27, 34–35, 71–73, 113 15, 132
—advertising (*see* advertising)
—affect and (*see* affect)
—American presidency and, 21
—cable, 2, 15, 26, 113
—campaign and, 16, 19–21, 30
—comedy, 36, 71, 91, 137; cognition and (*see* cognition); marginally attentive and (*see* marginally attentive); political party

identification and (*see* political party identification)
—commercials (*see* advertising)
—debate (*see* debate)
—democratic outcomes and (*see* democratic outcomes)
—entertainment talk show, 35–37, 71, 91–93, 137
—entertainment television, 22, 36, 61, 115
—marginally attentive and (*see* marginally attentive)
—late-night entertainment talk show, 2, 27–28, 23, 91–95, 132
—local news, 30, 37, 137
—network news, 2, 25–27, 29–31, 37, 40, 57–59, 61, 87, 131, 137
—newsmagazines, 34–37, 74, 89, 92–93, 137
—political party identification and (*see* political party identification)
—prime-time political drama, 34–35, 37, 74, 99, 137
—talk shows, 22, 89, 92–93, 137
television comedy. *See* television
television news. *See* television
television talk shows. *See* television
This Week with George Stephanopoulos, 95
thoughts. *See* cognition
Time, 33, 137
Tonight Show. *See* Leno, Jay
Torres, M., 124
tranquil. *See* affect
Tulis, Jeffrey, 14–15
Turrow, J., 43
two-step flow, 29, 60

Uncle Tom's Cabin, 12
Uncovered: The War in Iraq, 96
United Coal Worker's Union, 14
U.S. Constitution. *See* Constitution of the United States of America
U.S. News & World Report, 33

Valentino, N., 115
validity, 134
van Buren, Martin, 11
variance, 127*n*3
video malaise, 114, 122
volunteer association. *See* association
voting, 50–51, 111; likelihood of (*see* democratic outcomes); psychological theory of, 50–51, 84. *See also* democracy; Rational Choice Theory

Waldman, P., 89–92
Washington, George, 10
Watergate, 21, 89
Wayne, Stephen, 11
Weaver, D., 117
website. *See* Internet
Webster, J. G., 27
welfare state, 15
West, D., 132
West Wing, The, 35, 73–74, 95, 137
Whig party, 11
Wilkins, K. G., 115, 22
Will, George, 29, 40
Williams, B. A., 71–73
Wilson, Woodrow, 14–15
Winfrey, Oprah, 90
Worchel, S., 73
World According to Bush, The, 67, 96
World War II, 15–16, 131
World-Wide Web (WWW). *See* Internet
Wu, W., 117
WWW. *See* Internet
Wyer, Jr., Robert S., 49–50

Xenos, M. A., 29, 125

yard signs. *See* advertising
yellow journalism. *See* journalism
Young, Cathy, 81, 96
Yum, J. O., 100

Zaller, J., 135
Zajonc, Robert B., 49, 53, 69, 75

About the Authors

Michael Pfau is professor and chair of the Department of Communication at the University of Oklahoma and an active scholar in communication. Pfau's research and writing focuses on the influence of the mass media in a variety of contexts and on uses of the inoculation strategy to confer resistance to influence. Pfau has authored more than one hundred monographs and book chapters that have appeared in most of the leading journals in communication, including *Communication Monographs, Communication Research, Human Communication Research, Journal of Communication, Journal of Broadcasting & Electronic Media*, and many other venues. Pfau is the current editor of the *Journal of Communication*. He is past recipient of the National Communication Association's prestigious Golden Anniversary Monographs Award in recognition of "monographs that have made a significant contribution to the discipline." He has co-authored/co-edited six books, most recently *Handbook of Persuasion* (2002) and *With Malice toward All? The Media and Public Confidence in Democratic Institutions* (2001r).

J. Brian Houston is program director for the Terrorism and Disease Center of the University of Oklahoma Health Sciences Center. He was a doctoral student in the Department of Communication at the University of Oklahoma at the time this book was written. His scholarly interest emphasizes the interaction of media use with people's perceptions of citizenship and the democratic process. He has co-authored articles in *American Behavioral Scientist* and *Communication Monographs*, and he has presented numerous academic papers at professional conferences.

Shane M. Semmler was a doctoral student in the Department of Communication at the University of Oklahoma at the time this book was written. His scholarly interest is mass media, social influence, and information processing. He has presented numerous academic papers at professional conferences.

Date Due